Kafka's 'Landarzt' Collection

Australian and New Zealand Studies in German Language and Literature

Australisch-Neuseeländische Studien
zur deutschen Sprache und Literatur

Etudes parues en Australie et Nouvelle-Zélande
en relation avec la philologie allemande

edited by
Gerhard Schulz (Melbourne)
and John A. Asher (Auckland)

Vol. 13

PETER LANG
New York · Berne · Frankfurt am Main

Gregory B. Triffitt

Kafka's
'Landarzt' Collection

Rhetoric and Interpretation

PETER LANG

New York · Berne · Frankfurt am Main

Library of Congress Cataloging in Publication Data

Triffitt, Gregory B.,
  Kafka's 'Landarzt' Collection.

  (Australian and New Zealand Studies in German Language
and Literature; v. 13)
    Bibliography: p.
    1. Kafka, Franz, 1883–1924.   Landarzt.   I. Title.
II. Series.
PT2621.A26L337   1985   833'.912   85-6793
ISBN 0-8204-0204-4
ISSN 0171-6867

CIP-Kurztitelaufnahme der Deutschen Bibliothek

Triffitt, Gregory B.:
Kafka's 'Landarzt' Collection: Rhetoric and
Interpretation / Gregory B. Triffitt. – New
York; Berne; Frankfurt am Main: Lang, 1985. –
  (Australian and New Zealand Studies in German
  Language and Literature; Vol. 13)
  ISBN 0-8204-0204-4

NE: Australisch-neuseeländische Studien zur
deutschen Sprache und Literatur

© Peter Lang Publishing, Inc., New York 1985

Printed by Lang Druck, Inc., Liebefeld/Berne (Switzerland)

For

my parents,

my family and my friends,

especially

D.J.

CONTENTS

Foreword 9

Bibliographical Note 11

1. Scholarship and the Collection 13

2. Issues in Kafka Interpretation 19
   Allegorik 19
   Parabolik 36
   Einsinnigkeit 46
   Paradoxie 88

3. Towards a Rhetoric of the Collection 101
   Structure 102
   Point of View 109
   Symbol 121

4. *Ein Landarzt. Kleine Erzählungen:* An Interpretation 125
   Introduction 125
   Der neue Advokat 127
   Ein Landarzt 129
   Auf der Galerie 138
   Ein altes Blatt 142
   Vor dem Gesetz 146
   Schakale und Araber 150
   Ein Besuch im Bergwerk 154
   Das nächste Dorf 154
   Eine kaiserliche Botschaft 162
   Excursus: The Law 165
   Die Sorge des Hausvaters 171
   Elf Söhne 176
   Ein Brudermord 179

Ein Traum 184
Ein Bericht für eine Akademie 189
Conclusion 198

Notes 203

Bibliography 223

FOREWORD

Despite the hundreds of commentaries on the individual pieces comprising the *Landarzt* collection, very few scholars have concerned themselves with the work as a totality, and none of them has adequately accounted for the quite specific ordering of the pieces, although Kafka, himself, clearly set considerable store by the matter, as is evident from his letters to his publisher and his eventual withdrawal of the piece *Der Kübelreiter* before publication. The overriding aim of this study is to make good the omissions of previous scholars, not only by providing detailed analyses of all the texts as they occur in the collection, but also by defining the structural-thematic principles which underlie their sequence, modify their meaning through contextual interaction, and unite them into a coherent whole.

As a preliminary to interpretation, however, an attempt is made to isolate and describe the main features of Kafka's fictional rhetoric, particularly as exemplified by the collection. In part, this is undertaken through a critical survey of previous Kafka scholarship, concentrating on four dominant, historically successive attitudes to the interpretation of the author's work (*Eindeutigkeit, Vieldeutigkeit, Undeutbarkeit, suspensive Interpretation*) and the four main theoretical concepts associated with them (*Allegorik, Parabolik, Einsinnigkeit, Paradoxie*). Although this survey leads to the conclusion that most of the conflicting views about the meaning of Kafka's works can be attributed, not to the intrinsic nature of the texts, themselves, but to the inadequacy of the critical theories applied to them, it also seeks, more positively, to clarify all of the issues concerned, especially those factors which actually form part of Kafka's rhetoric, that is, parable, point of view and paradox. From these more general, theoretical considerations, the third chapter then proceeds specifically to analyse the principal elements of Kafka's rhetoric in the collection itself, namely, structure as indirect commentary, point of view as reinforcing structure, and symbol as

9

indicating the direction of meaning. Although limitations on length prevent this analysis from being more comprehensive, other important factors such as temporal perspective, irony and the grotesque have not been entirely ignored and are, in any case, mentioned or discussed at the appropriate places in the last chapter, where the preceding examination of Kafka's rhetoric provides the basis for a detailed interpretation of the collection as a unified, artistic whole.

For their generous assistance in the preparation of this study, the text of which was finalised in June, 1982, I would like to express my sincere and profound thanks to Professor G. Schulz (Melbourne), Professor P. Demetz (Yale) and Dr. R.N.N. Robertson (Oxford), all of whom offered very valuable suggestions for improvements; Professors J.H. Tisch and I.H. Smith (Tasmania); Mrs. U. Schlüter; Mrs. R. Lenck; Mrs. N. Gill; and, above all, my constant mentor and highly esteemed friend, Dr. T.P. Wojtowicz, whose serious illness since August, 1980, prevents him from even knowing that the work has actually been completed.

University of Tasmania   G.B.T.
February, 1984

BIBLIOGRAPHICAL NOTE

In order to reduce annotation to the absolute minimum, the following procedures have been adopted:

1. All references to and quotations from Kafka's writings and reported conversations have been identified in the text by bracketed inserts containing an abbreviated title and the relevant page number(s), e.g. (*Se* 123). The abbreviations used and the volumes to which they refer are as follows:

Se	= *Sämtliche Erzählungen*,	
	hrsg. Paul Raabe,	Frankfurt/M : Fischer, 1969
Pz	= *Der Prozeß*,	
	hrsg. M. Brod,	New York : Schocken, 1953
BkI	= *Beschreibung eines Kampfes*,	
	hrsg. M. Brod,	New York : Schocken, 1946
BkII	= *Beschreibung eines Kampfes. Die zwei Fassungen*,	
	hrsg. M. Brod & L. Dietz,	Frankfurt/M : Fischer, 1969
Hv	= *Hochzeitsvorbereitungen auf dem Lande*,	
	hrsg. M. Brod,	New York : Schocken, 1953
Tb	= *Tagebücher 1910-1923*,	
	hrsg. M. Brod,	New York : Schocken, 1951
Br	= *Briefe 1902-1924*,	
	hrsg. M. Brod,	New York : Schocken, 1958
Bm	= *Briefe an Milena*,	
	hrsg. W. Haas,	New York : Schocken, 1958
Bf	= *Briefe an Felice und andere Korrespondenz aus der Verlobungszeit*,	
	hrsg. E. Heller & J. Born,	New York : Schocken, 1967
Bo	= *Briefe an Ottla und die Familie*,	
	hrsg. H. Binder & K. Wagenbach,	New York : Schocken, 1974
Gk	= Janouch, G.: *Gespräche mit Kafka*,	
	erw. Ausg.,	Frankfurt/M : Fischer, 1968.

2. All references to and quotations from secondary literature have been identified in the text by bracketed inserts containing the author's

surname (plus initial, when two or more scholars with the same surname need to be distinguished), the original year of publication and, where necessary, the relevant page number(s) of the edition used, e.g. (Frye, 1957:89f.), except when the text immediately preceding the quotation or reference clearly indicates the latter's author and publication date, e.g. "As Frye (1957) has said: ...", in which case the quotation or reference has been identified simply by 'op.cit.', 'ibid.' or 'loc.cit.', as applicable, plus the relevant page number(s) when required. Full details of the studies concerned are to be found in the bibliography.

These same two procedures have also been adopted in the notes, which, for practical reasons, have had to be placed at the end of the text.

1. SCHOLARSHIP AND THE COLLECTION

During the lengthy period that elapsed between the compilation of the *Landarzt* collection in July-August, 1917 (*Br* 256ff.), and its delayed publication at the end of 1919 (Binder, 1975:235), it is now well known that, on several occasions, Kafka had cause to write to his publisher and insist on the particular order he had given the individual pieces (*Br* 228, 245), an order which research has clearly shown not to be chronological according to date of composition (cf. Pasley/Wagenbach, 1964; 1965; Binder, 1975). It is also equally well known that, for some undisclosed reason, Kafka eventually decided, at the earliest during the autumn of 1918 (Binder, 1975: 233), to withdraw *Der Kübelreiter* from the collection, although it had been listed in the original table of contents between the title-piece and *Auf der Galerie* (*Br* 258). And the obvious inference to be drawn from these firmly attested facts is that Kafka regarded the collection, in its published form, as an organic unity, each piece being assigned to a fixed position in keeping with its intended, individual purpose vis-à-vis the collection as a whole (cf. Sokel, 1967:276).

Yet, despite the scores of commentaries on such works as *Ein Landarzt*, *Auf der Galerie* and *Vor dem Gesetz* (cf. Beicken, 1974; A. Flores, 1976), extremely few scholars have attempted to analyse the collection in its entirety. Furthermore, even among these few, by far the most common procedure has been to ignore the questions raised by the quite specific order of the texts and to limit discussion, instead, to the elaboration of an ostensibly unifying theme, on which, it is claimed, each separate piece provides an individual variation. The earliest example of this approach is to be found in the first scholarly account of the collection, that by Tauber (1941), who maintains: "Eine innere Gegebenheit macht die Einheit des Sammelbandes *Ein Landarzt* aus (...). Diese innere Gegebenheit ist der Verlust des Sinnes, des Ziels, der Substanz, des Maßes" (op.cit.:70). Twenty-one years later, in the next analysis of the whole collection, Politzer

(1962) reaches a rather different, though not incompatible conclusion: "The process of dehumanisation is, with many variations, the unifying theme of the *Country Doctor* stories" (op.cit.:92).

Unlike Tauber and Politzer, Kauf (1972) derives his alleged principle of unity from material extrinsic to the collection, namely, Kafka's correspondence with Martin Buber, founder and editor of the journal *Der Jude*. On 22nd April, 1917, Kafka wrote to Buber offering him twelve pieces for publication, but mentioning only two titles, *Der neue Advokat* and *Ein Landarzt*. Eventually, however, Buber rejected ten of the twelve, in the same way that he had previously rejected *Ein Traum* (*Bf* 704f.). The two works he did choose to publish as *Zwei Tiergeschichten* (cf. A. Flores, 1976:5) were *Schakale und Araber* and *Ein Bericht für eine Akademie*. At the end of his handwritten note offering the twelve pieces, Kafka remarked: "Alle diese Stücke und noch andere sollen später einmal als Buch erscheinen unter dem gemeinsamen Titel: 'Verantwortung'" (Kauf, 1972: 420). On the basis of this far from conclusive evidence, Kauf nevertheless deduces that "Kafka originally intended to publish the stories, or at least most of the stories, that were later to appear under the collective title of *Ein Landarzt* under the heading of *Verantwortung*" (op.cit.:423). Without thoroughly investigating Kafka's notion of responsibility, he then proceeds to analyse all the pieces of the collection as variations on this theme. Quite apart from the difficulties presented by *Ein Traum*, which he can explain only as "a foil to the other stories" (ibid.:432), this approach leads to a series of contrived and shallow interpretations, not the least of which is his assertion that *Elf Söhne* "suggests the difficulty, if not impossibility, of making value judgements. And if value judgements can be made only in the most tentative manner, how is it possible to lead a responsible life?" (ibid.:430).

The most recent attempt to interpret the *Landarzt* collection solely in terms of theme and variations is that by Neumann (1979).[1] This, too, depends heavily on extrinsic information, namely, the details of Kafka's life at the time he wrote the majority of the pieces, and thus tends to reduce the collection to a supposedly veiled autobiography. Otherwise its comments are so general as to be true of a whole range of literature, including virtually every *Bildungsroman*

14

ever written. It is for this reason that they can so readily assimilate the most disparate of other views, from the Zionist to the Marxist. In summary, Neumann's argument runs thus:

> Der *Landarzt*-Band scheint (...) der Versuch zu sein, Redeordnungen zu erproben, die der Frage: 'Wer bin ich?' und der Gegenfrage: 'Wer bist du?', 'Wer seid ihr?' angemessen sind. Er läßt sich als Mythos (Redeordnung) begreifen, der die für Kafkas Entwicklung wesentliche Lebens- und Selbsterfahrungs-Krise zu organisieren sucht, die die wenigen Monate der Arbeit im *Alchimistengäßchen* im Winter 1916/1917 begleitete. (...) Sicher ist, daß die im *Landarzt*-Band erprobte sprachliche Selbstfindung an die Frage des Verhältnisses zum Vater und die Tatsache, daß diesem das Buch gewidmet wird, geknüpft bleibt. (op.cit.:347)

Despite their failure to address the crucial question of order among the *Landarzt* pieces, all of the studies discussed so far do at least attempt to view the collection as a thematically unified whole. The same cannot be said, however, of the analyses by Osborne (1967), Flach (1967), Gray (1973) or Hibberd (1975). For, although they differ considerably in their approaches, none of these scholars provides any more than a series of disconnected, frequently tentative and generally superficial remarks about the texts in question.[2] Indicative of their stance is Hibberd's description of the fourteen pieces:

> They vary from a few lines to several pages in length; some are related in content, but there is no one clear, unifying theme. Signs of a happier outlook on life are few, but the first and last piece (and Kafka was concerned about their order) have a note of renunciation and whimsy. (op.cit.:82)

In sharp contrast to the preceding studies, by far the most detailed and, in some respects, still the most perceptive is that by the East German scholar, H. Richter (1962). Because of his ideological bias, it is true, Richter introduces a great deal of inappropriate political jargon and evaluation into his commentary, talking about *Ein altes Blatt*, for example, in terms of the "Machtlosigkeit des kleinen und mittleren Bürgertums, das stets ökonomisch und politisch von größeren Mächten abhängig ist und kaum selbständige Macht besitzt" (op. cit.:139). At other points, he also refers to Kafka as a sensitive "Vertreter der bürgerlich-humanistischen Intelligenz" (ibid.:164) and criticises him for ignoring the "Proletariat als kämpfende Klasse" (ibid.:165). Ultimately, therefore, he construes the whole collection as a set of variations on the socio-political theme of modern, capitalistic society's allegedly fundamental contradictoriness and senselessness, to which, in the long run, its citizens can accommodate themselves only by accepting their unalterable situation, even if with a degree of irony, as in *Ein Bericht für eine Akademie* (ibid.:159-166). Despite the obvious prejudice of his views, however, Richter does make one very important advance on all the studies mentioned so far. This consists in the suggestion that *Der neue Advokat* embodies a form of thesis about the situation and laws of Kafka's time, a thesis which is then tested in the subsequent pieces: "Das Vorhaben, den Beweis in den folgenden Stücken im einzelnen anzutreten, könnte Kafkas Konzeption des Zyklus zugrunde liegen" (ibid.:129). As the later, detailed analyses of the present study will attempt to show, this notion does, in fact, constitute one of the most basic principles of the collection's structure, but certainly not in the ideological sense or system of values expounded by Richter.

Although they disregard Richter's very significant hypothesis about *Der neue Advokat*, Binder (1975:235f.) and Kittler (1979: 212ff.) take critical appreciation of the collection a step further by suggesting that the whole work is "eingerahmt" (Binder, 1975:235) by the first and last pieces. Within this framework, they then propose, the remaining texts are arranged, often in pairs, according to links in motif, e.g. death in *Ein Brudermord* and *Ein Traum*, the "Vater-Perspektive" (Binder, loc.cit.) in *Elf Söhne* and *Die Sorge des Hausvaters*. As Kittler, who openly acknowledges his deep indebtedness to Binder, sums up their joint argument:

> Die Erzählungen der Sammlung *Ein Landarzt* sind also ähnlich angeordnet wie in der *Betrachtung*. Ihr Verknüpfungsprinzip ist das der Serie. Fast jeder Text greift ein Detail des vorhergehenden auf, es gibt aber auch Verbindungen zwischen Texten, die innerhalb der Sammlung weit auseinander liegen. Die letzten Stücke führen in die Nähe der ersten zurück. (op.cit.:213)

Regrettably, however, neither of these scholars provides anything approaching a detailed analysis of the collection's fourteen texts, so that their attempts to explain the work's underlying system of coherence lack any depth. Thus the concept of a framework, for example, is based solely on the observation that, in the first and last pieces, "sich Tiere in Menschen verwandeln" (Binder, loc.cit.). Even if this were true (and it certainly does not apply to the human-equine Dr. Bucephalus), it would still not account for the fact that Kafka insisted on placing *Der neue Advokat* at the very beginning of the collection, despite the latter's title, and *Ein Bericht für eine Akademie* at the end. Clearly, any adequate explanation of the collection's order must make the elucidation of this fact its first priority, although so far H. Richter is the only scholar to have even tentatively broached the matter. Yet, as later analysis will demonstrate, once the opening piece has been understood in its full implications, the remaining structural principles of the collection will tend to reveal themselves. But before that analysis can be undertaken, the immediate requirement is a sound critical theory from which to develop valid interpretative practice, and that entails a survey of the diverse approaches to Kafka's fiction, from *Eindeutigkeit* to *Vieldeutigkeit*, *Undeutbarkeit* and "suspensive Interpretation" (Steinmetz, 1977).

2. ISSUES IN KAFKA INTERPRETATION

Given the recent publication of two extremely comprehensive and erudite surveys of Kafka scholarship (Beicken, 1974; Binder, 1979), it may seem unnecessary to preface a new interpretation of the *Landarzt* collection with yet another critical review, especially one which cannot even aspire to a similar breadth of scope. However, despite the enormous value of those two works, they are not without their shortcomings. In particular, they fail, either totally or in part, to come to terms with certain literary concepts which are not only fundamental to the interpretative act in general, but also of outstanding importance in evaluating and focussing the history of Kafka criticism. It is with these concepts that the following discussion will attempt to deal.

Allegorik

Contrary to the impression conveyed by A. Flores' recent and very deficient list of Max Brod's contributions to Kafka scholarship (A. Flores, 1976:37f.), the first phase of Kafka's posthumous reception was dominated by his long-standing friend and literary executor. For, apart from preparing and publishing the first editions of *Der Prozeß* (1925), *Das Schloß* (1926), *Amerika* (1927) and *Beschreibung eines Kampfes* (1936), he also produced numerous short commentaries, including an afterword to each of the volumes just mentioned, and in 1937 the first edition of his biography (s. Järv, 1961:70ff.). Above all, however, Brod and, in the English-speaking world, Edwin Muir (cf. Crick, 1980) established a critical approach which was to be adopted by friend and foe alike. Essentially, this consisted in attempting to interpret Kafka's works by assimilating them to some existing, but extrinsic form of ideology: Judaism, Zionism, Christianity, Existentialism, Freudianism and so on (cf. Ackermann, 1950; Poltizer, 1950; Krusche, 1974:77ff., 130ff.; Beicken, 1974:175ff.; Beicken, 1979a).

In employing this interpretative method, Brod and his contemporaries were, of course, making certain crucial, though unproven assumptions, not only about the nature of Kafka's world-view, but also about the structure of his art, and it was not long before the fact was brought to their attention. Indeed, as early as 1948, E. Heller sought to oppose them by pointing out that they were treating Kafka's work as if it were allegory, whereas an examination of this concept and at least *Das Schloß* showed them to be wrong (E. Heller, 1948:209f.; cf. E. Heller, 1974:116f.). Not long afterwards, Anders (1951:39ff.), Martini (1954:321f.) and Wiese (1956:325) developed similar arguments, and their views were soon firmly supported in what, for years, was to be regarded as the standard work on Kafka's oeuvre, the comprehensive study be Emrich (1958:75ff.).

Yet, despite the well-founded objections of these scholars, they failed to stem the tide of allegorical interpretations, which still continues to flow, albeit in more subtle and circumspect channels. Why this should have been so, it is impossible to say with any certainty. However, among the many plausible explanations, one of the more obvious is that, in their interpretative practice, Anders and Emrich contradicted their critical theory. At an early stage in the former's study, for example, it is arbitrarily asserted that a considerable part of Kafka's work is actually about the Jews: "Ja, in den *Chinesische Mauer* genannten Stücken ist das Wort *Jude* durchweg durch das Wort *Chinese* ersetzt" (Anders, 1951:10). And in an equally unfounded, allegorical fashion, Emrich summarily equates the America of Kafka's novel with "der modernen Industriegesellschaft" in general: "Der geheime ökonomische und psychologische Mechanismus dieser Gesellschaft und seine satanischen Konsequenzen werden hier schonungslos bloßgelegt" (Emrich, 1958:227), while Klamm of *Das Schloß* becomes for him merely an "überpersonale Liebesmacht" (ibid.:312).

A more likely and substantial explanation, however, is to be found in the theoretical statements of these scholars. For although they are united in the view that Kafka's works are not to be regarded as allegories, they are at odds about possible valid alternatives. E. Heller, for example, favours symbolic interpretation, but Anders, Wiese and, to some extent, Martini reject this argument, while Emrich goes a step further in denying the validity of parabolic interpretations as well. But if Kafka's works are neither allegorical, nor symbolic, nor parabolic, then how is one to interpret them? To offer as an answer a series of metaphors taken literally (Anders, 1951:40ff.) or a "Gleich-nis- und Bilderwelt" (Emrich, 1958:81; cf. Emrich, 1960:249ff.) is simply to evade the issue, since none of these terms is necessarily incompatible with those which have been rejected. It can scarcely be a cause of wonder, therefore, if this line of argument should have given rise to more confusion than before, or that it should have been widely ignored.

From the viewpoint of later Kafka interpretation, however, by far the most influential aspect of the positions adopted by E. Heller, Anders, Martini, Wiese and Emrich was almost certainly not the points of difference among them, but rather the area of agreement. For, in their united rejection of an allegorical approach to Kafka's works, each of them had recourse to a definition of allegory which derived from early nineteenth century poetics, especially the value-laden antithesis between symbol and allegory enunciated by Goethe (s. Sörensen, 1972:126ff.). And from at least the late 1950's on-wards, this form of definition has been continually under attack, although even the latest edition of Frenzel's handbook on the sub-ject takes no cognisance of the fact (Frenzel, 1963,[4] 1978:14-23, 35-45). With varying degrees of detail and, in some cases, with reference only to Coleridge, who transposed Goethe's theory into English, Frye (1957:89f.; 1965:14), Honig (1959:44ff.), Fletcher (1964: 13ff.), Hayes (1968), Hopster (1971), Sörenson (1972:264ff.), Clif-ford (1974:8), Todorov (1977:235ff.), Quilligan (1979:15, 32) and Kobbe (1980:314ff.) have all examined this question, and they are unanimous in denying the validity of Goethe's distinction:

Immer deutlicher erkennt man heute die geschichtliche Relativität des im 19. Jahrhundert als absolut gesetzten Gegensatzes zwischen dem 'echt' künstlerischen Symbol und der als kalt und trocken verschrienen Allego-rie. Diese Einseitigkeit sowohl der klassischen als auch der romantischen Symboltheorien sowie die Bindung dieser Theorien an bestimmte ästheti-sche und weltanschauliche Voraussetzungen hatten schon Fr. Creuzer und Ferd. Solger gesehen (...). (Sörenson, 1972:266)

Regrettably, however, the unanimity shown by these scholars in criticising nineteenth century theory is singularly lacking in their attempts to supersede it. Indeed, Sörenson and Todorov, like Mac-Queen (1970), offer no explicit definition of their own at all, while Hayes and Hopster so limit themselves to theoretical discussion in the terms employed by Goethe that their alternative definitions are ultimately as arbitrary as those they are opposing. Clearly what is needed is not abstract debate about allegory, but a revised, value-free definition, based firmly on the re-examination of literary works which are universally accepted as constituting allegories or containing allegorical elements. And to find this, one has to turn a group of predominantly American scholars.

Confronted with the works of Frye, Honig, Fletcher, Clifford and Quilligan, the reader's initial reaction might well be one of utter bewilderment about the meaning of allegory, so radically do their analyses differ from one another and from traditional discussions of the term. Yet, amid their undeniably perplexing array of divergent interpretations, it is possible to find at least three fundamental criteria about which there is general, if not total agreement and, for the purposes of this study, they are sufficient to permit of a decision about the central issue of the present discussion, namely, whether Kafka is, even in the terms of contemporary critical theory, the allegorist which so many scholars, including those now under consideration, claim him to be.[1]

In his extremely influential essay of 1957, Frye has the following to say about the nature of allegory:

> We have actual allegory when a poet explicitly indicates the relationship of his images to examples and precepts, and so tries to indicate how a commentary should proceed. A writer is being allegorical when it is clear that he is saying 'by this I *also* (*allos*) mean that'. If this seems to be done continuously, we may say, cantiously, that what he is writing 'is' an allegory. (op.cit.:90)

By 1965, however, he had become less tentative:

> We have allegory when the events of a narrative obviously and continuously refer to another simultaneous structure of events or ideas, whether historical events, moral or philosophical ideas, or natural phenomena. (...) there are two main types of allegory: historical or political allegory, referring to

22

characters or events beyond those purportedly described in the fiction; and moral, philosophical, religious, or scientific allegories, referring to an additional set of ideas. (Frye, 1965:12)

Allowing for the mistaken notions that all allegorists are poets and that the Greek *allos* means 'also', when in fact it means 'other(wise)', it is nevertheless clear from Frye's remarks that he considers one fundamental characteristic of allegory to be a dual or parallel system of meanings, the text of the work providing the surface or primary meaning, but at the same time 'obviously and continuously' signalling a different (*allos*), secondary meaning, which must be grasped if the allegory is to be understood as such. In other words, however radically Frye may depart from conventional wisdom in some of his other utterances, here he is restating one of the most traditional descriptions of all allegorical method and structure, that embedded in the literal meaning of the term itself, namely, "speaking otherwise than one seems to speak" (S.O.E.D.). Furthermore, his definition is strongly echoed in other modern studies of the subject.

Honig (1959), for example, maintains that the allegorical narrative "builds up the sense of the distinction to be drawn among 'the levels of meaning'", that a "constant layering of meaning" is decisive in the narrative's effect, and that "this translative use of narrative method and cultural ideal (...) characterises the concept of allegory" (op.cit.:53). Similarly, but in terms much closer to Frye's, Fletcher (1964) explains that, put most simply,

allegory says one thing and means another. It destroys the expectation we have about language, that our words 'mean what we say'. When we predicate quality x of person Y, Y really is what our predication says he is (or we assume so); but allegory would turn Y into something other (*allos*) than what the open and direct statement tells the reader. (op.cit.:2)

Later in his study, he also states that allegories "are based on parallels between two levels of being that correspond to each other, the one supposed by the reader, the other literally presented in the fable" (ibid.:113). Much the same idea is then expressed by Clifford (1974): "allegory invites its readers from the outset to see the particular narrative as being also a series of generalised statements, and demands that concepts be identified simultaneously in their fictional and ideological roles" (op.cit.:7f.). Finally, even Kobbe (1980), who argues purely theoretically, appears to support Frye's definition, albeit in a somewhat opaque technical jargon:

> Die Allegorie ist die künstlerische Vertextung einer jeweils enzyklopädisch identifizierbaren Wahrnehmungsstruktur (einer Aktivität/eines Prozesses/ eines Zustandes von bzw. an Lebewesen oder Sachen). Es wird jeweils nur eine solche Wahrnehmungsstruktur verwendet, die — unabhängig von der künstlerischen Vertextung — als Prädikator innerhalb metaphorisher und/ oder metaphysischer Prädikationen (mit der zweistelligen Elementarform 'A ist p') fungieren kann. (op.cit.:326)

With the exception of Quilligan, then, most contemporary scholars tend to unite in regarding allegory as being characterised by the type of structure or method described by Frye. The first question, therefore, to be asked about Kafka's allegedly allegorical texts is whether they actually exhibit the structure these scholars attribute to them. And an answer to this question would seem, very obviously, to require a structural analysis of at least all the texts comprising the present collection. But since any such analysis would presuppose a considerable amount of interpretation, no matter how objective the analyst attempted to be, the whole undertaking would clearly be futile, for it would simply amount to placing yet another interpretation beside the many that already exist and arbitrarily declaring it to be the more accurate.

This does not mean, however, that the question is incapable of being decided. Rather, it implies that a different approach must be adopted, one which is more likely to produce valid results. And the most promising would appear to lie in an examination of Kafka's commentaries on his own works. After all, whether one accepts the views of Dante in his *Convivio* and the famous letter to Can Grande della Scala, or those of Spenser in his equally famous letter to Sir Walter Raleigh about *The Faerie Queene*, or those of contemporary theorists in the studies already mentioned, the fact remains that 'the making of allegory' is obviously a very conscious act. Consequently, one would naturally expect an author to be well aware of any intended allegorical structure in his works, and to furnish clear evidence of it in his commentaries on them.

Yet, among the admittedly infrequent and generally brief interpretations Kafka provides of his works in his letters (e.g. *Br* 116, 117f., 150; *Bf* 53, 87, 218, 278f., 394, 396f., 445, 561f.; *Bm* 14f., 20f., 214), his diaries (e.g. *Tb* 296f., 297, 481, 535f.) and his conversations with Janouch (e.g. *Gk* 43f., 52f., 53f., 55f., 132f., 247)[2], there is none that indicates any intention, on his part, to create a structure of the type now considered to be a defining characteristic of allegory. Nor, it needs to be added, does any of them substantiate the alternative allegorical criteria proposed by Quilligan (1979): "cosmically extended verbal echoing and wordplay" (op. cit.:41), a Biblical pretext — pre-text (ibid.:97ff.), etc. To demonstrate these points, the longest of his commentaries, that on *Das Urteil*, should serve:

Anläßlich der Korrektur des *Urteil* schreibe ich alle Beziehungen auf, die mir in der Geschichte klargeworden sind, soweit ich sie gegenwärtig habe. (...) Der Freund ist die Verbindung zwischen Vater und Sohn, er ist ihre größte Gemeinsamkeit. Allein bei seinem Fenster sitzend wühlt Georg in diesem Gemeinsamen mit Wollust, glaubt den Vater in sich zu haben und hält alles, bis auf eine flüchtige traurige Nachdenklichkeit für friedlich. Die Entwicklung der Geschichte zeigt nun, wie aus dem Gemeinsamen, dem Freund, der Vater hervorsteigt und sich als Gegensatz Georg gegenüber aufstellt, verstärkt durch andere kleinere Gemeinsamkeiten, nämlich durch die Liebe, Anhänglichkeit der Mutter, durch die treue Erinnerung an sie und durch die Kundschaft, die ja der Vater doch ursprünglich für das Geschäft erworben hat. Georg hat nichts; die Braut, die in der Geschichte nur durch die Beziehung zum Freund, also zum Gemeinsamen, lebt, und die, da eben noch nicht Hochzeit war, in den Blutkreis, der sich um Vater und Sohn zieht, nicht eintreten kann, wird vom Vater leicht vertrieben. Das Gemeinsame ist alles um den Vater aufgetürmt. Georg fühlt es nur als Fremdes, Selbständig-Gewordenes, von ihm niemals genug Beschütztes, russischen Revolutionen Ausgesetztes, und nur weil er selbst nichts mehr hat als den Blick auf den Vater, wirkt das Urteil, das ihm den Vater gänzlich verschließt, so stark auf ihn. Georg hat so viel Buchstaben wie Franz. In Bendemann ist 'Mann' nur eine für alle noch unbekannten Möglichkeiten der Geschichte vorgenommene Verstärkung von 'Bende'. Bende aber hat ebenso viele Buchstaben wie Kafka und der Vokal e wiederholt sich an den gleichen Stellen wie der Vokal a in Kafka. Frieda hat ebensoviel Buchstaben wie F. und den gleichen Anfangsbuchstaben, Brandenfeld hat den gleichen Anfangsbuchstaben wie B. und durch das Wort 'Feld' auch in der Bedeutung eine gewisse Beziehung. Vielleicht ist sogar der Gedanke an Berlin nicht ohne Einfluß gewesen und die Erinnerung an die Mark Brandenburg hat vielleicht eingewirkt. (*Tb* 296f.)

Much has, of course, been made of the last two paragraphs of this commentary, especially by those with a penchant for biographical and Freudian allegoresis (cf. Beicken, 1974:24ff.; Binder, 1975: 123ff.; A. Flores, 1976a). However, what many of such interpreters fail to point out is that the somewhat contrived nominal correspondences proposed by Kafka did not occur to him until 11th February, 1913, that is, almost five months after he had written the story. As he, himself, was to say of them in a letter to Felice on 2nd June, 1913: "das sind natürlich lauter Dinge, die ich erst später herausgefunden habe" (*Bf* 394). Furthermore, when Janouch, referring to the central character of *Die Verwandlung*, suggested a similar equation between the names 'Kafka' and 'Samsa', Kafka firmly rejected the idea: "Kafka unterbrach mich. 'Es ist kein Kryptogramm, Samsa ist nicht restlos Kafka. *Die Verwandlung* ist kein Bekenntnis, obwohl es — im gewissen Sinne — eine Indiskretion ist'" (*Gk* 55). It ist clearly wrong, therefore, to suppose that Kafka's attempt to equate Georg Bendemann and his fiancée, Frieda Brandenfeld, with himself and Felice Bauer (to whom, at the time, he was not engaged) testifies to an allegorical literary intention. Rather, in making these remarks, Kafka seems merely to have been indulging a personal idiosyncrasy, namely, the tendency to regard his works as being prophetic of his life, a further example of which is provided by his comment about the diagnosis of his tuberculosis, in part of a letter where he is addressing Brod: "Auch habe ich es selbst vorausgesagt. Erinnerst Du Dich an die Blutwunde im *Landarzt*?" (*Br* 160). That Kafka, in seeking to create such biographical correspondences, is tending to allegorise his texts cannot be denied. However, as Frye (1965:13) and Quilligan (1979:31f.) have both pointed out, allegoresis does not transform a work into an actual allegory. And, according to the structural principle enunciated by the majority of contemporary scholars, there is no evidence that, at the time of their composition, Kafka intended any of his works to be actual allegories.

A second defining characteristic of allegory about which recent studies reveal general agreement is the nature of its purpose or aim and, by implication, its source. This, most scholars now maintain, is to be described as ideological or idealistic. Honig (1959), for example, regards allegory as communicating "a vital belief" (op.cit.: 12) and "serving the expression of ideological aims" (ibid.:179), while Fletcher (1964) believes that it has "an ideal character" (op. cit.:349) and is "classically used for didactic and moral suasion" (ibid.:120). Similarly, Clifford (1974) observes that, in allegory, "the structure of the fiction is dominated or preceded by the ideological structure", so that it becomes "overtly moralistic or didactic" (op.cit.:7). Finally, Quilligan (1979), who generally condemns and studiously avoids notions associated with the traditional definition of allegory, nevertheless shows a close affinity with the views already quoted, when she asserts that "all allegories incorporate the Bible into their texts" (op.cit.:96) and, soon afterwards, abandons the Bible in favour of "any text which offers a legitimate language in which to articulate the sacred" (ibid.:100). Earlier she also declares that the experience of allegory brings the reader to a consciousness of "his relation to the only 'other' which allegory aims to lead him to, a sense of the sacred" (ibid.:29). In other words, she, too, considers that allegory proceeds from, and strives to guide the reader towards, a form of ideological or idealistic awareness. It is simply that she would rather ignore the obvious political allegory in, for example, Dryden's *Absalom and Achitophel* or Swift's *Tale of a Tub*, and limit this awareness to the religious.

Given this broad consensus, the question now becomes whether Kafka actually accepted or adhered to some coherent system of 'vital beliefs', some ideology or form of idealism, since if he did not, it would obviously be impossible for him to proceed from it or to attempt to persuade his readers of it. And, despite the contrary views of Zionists, theologians of crisis, Existentialists, Freudians, Marxists and so on, the clear answer to this question, on the basis of available biographical and literary evidence, is that he did not.[3] Certainly his works, both literary and otherwise, imply a set of personal values, even an individual view of life. But the same may be said of any number of writers, including many that no-one would ever consider calling allegorists, for the simple reason that a set of personal values does not amount to an ideology. Indeed, in

Kafka's case, it does not even amount to an individual system of 'vital beliefs', let alone a form of idealism (cf. Foulkes, 1967). As he, himself, put it, on 25th February, 1918, in a statement that no allegorist could ever have written:

Es ist nicht Trägheit, böser Wille, Ungeschicklichkeit — wenn auch von alledem etwas dabei ist, weil 'das Ungeziefer aus dem Nichts geboren wird' — welche mir alles mißlingen oder nicht einmal mißlingen lassen: Familien-leben, Freundschaft, Ehe, Beruf, Literatur, sondern es ist der Mangel des Bodens, der Luft, des Gebotes. Diese zu schaffen ist meine Aufgabe, nicht damit ich dann das Versäumte etwa nachholen kann, sondern damit ich nichts versäumt habe, denn die Aufgabe ist so gut wie eine andere. Es ist sogar die ursprünglichste Aufgabe oder zumindest ihr Abglanz, so wie man beim Ersteigen einer luftdünnen Höhe plötzlich in den Schein der fernen Sonne treten kann. Es ist das auch keine ausnahmsweise Aufgabe, sie ist gewiß schon oft gestellt worden. Ob allerdings in solchem Ausmaß, weiß ich nicht. Ich habe von den Erfordernissen des Lebens gar nichts mitge-bracht, so viel ich weiß, sondern nur die allgemeine menschliche Schwäche. Mit dieser — in dieser Hinsicht ist es eine riesenhafte Kraft — habe ich das Negative meiner Zeit, die mir ja sehr nahe ist, die ich nie zu bekämpfen, sondern gewissermaßen zu vertreten das Recht habe, kräftig aufgenommen. An dem geringen Positiven sowie an dem äußersten, zum Positiven umkip-penden Negativen, hatte ich keinen ererbten Anteil. Ich bin nicht von der allerdings schon schwer sinkenden Hand des Christentums ins Leben ge-führt worden wie Kierkegaard und habe nicht den letzten Zipfel des davon-fliegenden jüdischen Gebetmantels noch gefangen wie die Zionisten. Ich bin Ende oder Anfang. (*Hv* 120f.; cf.*BkI* 281f.)

According, then, to the two fundamental criteria accepted in most modern studies of the subject, there is no justification whatever for the still common view that Kafka wrote allegories or for those numerous interpretations which treat his works as if they were allegories. Unfortunately, however, that is not an end to the matter. For, in his essay of 1957, Frye also advanced a related, radical view of interpretative commentary, which has since been fully endorsed by Honig (1958:285), Fletcher (1964:8), Clifford (1974: 33) and Quilligan (1979:15f.), and runs thus:

It is not often realised that all commentary is allegorical interpretation, an attaching of ideas to the structure of poetic imagery. The instant that any critic permits himself to make a genuine comment about a poem (e.g. 'In *Hamlet* Shakespeare appears to be portraying the tragedy of irresolution') he has begun to allegorise. (Frye, 1957:89)

Assuming, as it does, that all interpretative commentary employs the same methodology, this statement would, if it were true, justify any and all interpretations of Kafka's works, since it allows of no criterion by which to distinguish the valid from the invalid. And even if, as Frye (1965:13) later admits, this would not turn structurally non-allegorical works into genuine allegories, such a distinction would make no material difference at all to the possible range and variety of equally valid, even if totally conflicting and mutually exclusive interpretations permitted by his theory. Unless, therefore, the continuing babel among Kafka scholars is simply to be sanctioned, it must be shown that Frye's view and its underlying assumption are false.

One simple means of achieving this end is to compare several different interpretations of the same literary text, e.g. the title-piece of the present collection. Towards the end of his analysis, Brinkmann (1961) comments thus:

Nicht das Absurde, das Widersinnige und Widervernünftige triumphiert hier. Vom Ende her fällt (...) aus manchen bis dahin verborgenen Türen das Licht auf die Vorgänge. Es sind die schreckhaften Visionen der Existenzangst, die Widersprüche zwischen dem gewollten, motivierten, dem zweckvoll ausgerichteten Leben und der Wirklichkeit, die sich hier in den sich jagenden Bildern vom Landarzt kundgeben, der vor dem unlösbaren Widerspruch des eigenen Planens und großen Wollens im Dienste der Menschheit und der aus der Unzulänglichkeit des Menschen unberechenbaren Gegenmächte, die ihn zu vernichten drohen und die er als Verhängnis, als ausweglose Kette des Schicksals erlebt, steht. (op.cit.:41)

Five years later, Sokel (1966) provides a very different picture:

Images and plot of this tale enable us to see Kafka's works as pieces of an autobiography in metaphoric disguise. The 'call' of the night bell is a translation into sensory terms of Kafka's 'call' to literature, which he understood as an art of healing and self-preservation, a 'doctor's' art. (...) 'A Country Doctor' presents in the hieroglyphic language of dreams a clear and exact presentation of Kafka's inspirational process and the problems it posed for his life. (op.cit.:6f.)

Tiefenbrun (1973) varies the meaning even more radically:

> Kafka indicated within the totality of his writings that he was extremely ambivalent about his homosexual orientation. In 'The (sic!) Country Doctor', he regards it as a pigsty which provides him with unearthly horses which transport him figuratively; however, his homosexual inclinations also banish him to an icy realm in which he must live in uncompromising loneliness. (op.cit.:20)

Finally, Bridgwater (1974) construes the work thus:

> It is all too easy, when reading *Ein Landarzt*, to *mis*apply a Christian admiration for self-denial to the country-doctor's behaviour. To do so is necessarily to misinterpret the story. The simple fact of the matter is that the would-be 'Heiland' is in a 'heillos' position at the end of the story. (...) Essentially Kafka's story is concerned with Nietzsche's distinction between the Christian-ascetic view of self-denial as a virtue, and the Dionysian view of it as folly. (op.cit.:114f.)

Whatever one may consider to be the individual merits of these four interpretations, the clear and undeniable fact is that they are not methodologically identical. On the contrary, whereas the first moves from a consideration of the particular figures and events of the story to a generalisation of their significance, the last three proceed from the assumption that, although Kafka is creating a specific set of meanings within the story, he is actually intending or signalling a quite different, though equally specific set of meanings outside the story. Thus the interpretative method of the last three consists in replacing the particular, literal terms of the work with another, equally particular set of terms borrowed from autobiography, psychoanalysis and philosophy, respectively. In other words, whereas the last three interpreters quite arbitrarily treat Kafka's text as if it were an allegory, the first one does not. And from this it follows that Frye's notion of commentary is to be totally rejected. So, too, are all commentaries which assume Kafka's works to be allegorical when, even according to the criteria of the most recent, allegorical theory, they demonstrably are not.

Deserving of special mention, in this context, are those increasingly prevalent interpretations which reduce Kafka's oeuvre to a series of covert variations on the implicitly egotistic themes of Kafka writing about Kafka's reading[4] and Kafka writing about Kafka's writing.[5] Indeed, one example of this last approach has proven to be so influential and is still so widely accepted that it merits a detailed critique, particularly since it has also been adopted as an ostensibly reliable basis for dating the composition of several works in the present collection (Pasley/Wagenbach, 1964:157). The commentaries in question are, of course, those of Pasley.

As is now well known, in his biography of Kafka, Brod made the following remarks about the piece called *Elf Söhne*:

> Das Prosastück 'Elf Söhne' (...) ist meines Erachtens als Wunschbild einer Vaterschaft, einer Familiengründung zu verstehen, die dem Vorbild des Vaters etwas Gleichartiges, das heißt, ebenso Patriarchalisch-Großartiges, in aller Lebensschlichtheit ans Mythische Grenzendes entgegenhalten kann. Dieser Erklärung widerspricht es nicht, daß mir Franz einmal sagte: 'Die elf Söhne sind ganz einfach elf Geschichten, an denen ich jetzt gerade arbeite'. (Brod, 1954:145f.)

Rejecting Brod's commentary, however, Pasley decided to take Kafka's explanation quite literally and search for some clue to the allegedly literary identity of these sons. This he eventually found in a list of works originally contained in the so-called sixth octavo notebook (*Hv* 447). There the title *Elf Söhne* appeared as the last in a series of twelve pieces, the other eleven being, in order: "*Ein Traum, Vor dem Gesetz, Eine kaiserliche Botschaft, Die kurze Zeit* (d.h. *Das nächste Dorf*), *Ein altes Blatt, Schakale und Araber, Auf der Gallerie* (sic!), *Der Kübelreiter, Ein Landarzt, Der neue Advokat* und *Ein Brudermord*" (Pasley, 1965:22). These pieces, he therefore concluded, were the sons being discussed in *Elf Söhne*, and their order, he attempted to show, corresponded to that of the sons as portrayed by their father.

Pursuing the metaphor of literary paternity, Pasley then moved on to *Die Sorge des Hausvaters*. Here further clues were provided by the worry Kafka suffered because of his inability to complete so many works, as well as the fact that the central character of the piece is referred to as a child. From this and other extrinsic evidence (e.g. Italian 'gracchio' = Czech 'kavka'), he proceeded to identify Odradek with the fragmentary work, *Der Jäger Gracchus*. Finally his attention was drawn to *Ein Besuch im Bergwerk*, where "eine scheinbar willkürliche und gar sinnlose Aufzählung einzelner Figuren, die dennoch eine zusammenhängende Gruppe bilden" (op.cit.:31) reminded him of *Elf Söhne*. However, this time there was no question of a father-son relationship, but rather of an inferior worker portraying his superiors. Translated into literary terms, this became Kafka being visited by ten authors represented in Wolff's *Der neue Roman, ein Almanach* (1917), writers such as Heinrich Mann, Hofmannsthal, Sternheim and Brod, all of whom Kafka considered his betters. And the self-important *Kanzleidiener* accompanying the engineers is identified with the employee of Wolff's press who provided 48 pages of editorial information at the end of the almanac.

Since the publication of Pasley's startling theories, there has, of course, been no lack of opposition to them. Politzer (1965), for example, regards them as reducing Kafka's work to the "Niveau eines Gesellschaftsspiels 'Wer ist Wer bei Kafka?'" (op.cit.:151). In a similar vein, but referring only to *Elf Söhne*, David (1971) rejects Pasley's commentary as "eine positivistische Interpretation" that robs the text of "jeder tieferen Bedeutung" und reintroduces the allegorical methods of earlier Kafka criticism (op.cit.:249), although it should be pointed out that his alternative interpretation is methodologically little better, since it, too, becomes allegorical in arbitrarily identifying the eleventh son with Kafka and the religious belief that eleven represents "die Sünde" (ibid.:259). Gray (1973) also limits his remarks to *Elf Söhne*, maintaining that Pasley's "suggestion, if true, does little honour to Kafka, and attributes to him a mode of writing found nowhere else" (op.cit.:127). Beicken (1974: 146f.), on the other hand, agrees with Kobs (1970:80) in endorsing Pasley's explanation of *Elf Söhne*, because it is allegedly attested by Kafka. But both reject the other two 'mystifications' as unproven, allegorical theses, a view also shared by Hillmann (1967) and Krusche (1974:82), at least in the case of *Die Sorge des Hausvaters*.

Despite these criticisms, however, Pasley (1971) has more recently defended his position and even extended the significance of his explicative procedure, while Mitchell (1974) and Böschenstein (1980), following suggestions in Kobs (1970:80) and Binder (1975: 223), respectively, have provided variations on Pasley's version of *Elf Söhne*, employing the same "allegorisch-genetische" method (Hillmann, 1967:206), but reversing, with slight divergences, the order of the literary 'sons' on Kafka's list. For the rest, acceptance has been general, and no-one at all has proposed re-examining the dates of composition derived from such extraordinary interpretations. Yet, quite apart from the preceding arguments of this study about Kafka and allegory or allegoresis, there are several, very good reasons for submitting that, even in the case of *Elf Söhne*, the only work of the three where there is any justification whatever for Pasley's approach, his views are misguided and should be rejected.

When Kafka explained to Brod: "Die elf Söhne sind ganz einfach elf Geschichten, an denen ich jetzt gerade arbeite", he also tacitly confronted the would-be interpreter with two central problems. The first and more specific, based on a literal understanding of his statement, consists in the challenge to discover which stories he could possibly have had in mind. And since that issue has already been settled by Pasley, at least to the satisfaction of the vast majority, it would seem unnecessary to pursue the matter further. However, if the actual wording of Kafka's explanation is considered more carefully, it becomes apparent that Pasley's solution cannot possibly be correct. For, implicit in Kafka's remark are not only the facts that he had already written *Elf Söhne* and that Brod had read it, but also the clear indication that the stories allegedly representative of the sons were, at that stage, incomplete or at least not yet in a form the author regarded as final. However, according to reliable evidence from other sources (Pasley/Wagenbach, 1964:164; 1965:67; Binder, 1975:223f.), it is known that *Elf Söhne* was almost certainly composed towards the end of March, 1917, which must be regarded as the *datum ante quem* for the conversation between Kafka and Brod. Yet, by that time, two of the pieces in the list adopted by Pasley were not only complete; each of them had also appeared in print no fewer than three times. The works in question are *Vor dem Gesetz* and *Ein Traum*. As Dietz (1982) has just demonstrated, the former was first published in the journal *Selbstwehr*, in September, 1915, then in the literary almanac *Vom jüngsten Tag*, 1916 (actually 1915) and in a second, revised edition of the same anthology, printed in November, 1916 (op.cit.:62, 74, 82), while *Ein Traum* was published in two separate literary journals during 1916, *Das jüdische Prag* and *Der Almanach der neuen Jugend auf das Jahr 1917*, then in the *Prager Tagblatt* of 6th January, 1917 (ibid.:83f.). In the light of this information, it would obviously be nonsensical for Kafka, at some time after the end of March, 1917, to refer to either of these works as "Geschichten, an denen ich jetzt gerade arbeite". Consequently the list adopted by Pasley and his resultant series of ostensible identifications must both be rejected, while the related dates of composition clearly need to be reconsidered.

The second, more general problem raised by Kafka's statement is the necessity to decide whether it is to be taken literally or not. In other words, given the fallacy of Pasley's argument, should scholars continue to cast about for a group of stories that Kafka evidently had in mind, or should they construe his remark to Brod in some other way? To answer this question with complete certainty is now, of course, impossible. However, there are certain indicators which make it very inprobable, indeed, that Kafka meant his words to be taken literally. Not the least among these is the fact that Brod, himself, did not understand him in this fashion. After all, he was not only present when Kafka passed the remark, but has also reported that, even when Kafka was discussing his will, the two of them spoke "in jenem scherzhaften Ton (...), der unter uns üblich war, jedoch mit dem heimlichen Ernst, den wir dabei stets einer bei dem andern voraussetzten" (*Pz* 318). It would not seem unreasonable, therefore, to suspect a degree of irony or 'jocular seriousness' on this occasion as well.

Much weightier evidence against a literal interpretation, however, is to be found in Kafka's conception of the creative writer and of literature as art. At the end of September, 1917, he noted in his diary that he would find true happiness as an author only if he could raise "die Welt ins Reine, Wahre, Unveränderliche" (*Tb* 534), and years later, in his exchanges with Janouch, he attributed this aim to the creative writer in general: "Literatur bemüht sich, die Dinge in ein angenehmes, gefälliges Licht zu stellen. Der Dichter ist aber gezwungen, die Dinge in den Bereich der Wahrheit, Reinheit und Dauer emporzuheben" (*Gk* 84). Indeed, lasting truth and its light are frequently associated, in his recorded comments, with the nature and purpose of creative writing: "Dichtung ist immer nur eine Expedition nach der Wahrheit (...). Die Wahrheit ist das, was jeder Mensch zum Leben braucht und doch von niemand bekommen oder erstehen kann. Jeder Mensch muß sie aus dem eigenen Inneren immer wieder produzieren, sonst vergeht er. Leben ohne Wahrheit ist unmöglich" (*Gk* 224); "Unsere Kunst ist ein von der Wahrheit Geblendet-Sein: Das Licht auf dem zurückweichenden Fratzengesicht ist wahr, sonst nichts" (*Hv* 46, 93f.); "Die Kunst fliegt um die Wahrheit, aber mit der entschiedenen Absicht, sich nicht zu verbrennen. Ihre Fähigkeit besteht darin, in der dunklen Leere einen Ort zu finden, wo der Strahl des Lichts, ohne daß dies vorher zu erkennen gewesen wäre, kräftig angefangen werden kann" (*Hv* 104). From these and other examples that could be quoted (e.g. *Br* 27; *Tb* 563f.; *Bf* 595; *Gk* 74f., 191, 231), it must surely follow that, unless Kafka was being totally untrue to himself, he could not possibly have indulged in the form of literary mystification which is now so widely attributed to him. But in case there should still be some lingering doubt, one final sentence from his alleged conversations with Janouch may help to dispel it: "Die Kunst ist nicht eine Frage der rasch dahinschwindenden Verblüffung, sondern des lange wirkenden Beispiels" (*Gk* 220).

Assuming, then, that Kafka's remark to Brod was not intended to be taken literally, what meaning, if any, is to be attached to it? The only valid means of answering this question is to undertake a detailed, non-allegorical analysis of the text in question, since, from the literary point of view, it is the work that gives significance to Kafka's explanation and not vice versa. And although such an analysis will be provided later in this study, it now becomes necessary to anticipate its findings, if this discussion, itself, is not to conclude in mystification.

Like *Die Sorge des Hausvaters*, *Elf Söhne* implicitly challenges the notion of fatherhood as an unequivocal and enduring existential value. This it does by indirectly presenting a father whose loving dissatisfaction with his children derives not so much from the particular faults of each son as from the father's own knowledge that, in them, he has failed to overcome himself. The positive fulfilment he had evidently hoped to find in procreation has been denied him. In his sons he has merely propagated his own imperfection.

To anyone familiar with Kafka's constant criticisms of his own work, the ironic meaning of his statement will now be only too apparent. So will the futility of attempts to identify the individual sons with particular texts, since at various times Kafka was inclined to incinerate the lot. As for the specific number of eleven sons and eleven stories, an explanation will be offered in the appropriate place. At this juncture, the crucial point to be reiterated is that Pasley's admittedly ingenious and profoundly influential interpretations of Kafka's three works are simply an extreme form of that pervasive, but entirely ill-founded, critical method which either deems Kafka's literary texts to be actual allegories or arbitrarily treats them as if they were. Once and for all, it should be acknowledged that there is no reliable evidence to support this allegorical theory or practice and that, regardless of the multifarious forms it may assume, it should finally be abandoned by serious Kafka interpreters (cf. *Bf* 596; *Gk* 205).

Parabolik

At the same time as E. Heller, Anders and Emrich were attempting to reduce the confusion in Kafka studies by rejecting what they regarded as false interpretative methods and proposing various alternatives, another group of scholars began to adopt a radically different approach. Led by Politzer, who, within a decade of Kafka's death, had asserted that analysis of *Vor dem Gesetz* demonstrated "die Unmöglichkeit eines eindeutigen Ergebnisses" (Politzer, 1934:77), these writers inclined increasingly to the belief that the reason for the ever widening range of views about Kafka's works lay not so much in the preconceptions of misguided ideologues as in the actual nature or structure of the texts themselves. In other words, whereas previous interpreters, whether allegorical or not, had tacitly assumed that each of Kafka's works could have but one meaning and that the task of explication consisted in uncovering and defining that particular meaning, this school of thought maintained, to the contrary, that all of the works were actually and inherently *mehrdeutig, vieldeutig* or ambiguous and thus open to a potentially infinite number of valid, divergent readings.

Although this theory had been anticipated in earlier statements by Politzer (1934; 1939; 1946; 1950), Bense (1952:90), Martini (1954:303) and even Emrich (1954:230), its first explicit proponent seems to have been Busacca (1958). Discussing *Ein Landarzt*, Busacca argued that the story was structured according to a "comparatively simple" system of "*primary* relations" (op.cit.:49) based on two age-old notions about the nature of earthly reality:

> The world assumed by Aesop is rational and orderly. The only variables are the sentient beings. But such a construction of the world has, in human history, stood only as Working Hypothesis A. Working Hypothesis B, equally ancient, assumes a world in which tragedy is natural and inevitable, assumes that order is not a fact of nature but a limited and fallible human construct. In the 'B' world, which is perhaps as valid as the 'A', any rationale of behaviour which assumes a thoroughly orderly universe must be more or less mistaken, tragic to participate in, comic to view — if viewed, with detachment, from a 'B' world standpoint.
> Franz Kafka, who properly regarded his writings as comic, is clearly of the 'B' world. (ibid.:45f.)

Having thus defined the 'primary relations', Busacca then gives his explanation of the story: "A man glimpses the 'B' world, and is shocked out of 'rationalistic complacency', out of the 'A' world, for the shock transforms his sense of his own human role, jolts him into a new ontology" (ibid.:49). And since this system of 'primary relations' is, of necessity, very general, it allows of many specific interpretations: "Taken as *oracle* (...), if one picks vocabulary from the 'B' world, or as *slide rule*, if from the 'A', the story may be particularised, for those who insist upon particularisations, in the contexts of numberless analogues; for once the primary *relations* are apparent, there is no problem in providing *termini*" (ibid.:51). Furthermore, all of these "analogues offered by the explicators are perfectly sound; what is ridiculous is the insistence of each explicator that the others are wrong" (ibid.:46).

However extreme Busacca's views may appear, even today, they were nevertheless very quickly and firmly supported by the much more detailed, wide-ranging studies of Pongs (1960), Dentan (1961) and Politzer (1962; 1965). For, despite obvious differences among these three scholars in their approach, terminology and degree of tolerance towards previous interpretations (cf. Politzer, 1962:10f.), they were unanimous in affirming the notion that the very essence of Kafka's works resided in their intrinsic *Vieldeutigkeit*, and that this quality derived from what a contemporary grammarian might term their 'deep structure' or as Hillmann (1964:165; 1967:208ff.), borrowing from Mahler (1958:46ff.), was to put it, the *Modell* they embodied. Thus there became established a mode of critical theory and practice which was to dominate Kafka scholarship throughout the 1960's and beyond, as is witnessed by the writings of Garaudy (1963:177), Altenhöner (1964:67f.), Hillmann (1964:166; 1965: 270; 1967:210), Hasselblatt (1964:144f.), P. Heller (1966; 1974), Fingerhut (1969:299), Gaier (1969) and Sussman (1977:49).

Yet, for all the valuable insights provided by these scholars, not least in their attempts to define the actual structure of Kafka's works, their central argument is profoundly flawed. Quite apart from the unjustified relativism implicit in their regarding all forms of Kafka interpretation as being equally valid or invalid, they also assumed that Kafka's work was essentially static, a long series of variations on one basic, abstract structure of relations or ideas, when their own analyses clearly show that it is not. By far their most serious error, however, was their failure to realise that, in proposing *Modelle* of Kafka's works, they were also engaging in interpretation and thus falling victims to their own argument. For if it is true that Kafka's works are inherently *mehrdeutig*, *vieldeutig* or ambiguous and that all interpretations of them are therefore equally valid or invalid, then the second of these propositions must apply to the first as well, since that, too, is an interpretation. Consequently, the argument is self-defeating. The same conclusion can be reached in another way as well. To maintain that Kafka's works are intrinsically *vieldeutig* is simultaneously to assert, at least in the terms of these scholars, that the works are incapable of being reduced to a single interpretation. Yet, in order to assert that the works are *vieldeutig*, one must do

38

precisely what, according to these scholars, their own proposition precludes, that is, one must reduce the works to a single interpretation, namely, that they are *vieldeutig*. Thus, as already pointed out, such an argument is logically impossible and should be totally repudiated. So, too, should the use of that now ubiquitous, but generally quite inappropriate term 'parable', which these scholars popularised as a description of some, if not all of Kafka's literary structures in their allegedly inherent *Vieldeutigkeit*.

The first to designate one of Kafka's works a parable seems to have been Politzer (1939), but critical discussion of the term's applicability did not begin until the 1950's, when the studies of Heselhaus (1952) and Heldmann (1953) appeared. And according to both of these scholars, the nature of the parable resides essentially in its content, which relates the contingent and human to the absolute, divine. Referring to the various transformed beings in Kafka's works, Heselhaus puts the matter thus:

> Die Kafkasche Metamorphose ist weder märchenhaft noch mythisch: sie gehört in einen theologischen Bereich. Ich würde sie (...) als *parabolische* Metamorphose bezeichnen; d.h. sie weist schon als Phämomen, als bloßes Geschehnis über sich hinaus.(...) Die Geschlagenheit der Kreatur, die Erfahrung des Menschenseins als eines kreatürlich-gefährdeten Zustandes wird das Tor zum Absoluten, indem der sinnbildliche Charakter — die Bezogenheit des Menschen auf ein Höheres, Absolutes — in der Sprache, in den Bildern, im Vorgang des Erzählten faßbar wird. (op.cit.:366)

In a very similar vein, Heldmann asserts: "Es wird nämlich die Erfahrensweise eines bestimmten Verhältnisses des Menschen zum Absoluten sichtbar. In Anlehnung an diese — in der Parabel vorherrschende — Thematik soll die Erfahrensweise dieses Verhältnisses: das Parabolische genannt werden" (op.cit.:7).

Despite the obvious weaknesses in these statements, which, if they were correct, would render virtually all religious art parabolic, the criterion of content remained a frequent means of attempting to define the concept under consideration. Emrich (1958), for example, maintained that parables were possible only "vor dem Hintergrund einer fest umrissenen Religion, Philosophie oder Weltanschauung. Der Hintergrund der Kafkaschen 'Parabeln' aber ist leer" (op.cit.:77). Pongs (1960) disagreed with Emrich, but apart from acknowledging the didactic purpose of the genre, still discussed it very largely in terms of content: "Wie einst parabola die Gleichnisreden Jesu bezeichneten, erwächst hier die gleichnishafte Lehrform, einer absurden Zeit ihr Gleichnis des Absurden vor die Augen zu bringen, damit sie sich selbst in den Fängen des Bösen erkennt, ein lichtloses Geschlecht in der Welt als Labyrinth" (op.cit.:53; s.a. 60ff.). Finally, Politzer (1962), while adding the ostensibly structural notion of *Vieldeutigkeit*, also equated the parable with a particular set of ideas:

> All that Kafka ever wrested from the silence surrounding him was the insight 'that the incomprehensible is incomprehensible, and this we already knew'. The phrase is taken from a longer aphorism with the revealing title, *On Parables*.(...) (Kafka's) parables are as multilayered as their Biblical models. But, like them, they are also multifaceted, ambiguous, and capable of so many interpretations that, in the final analysis, they defy any and all. (op.cit.:21)

Recognising the fallacy of attempting to define a literary genre exclusively or even primarily according to its thought-content, Mahler (1958) sought to provide a more adequate justification for applying the term 'parable' to the works of Kafka and other modern writers. Accepting, like Heselhaus (1966:9), the definitions in Jülicher's unfortunately quite outdated two-volume study *Die Gleichnisreden Jesu* of 1888/89 (cf. McDonald, 1966:1827) and adopting Kahler's view (1953) that the modern novel was transforming itself "*zur Parabel*, zur Beispielsgeschichte, deren Vorgang von vornherein nur das Modell einer spirituellen Erfahrung, wenn nicht gar einer Lehre ist" (op.cit.:34), Mahler undertook a structural analysis of the genre and arrived at the following conclusions:

> Dieser Typ der Erzählung, die modellhaft eine Fülle von prinzipiell gleichgebauten Situationen analogieartig enthält und sozusagen eine Ur-oder Elementarsituation repräsentiert, die in unzähligen Alltagssituationen mehr oder weniger aufleuchten kann, soll hier (im Anschluß an Jülicher) parabolische Erzählung oder Parabel genannt werden. Wichtig ist, daß das Detail nicht identifiziert werden darf. Weil die Parabel nur der geistigen Wirklichkeit des Problems, bzw. des 'Sinnes' verpflichtet ist und von diesem ihre

Realität — aus zweiter Hand — bezieht, ist sie uneigentliche Darstellung, als solche der 'Natur' nicht verpflichtet und eine nichtrealistische Erzählform wie auch die Allegorie. Der bedeutendste und auch ausschließlichste Vertreter dieser Gattung in der Moderne ist Franz Kafka. (op.cit.: 46f.)

Later, he also speaks of the "Vieldeutigkeit und Allgemeinheit im Besonderen der dargestellten Situation, die der Gattung Parabel eigen ist" (ibid.:74).

Despite certain important refinements to Mahler's theory proposed by Hillmann (1964:163ff.), Sokel (1967), Fülleborn (1969) and especially Elm (1976), the actual substance of his definition has gained almost universal acceptance, as is witnessed not only by the currency his broad sense of the term has gained among the vast majority of Kafka scholars, but also by the continuing flow of publications which directly or indirectly support his arguments, e.g. Eastman (1960), Wiese (1962), Auden (1963), Henel (1963), Deinert (1964), Brandstetter (1966), Brettschneider (1971), Lawson (1972), H. Kraft (1972), Wäsche (1976) and Pascal (1974; 1977; 1980).[6] At least one scholar, however, ultimately came to the realisation that, before Mahler's definition could be allowed to stand, it needed to be thoroughly tested against the findings of more recent Biblical scholarship, since it was, after all, on the conclusions of much earlier Biblical analysis that its validity so heavily depended. Consequently, Philippi (1969) undertook a review of relevant exegetical studies by contemporary German, evangelical theologians, especially Linnemann, Bultmann and Fuchs. And the principal outcome of his survey was a revised distinction between the terms *Gleichnis* and *Parabel*, according to their structure, content and purpose:

Das Gleichnis — bisher von uns in dem weiten Sinn gebraucht, der eine recht undifferenzierte Verwendung der Begriffe Gleichnis und Parabel erlauben konnte — unterscheidet sich, gebraucht man den Begriff in einem engeren, spezifischeren Sinn, als wir es bisher mit der Tradition getan haben, deutlich von der Parabel. Es baut auf dem Vergleich auf, bei dem etwas für ein anderes eintritt. Es erweitert ihn zum Satz, zur Erzählung. Es schildert vor allem 'einen typischen Zustand oder typischen bzw. regelmäßigen Vorgang'. In jedem Fall beruft es sich auf Allgemeingültiges. Das

Bild ist aus der alltäglichen, jedem zugänglichen Wirklichkeit genommen; es besitzt die Autorität des allgemein Bekannten (op.cit.:314).
Die Parabel führt ein Verhalten, das die Situation erfordert, an einem entsprechenden, aber nicht deckungsgleichen vor. Die Erzählung nötigt zur Wertung: Sie soll von ihrem Zentrum her auf eine andere Ebene, vom 'Bild' auf die 'Sache' übertragen werden. Ihre Anschaulichkeit fingiert Realität. Die *analogia*, Entsprechung zur Sache verlangt, diese aufzufinden, zu ihr überzugehen.
Dabei hat die Parabel nur einen zentralen Vergleichspunkt, ohne Vergleichspartikel zu benutzen. Die (erzählte) Wirklichkeit wird von einem vorausliegenden her auf einen von einer Argumentationsabsicht gesteuerten Ablauf reduziert, Seitenkomplexe werden weitgehend ausgeschaltet. (...) Die Parabel ist eine Form des Denkens so sehr wie eine des Erzählens. Sie muß bewußt gebraucht werden; sie hat ein Ziel, das sie erkennbar machen will. Sie lehrt aber nicht, sondern fordert zum Vollzug auf. (ibid.325f.)

The first point that needs to be made about this distinction is that it does not have the support of at least one of Philippi's main authorities, Fuchs (ibid.:314). The second and far more important point, however, is that, if one applies Philippi's criteria with any rigour to those passages designated as parables in the synoptic gospels of *The Jerusalem Bible* (1966), then not just a few, but a clear majority of them fit into neither of his categories. For some, including the famous story of the good Samaritan (Lk 10:29-37), are *parabolisch* in their content and lack of a *Vergleichspartikel*, but nevertheless quite openly teach (e.g. Mk 12:1-12; Lk 16:1-8, 18:9-14, 19:11-17, 20:9-19), while others are *parabolisch* as regards *Vergleichspartikel* and explicit teaching, but are *gleichnishaft* in content (e.g. Mt 13:4-9; Mk 4:1-9; Lk 8:4-8). Similarly, some are *gleichnishaft* in containing a *Vergleichspartikel* and an overt lesson, but are more *parabolisch* in content (e.g. Mt 13:24-30, 22:1-14, 25:1-13, 15:14-30), while others are *gleichnishaft* in content and teaching, but lack a *Vergleichspartikel* (e.g. Mt 21:28-32; Mk 4:21-23, 4:24-25; Lk 8:16-18). Obviously, then, Philippi's proposed distinction is invalid and should be rejected, despite the accurate insights his article otherwise affords. However, if one combines certain of these insights with those of some contemporary, English-speaking exegetes (Navone, 1964; McDonald, 1966; Galloway, 1967), there emerges a sufficiently clear image of the parable to finally demonstrate whether and to what extent

Kafka's works may truly be described as exemplifying this genre.

In the joint, though not always unanimous view of these scholars, a parable is a brief, essentially narrative statement, sometimes no longer than a single sentence (e.g. Mt 13:33, 44-46), which serves to teach one quite specific point by means of self-evident analogy or "a developed comparison" (Galloway, 1967:1954). Although this indispensable analogical framework (cf. Philippi, 1969:314f.) need not take the direct form of an explicit simile ("The kingdom of heaven is like ..."), it must nevertheless be unequivocally established by the immediate context, if the parable is to achieve its overtly didactic purpose (cf. parables of the good Samaritan, the prodigal son, etc.). Furthermore, because each parable is intended to clarify only a single point, all its content is subordinated to that particular end. Consequently, any attempt to elaborate parallels between the details of the things compared is alien to its nature and results in allegoresis, at least one example of which is provided by the synoptic gospels, themselves (Mt 13:18-23; Mk 4:13-20; Lk 8:11-15), and has been explained by Galloway (1967) as "a later formulation by which the early church adapted the teaching of Christ to contemporary needs in a perennially valid way" (op.cit.: 1959; cf. McDonald, 1966:1823, 1826; Navone, 1964:924).

If one accepts this current definition (cf. Elm, 1976:492ff.), it will be obvious that to classify all or even most of Kafka's works as parables or 'parabolische Erzählungen' is simply to misunderstand the nature of the genre in question, a view towards which Binder (1966:197; 1979b:58ff.) also inclines. For, of the collected texts now published, only two satisfy all the criteria of the parable: *Vor dem Gesetz* in its original context of *Der Prozeß* (*Pz* 255f.) and *Eine kaiserliche Botschaft* in its original context of *Beim Bau der chinesischen Mauer* (*BkI* 77f.).[7] Removed from their original contexts, however, as they are in the *Landarzt* collection, even these two works cease to be parables.

In the face of these conclusions, it might easily be objected that a definition of the parable based on New Testament studies is irrelevant to Kafka, since he was not writing in the Christian tradition. Consequently, it needs to be pointed out that the above definition is not based exclusively on the evidence of the gospels, but also encompasses the theory and practice of Hellenic, Old Testament and Rabbinical literature as surveyed by Galloway (s.a. Heselhaus, 1966). And since these traditions are the very sources of our term 'parable', they must be relevant to its definition at any time and with reference to any writer.

Some scholars, however, maintain that Kafka and many other modern writers have radically modified this tradition by creating an "open parable" (Eastman, 1960; H. Kraft, 1972:61). What is to be made of their claims? Again, the answer is quite straightforward. Such a modification is manifestly and completely irreconcilable with the nature of the genre at issue. For a parable which is not 'a developed comparison', which lacks a self-evident and quite specific analogical framework, is simply no parable at all. Consequently, this and similar theories about the so-called modern parable (Elm, 1982) must be regarded not only as unproven, but also as unprovable.

Finally, there remains the related matter of Kafka's piece entitled *Von den Gleichnissen* (*BkI* 95), which was probably composed between the end of 1922 and the middle of 1923 (cf. Pasley/Wagenbach, 1964:74; Binder, 1975:299). Apart from Politzer (1962; 1965), many scholars have provided commentaries on this text (s. Beicken, 1974:168ff.) and, like Politzer, they have all assumed that, in using the term *Gleichnis*, Kafka intends 'parable' in the Biblical or some allegedly modern sense.[8] However, from the one example of *Gleichnis* given in the text, this assumption would appear to be unfounded.

> Viele beklagen sich, daß die Worte der Weisen immer wieder nur Gleichnisse seien, aber unverwendbar im täglichen Leben, und nur dieses allein haben wir. Wenn der Weise sagt: 'Gehe hinüber', so meint er nicht, daß man auf die andere Seite hinübergehen solle, (...) sondern er meint irgendein sagenhaftes Drüben, etwas, das wir nicht kennen, das auch von ihm nicht näher zu bezeichnen ist und das uns also gar nichts helfen kann. (*BkI* 95)

Provided one does not approach these words with a preconceived notion about the meaning of *Gleichnis*, it is clear that the expression 'Gehe hinüber' is intended as an example of the supposedly useless *Gleichnisse* of the wise, and that such an expression has as little in

44

common with the traditional notion of the parable as do Goethe's lines from the conclusion to *Faust II*: "Alles Vergängliche/ist nur ein Gleichnis" (1. 12104f.). Furthermore, from the ensuing commentary in the text, it becomes apparent that what the speaker has in mind is not, as Gaier (1969:294) believes, similes, but rather metaphors, or, more generally, the figurative use of language. In other words, the meaning being attached to the term *Gleichnis* in this context is very close to the following definition provided by one of Kafka's favourite references (cf. *Br* 169; Brod, 1954:130, 259; Wagenbach, 1958:90f.), namely, Grimm's *Deutsches Wörterbuch*: "'Sinnbild', 'Abbild' für ein Verhältnis tieferer Bedeutsamkeit besonders dort, wo ein Sichtbares ein Unsichtbares, ein Greifbares ein Ungreifbares ausdrückt, ein äußerer Gegenstand oder Vorgang bildhaft oder gestalthaft einen inneren verkörpert, repräsentiert". That this meaning of *Gleichnis* was current in Kafka's day is demonstrated by the sources quoted in Grimm, and its continuing currency is attested by Emrich (1958), who emphatically denies that Kafka's works are *Parabeln*, but readily grants them "einen Gleichnischarakter" (op.cit.:81). Viewed in this light, *Von den Gleichnissen* becomes a statement not about the nature of parables, but about the nature of language and, as such, it is anticipated by the diary entry of 6th December, 1921: "Die Metaphern sind eines in dem vielen, was mich am Schreiben verzweifeln läßt" (*Tb* 550), as well as the aphorism of 18th December, 1917: "Die Sprache kann für alles außerhalb der sinnlichen Welt nur andeutungsweise, aber niemals auch nur annähernd vergleichsweise gebraucht werden, da sie, entsprechend der sinnlichen Welt, nur vom Besitz und seinen Beziehungen handelt" (*Hv* 45, 92).

From the deliberations of this section, then, three main conclusions follow. First, the claim that Kafka's works are inherently *vieldeutig* and that all interpretations are therefore equally valid or invalid is a self-defeating argument and logically impossible. Second, with the exception of *Vor dem Gesetz* and *Eine kaiserliche Botschaft* in their original contexts, none of Kafka's works can be designated a parable without simultaneously contradicting the essential meaning of that term. Third, Kafka's use of the word *Gleichnis* bears no relation whatever to the traditional and still current understanding of the literary genre 'parable'. All of the widely held views opposed to these conclusions are therefore in need of revision.

Einsinnigkeit

Even before Kafka's works had been expounded as parabolic and inherently *vieldeutig*, yet another alternative to their allegorisation had been conceived and enunciated. This time the aim was to achieve true philological rigour, the scholar's overriding concern being not with speculative interpretation, but with the precise analysis and description of literary form. More specifically, the exponents of this critical method sought to provide a genuinely sound basis for the understanding of Kafka's texts by defining the actual nature and implications of the author's narrative technique, above all his use of perspective or point of view.

Initiating this approach, Beißner (1952) made the following crucial assertion: "Kafka erzählt, was anscheinend bisher nicht bemerkt worden ist, stets einsinnig, nicht nur in der Ich-Form, sondern auch in der dritten Person" (op.cit.:28). What this means, in Beißner's view, is that each of Kafka's works is narrated exclusively through its central character: "nichts wird ohne ihn oder gegen ihn, nichts in seiner Abwesenheit erzählt, nur seine Gedanken (...) weiß der Erzähler mitzuteilen" (loc.cit.). Since "die innere Welt" is, therefore, the subject of Kafka's stories and the narrator does not adopt the stance of a dispassionate observer, "so bleibt ihm kein anderer Platz als in der Seele seiner Hauptgestalt: er erzählt sich selbst (...)" (ibid.:29). As a consequence, none of Kafka's narrators, whether first-person or third-person, ever seems to know more than his characters or the reader at any given moment in time: "Der Erzähler (...) ist nirgends dem Erzählten voraus, auch wenn er im Praeteritum erzählt. Das Geschehen erzählt sich selber im Augenblick, in paradox praeteritaler Form (...)" (ibid.:32). Thus the narrator is "nicht nur mit der Hauptgestalt eines (und er ist es bei Kafka auch dann, wenn er in der dritten Person erzählt), sondern auch mit dem Erzählten" (ibid.:34). It is because Kafka's narrators lack any distance from the figures and events of their narratives that one finds in the latter "keine Reflexion über die Gestalten und über deren Handlungen und Gedanken. Es gibt nur den sich selbst (paradox praeterital) erzählenden Vorgang" (ibid.:35). Finally, owing to the identity between the narrator and the narrated in Kafka's works, the author transforms "nicht nur sich selbst, sondern auch den Leser in die Hauptgestalt. Er tritt keinen Augenblick aus dem auf das Innerseelische der Hauptgestalt gerichteten und um dieses Innerseelische erweiterten Zusammenhang heraus und entläßt auch den Leser nicht daraus, läßt ihn nicht los" (ibid.:36).

Despite the quite remarkable nature of Beißner's enterprise in his analysis of Kafka's oeuvre and the even more remarkable manner in which some of his conclusions are expressed, neither his first monograph nor its successor (Beißner, 1958) attacted much critical attention. Indeed, apart from Martini (1954:292ff.), Wiese (1956: 327f.) and Pascal (1956:249), all of whom accepted his theory in varying degrees, no other major scholar was to take cognisance of it for at least a decade, so that even Politzer (1962) still made no reference to it or its sequel in Walser (1961). The most likely reason for this neglect was Beißner's apparent failure to demonstrate the relevance of his theories to the task of interpretation. Yet, from the very beginning, the link between the two had always been present, as Martini (1954) clearly perceived, when he construed *Einsinnigkeit* as placing the phenomena of Kafka's world "in einen autonomen Raum der Existenz", inaccessible to human interpretation (op.cit.: 307), and as thus accounting for the essential mysteriousness and *Vieldeutigkeit* of the works (ibid.:303). For his part, however, Beißner originally drew the inference that, if his theory were correct, then the texts should be interpreted as studies in delusion. Thus *Die Verwandlung* presented "die traumhaft verzerrte Einsamkeit des erkrankten Helden, der sich in ein ungeheueres Ungeziefer verwandelt wähnt" (Beißner, 1952:36), while in *Der Prozeß* it was, in his opinion, all too evident, "daß alles, daß der ganze Prozeß ein innerseelisches Wahnbild eines in *vollständiger Erschöpfung* isolierten Geistes ist" (ibid.:39f.). But in his last two monographs, Beißner (1963;1972) considerably modified this position. Drawing on various frequently quoted passages from Kafka's diaries (e.g. *Tb* 420) and notebooks (e.g. *Hv* 72), he now concluded that the works were the representation of the author's "traumhaften, innern Lebens" (1963:

18f.), that their images were "Traumassoziationen" (ibid.:29), and that Kafka had created this "innere Welt", which can only be lived and not described (loc.cit.), in opposition to "der gottverlassenen modernen Zeit" (ibid.:33), as a defence against the contemporary "äußere Welt der Trümmer (...); gegen sie stellt Kafka seine unzerstörbare, innere, erschriebene Welt: sein traumhaftes, inneres Leben" (1972:11). Just how this made the works relevant to anyone but Kafka, except as a form of ultimately inexplicable, nightmarish escape (cf. Beißner, 1963:29), Beißner unfortunately did not indicate.

Ironically, the work that finally gave currency to Beißner's theories was one which considerably revised, even radicalised his ideas and had originally been submitted to him as a doctoral dissertation ten years earlier, namely, Walser's study (1961) of the three novels. Agreeing with Beißner that Kafka dispenses with the "erscheinenden Erzähler" (op.cit.:22) and places "den Gesichtspunkt der Perspektive seines Erzählens in den Helden" (ibid.:23), so that the reader experiences everything "mit ihm und durch ihn" (ibid.: 49), Walser nevertheless departs from Beißner in preferring to describe the relationship between author and central character as one of congruence rather than identity:

> Wir vermeiden es, von Identität zu sprechen, weil uns daran liegt, die Dekkung von Autor und Held technologisch zu sehen. Kongruenz heißt nicht, was Identität heißen könnte, daß der Held mit dem Autor meinungsidentisch ist. In der Kongruenz decken sich Autor und Held, wenn man es recht versteht, nur äußerlich, das heißt: erzählungstechnisch. (ibid.:135)

Regrettably, however, Walser never once explains the grounds for his distinction, that is, the criteria by which he has decided that the congruence between author and 'hero' is limited merely to the perceptual; yet the point is crucial to the remainder of his arguments about the nature of Kafka's works.

Similarly, although Walser agrees that everything constituting the three novels is filtered through the central character, he does not believe, like Beißner, that this creates an 'interior world' representing the psyche of either the 'heroes' or the author. On the contrary, taking into account the nature of time, space and character in these works, Walser is convinced, "daß es sich nicht um eine abgebildete, die vorhandene Wirklichkeit adäquat repräsentierende Welt handelt" (ibid.:140). Rather, Kafka's novels embody "eine Welt, die dem Bewußtsein gegenüber, das sie erschuf, Unabhängigkeit erlangt" (ibid.: 114), an ontologically autonomous world that is 'intrasubjective' (loc.cit.), even 'transcendental' (ibid.:103), and distinguished "vorwiegend durch ihre Geschaffenheit" (ibid.:49).

Within such an autonomously "organisierten Welt" (ibid.:58), Walser maintains, everything is subordinated to "Funktionalismus" (ibid.:59). This applies not only to the whole "Gegenwelt" encountered by the 'hero' and the circumstances in which he encounters it (time and space), but also to the 'hero' himself. For while the former exists solely for the purpose of "Aufhebung" (ibid.:79ff.), the latter's overriding function is self-assertion:

> Die Relation, in der die Ordnungen zueinander existieren, ist die Aufgehobenheit. Diese ist prinzipiell vorhanden. Sie wird von den Helden immer wieder durch die Behauptung ihrer eigenen Existenz gekündigt. Die K.s sind wesentlich auf nichts anderes als diese Behauptung hin angelegt: Behauptung ist ihr fundamentaler Existenzbeweis; der der Gegenordnung ist die Entfernung (als Vollzug). (ibid.:86)

Furthermore, "da die Gegenordnung unerschöpflich an aufhebender Kraft ist" (loc.cit.), the struggle of Kafka's 'heroes' "gegen das Aufgehobenwerden" is "endlos" (loc.cit.).

> Das heißt also, als allgemeinste Aussage über Kafkas Romane, daß *Tun* seinen pragmatischen Sinn verliert; jedem Tun ist seine Aufhebung immanent, weil es bei Kafka nur Tun von einander fremden Ordnungen gibt, und diese heben ihnen seinsfremde Tätigkeit eo ipso auf. Darum wird die Wiederholung zu einer Notwendigkeit. (ibid.:87)

The "Sinn" of Kafka's novels is therefore "eigentlich Sinnlosigkeit" (ibid.:117). Thus, in the same way that Beißner (1952:6ff.) had begun by denouncing allegorical 'translators' of Kafka's works, but had ultimately arrived at a form of biographism, if not Freudianism, Walser, too, rejects all "dichtungsfremden Kommentare" (op.cit.:11) on the very first page of his text, but eventually reaches exactly the same conclusion as Camus, who allegorises Kafka's oeuvre in terms of absurdist philosophy (Camus, 1948). And yet Walser steadfastly as-

49

serts that his analysis has in no way involved interpretation (op.cit.: 129)!

Immediately after the publication of Walser's study, though not always in response to it, *Einsinnigkeit* became increasingly the subject of critical discussion. Some scholars simply accepted the notion, at least in its technical aspects, without demur (Rhein, 1964:22; Jahn, 1965:6, 104; Pasley, 1966:7ff.). Fietz and Schillemeit, on the other hand, attempted to show that *Einsinnigkeit* actually implied *Undeutbarkeit*, that Kafka's works displayed "die Verabsolutierung des einsamen, subjektiven Erlebnisses", which is "in sich wertfrei, d.h. moralisch nicht mehr faßbar" (Fietz, 1963:75) or that "die Wirklichkeit, um die es in Kafkas Dichtung geht, ist keine andere als sie, die Dichtung selbst" (Schillemeit, 1966:579). Evidently it did not occur to either of them that, in regarding something as *undeutbar*, one is simultaneously and necessarily engaging in *Deuten*, so that their underlying argument is self-defeating.

By far the majority of scholars, however, sought to disprove the theories of Beißner and Walser by establishing the presence of a concealed, authorial or omniscient narrator. Wiese (1962) detected "eine Distanz zum Erzählten" indicating the "Dichter Kafka" behind the narrative (op.cit.:326), while Allemann (1963) believed Kafka's use of perspective to be "im Grunde rein funktional bestimmt, durch die eigentümliche Sehweise des verborgenen Erzählers" (op.cit.:240). Re-interpreting the so-called *Versehen* or *Verfehlungen* mentioned by Walser (1961:32, 137) and linking them with Kafka's use of summary, Leopold (1963) and Kudszus (1964; 1970) endeavoured to demonstrate the existence of important, authorial breaks in the "single limited perspective" (Leopold, 1963:31), but Beißner (1972) was inclined to dismiss such arguments as "törichte Beckmesserei" (op.cit.:39). Philippi and Langguth concentrated their attention, instead, on such narrative elements as the account of physical actions and the use of dialogue (cf. Sokel, 1964:396), from which they deduced that, although "the internal drama of the narrative (...) is all seen through K.'s eyes" (Langguth, 1968:52), the events which constitute "das Gerüst der erzählten Welt" (Philippi, 1966:21) are nevertheless presented in a manner that is "perspektivisch völlig neutral" (loc.cit.; cf. Langguth, loc.cit.). Finally and for a variety of reasons, a significant number of other scholars arrived at the conclusion that, while works like *Das Urteil*, *Die Verwandlung* and the three novels provided unmistakable evidence of *Einsinnigkeit*, the remainder of Kafka's texts employed a more distanced, external perspective (*Außensicht*) or a combination of the two.[9]

In all of this discussion about the nature of Kafka's narrative perspective, however, a few scholars also suggested or actually stated a principle which has been widely overlooked in reviews of their studies (cf. Beicken, 1971:58ff.; 1974:137ff.), but which will prove to be of considerable, even crucial importance in the final assessment of *Einsinnigkeit*. Sokel (1964), for example, when distinguishing between Kafka's allegedly dreamlike-expressionistic stories and his later works, had the following to say about the latter: "Zwischen den Leser und die Perspektive der Gestalt schiebt sich die bewußte Ironie, die der traumhaften Wirkung entgegensteht" (op.cit.:21). Similarly, in his study of 1966, Sokel maintained that, even in works like *Das Urteil*, *Die Verwandlung* and *Der Prozeß*, the "protagonist's perspective, to be sure, operates for the purpose of blocking access to and comprehension of the truth, but the truth emerges through the defeat of the protagonist's consciousness" (op.cit.:12). In the same year, Binder (1966), commenting on the difficulties facing the interpreter of Kafka's works, remarked:

> Wie kann man solche Fehlinterpretationen vermeiden, wo einen Fixpunkt für sachgemäße Interpretation finden, wenn das Vorverständnis des empirisch Gewohnten fehlt? Die Antwort lautet: *Man muß die Funktion der Motive innerhalb des Erzählgefälles und an der Erzählstruktur die Meinungen der Figuren messen.* (op.cit.:121)

The following year, Henel (1967), who attempted to reinterpret Kafka's *einsinnige* works as the confrontation between a guilty man and his conscience projected as *Gegenwelt*, nevertheless stated:

> Aber trotz der einseitigen Perspektive weiß der aufmerksame Leser über den Helden Bescheid, denn er sieht mit ihm auf die Welt, in der sich die innere Situation des Helden spiegelt. Als außenstehender Beobachter kann er diese Reflexionen objektiv interpretieren, während der Held auf sie mit Ärger reagiert (...). (op.cit.:259)

Finally, in 1969, Fingerhut, discussing some of Kafka's animal stories, observed:

> Das Groteske entwickelt sich in Kafkas Umformungen zu dem eigentlichen Pendant des Märchenhaften. Aufgebaut aus der gleichen Mischung von Realem und Phantastischem, erzählt aus der gleichen Einsinnigkeit der Perspektive, bedient es sich der Harmonie jener Erzählgattung, um den Leser aus der Illusion einer im Kunstwerk erstellten, heilen Welt zu reißen (...). (op.cit.:168, s.a. 182)

Common to all of these views is at least the implied notion that, even when Kafka employs the technique of so-called *Einsinnigkeit*, he can still distance the reader from the work and convey his own authorical attitudes by means of indirect or implicit commentary (cf. Booth, 1961:272ff.; Chatman, 1978:228).

For the time being, however, this very significant point was generally ignored, as a third phase in the affirmation of *Einsinnigkeit* was established by another member of the Tübingen school, Kobs (1970). Amplifying and refining the approach of Walser, who tried to show that the very language of Kafka's works validated his concepts of *Einsinnigkeit* and *Aufhebung* (Walser, 1961:92ff.), Kobs actually begins his study with an essay in detailed linguistic examination. Taking the brief, early piece, *Die Bäume*, and submitting it to what Glinz has dubbed "inhaltsbezogene Textanalyse" (Kobs, 1970:56ff.), Kobs reaches the conclusion that the work's ultimate effect is to create an impenetrable 'paradoxical circle' (op.cit.:7-19), resulting from an "Übermaß an scharfsinniger Argumentation" (ibid.: 11). In his view, the essential nature of the text is consequently to be described as "objektive Hermetik" (ibid.:33,46), a characteristic he attributes to all of Kafka's other brief, more aphoristic works as well (ibid.:33).

Although this first major argument in Kobs' study explicitly excludes the question of narrative perspective and will therefore not be critically assessed until later, in the consideration of *Paradoxie*, it nevertheless remains extremely relevant to the present discussion, since it provides a correlative to Kobs' understanding of *Einsinnigkeit*, which he elaborates with particular reference to *Amerika* or *Der Verschollene*. Disagreeing with Walser's conception of time in

Kafka's novels and deducing from this that the convergence between narrator and 'narrating medium' or *Perspektivgestalt* is not a purely technical matter (ibid.:25f.), he then proceeds to construe *Einsinnigkeit* as meaning, "daß alles, was erzählt worden ist, in der Art, wie es erzählt worden ist, nur in der Vermittlung durch Karls Bewußtsein hat erzählt werden können" (ibid.:32). What this implies, he believes, is that, in the novels, there are "keine absoluten Sätze und keine unbezweifelbare Wirklichkeit. Nicht Fakten werden hier erzählt, sondern Eindrücke" (ibid.:33).

Developing this point further, Kobs then maintains that, since Karl Roßmann's account of 'facts' can be shown to be full of inconsistencies and his evaluation of people and events is possibly even more unreliable, the potential interpreter is left in an impossible position, because the narrator, having been reduced "auf die Funktion eines nur registrierenden Organs" (ibid.:32), fails to provide him with any unequivocal criterion by which to judge what constitutes truth in the narrative (loc.cit.). Thus the principle of *Einsinnigkeit* achieves "für die größeren Werke erzählenden Inhalts dasselbe wie der paradoxe Zirkel für die kleine Prosa von der Art des Stükkes *Die Bäume*" (ibid.:33). Indeed, the only difference between the two lies in that "zwischen der 'objektiven Hermetik' des paradoxen Zirkels und der 'subjektiven' der einsinnigen Darstellung" (ibid.: 46). In both cases, however, "ist die Frage nach dem Sinn 'aufgehoben' in der doppelten Bedeutung des Wortes" (ibid.:19). As a consequence, the would-be commentator on the shorter works must be content to show, "weshalb jedes Erklären seinen Gegenstand verliert, weshalb das Streben nach positiven Bestimmungen in paradoxe Zirkel umschlägt, weshalb schließlich der Bereich jenseits des Zirkels sich der Formulierbarkeit entzieht" (loc.cit.), while the interpreter of the longer narratives remains the captive of an "einsinnig erzählte(n) Welt" and "kann bestenfalls ihr Sosein als Funktion der Sehweise erklären, nicht aber aus ihr heraustreten, ohne auf inhaltliche Aussagen verzichten zu müssen" (ibid.:53).

Despite its obvious indebtedness to Beißner and especially Walser, Kobs' study undeniably constitutes an original and ingenious contribution to Kafka scholarship. Yet, notwithstanding its obvious merits, one may seriously question its alleged superiority to its predecessors. Certainly it avoids the type of allegoresis into which Beißner eventually strays, as well as the implicitly absurdist position of Walser and the self-defeating theories about *Undeutbarkeit* suggested by Fietz and Schillemeit. However, in the final analysis, it remains extremely doubtful whether its own underlying implications are any more valid, let alone illuminating, than those it has sought to correct. For it should not be overlooked that Kobs' ultimate conclusions unmistakably indicate that, at least in the case of Kafka, the notion of literature and literary interpretation is to be radically revised. Indeed, if his views are accepted at all, there remains no logical alternative to the inference that, for Kafka, literature is nothing more than the art of communicating how not to communicate, while the interpretation of his work becomes a mere exercise in proving this to be the case. In other words, for all his attempted philological rigour and his utter rejection of allegoresis (ibid.:20ff.), Kobs, like Beißner and Walser before him, actually ends up adopting a position identical with that of certain allegorical commentators, namely, those abovementioned, increasingly numerous scholars who, on largely biographical evidence, interpret Kafka's works as the author's writing about the author's writing. That Kobs can nevertheless regard his findings as being "ebenso tröstlich wie trostlos" and as preventing "den Einbruch des Absurden" (ibid.:29) serves only to reveal the fundamental irrationality of his approach.

Given the ultimate implications of Kobs' arguments, it is perhaps not surprising to find little direct support for them in more recent studies. What is surprising, however, is that most of those who do confirm his views make no mention whatever of his work. One such is Thorlby (1972), who maintains that Kafka's oeuvre represents "the process of describing the world when no convention is available to tell us what it means, not even a convention that will enable us to distinguish what is there from what we think is there" (op.cit.:98). From this he then concludes, in terms strongly reminiscent of Kobs' final position: "Kafka's writing is directed against the absurdity not of the world, but of writing. It reflects its own activity, its own reality — and utter artificiality" (loc.cit.).

Rolleston (1974) also ignores Kobs' study, but nevertheless offers a closely related interpretation constructed on two main premisses:

54

"the rigorous insistence on the hero's perspective" (loc.cit.:102), that is, Beißner's *Einsinnigkeit* (ibid.:xiv), at least in the works predating 1915 (ibid.:17, 26,102), and a "theatrical metaphor" (ibid.:xv) or "theatrical analogy" (ibid.:40) derived from Beck's analysis (1971) of the influence exerted on Kafka by a troupe of Yiddish actors during the last months of 1911 (cf. *Tb* 79ff.). Combining these two notions, Rolleston distinguishes between earlier works, in which "the Kafka hero tries to incorporate the world into his own mental theatre, to become the spectator of his own drama" (ibid.:143), and later works, where the 'hero' attempts "to re-enter the world through the alignment of private role with public function" (loc.cit.; s.a.202f.). In both cases, however, the outcome is essentially the same, for the texts are so structured that "each culminates in a parablelike clarity that serves only to generate questions without end" (ibid.:67), as they describe "an inexorable circle back into the smallest details of the immediate events, opening a void beneath every thought or statement" (ibid.:100), or else "the unmediated focussing on the 'facts' of a story results in a dialectical calling into question of both the narrator and his world, so that the reader comes to feel (...) that he has witnessed only an *absence* of reality, a narrative running into the sands of language without content" (ibid.:103). Thus, at the end of each work, "the attention of all participants is redirected to the stage, than which nothing more 'real' can be conceived after all" (ibid.:41) and "the metamorphosis of the theatre, so indefatigably imagined, never takes place" (ibid.:143). However much Rolleston may appear to depart from these admittedly arbitrary and fanciful theories in his subsequent essays (Rolleston, 1976; 1976b; 1979), his firm link with Kobs still remains quite unmistakable in his continuing insistence on the essentially closed or hermetic quality of Kafka's works. As he says of *Der Prozeß*: "The problem is simply that the text cannot be translated directly into, or even adequately evoked by, any other terminology" than that of the text itself (Rolleston, 1976:5).

Another scholar who makes no reference to Kobs, but clearly agrees with him, is Krusche (1974). In his commentary, the method consists of a threefold transition:

von der Analyse der charakteristischen Erzählformen Kafkas zu den unter dem Begriff des 'Reduktiven' zusammengefaßten Deutungen, von der Untersuchung der Motivgestaltung zu den unter dem Begriff des 'Spekulativen' gebündelten Interpretationen und von der Erörterung der Sozialfunktion des Künstlers Kafka zur Analyse des Kunstbegriffs, wie er in großen Teilen der bisherigen Kafka-Literatur sich zeigt. (op.cit.:7)

And, having completed these processes, he concludes:

(Kafka) begibt sich in die paradoxe Situation eines Menschen, der sich fortwährend und in höchster Eindringlichkeit, Einprägsamkeit und formaler Verbindlichkeit — unter den Bedingungen natürlich künstlerischer Gestaltung — mitteilt und all seiner Mitteilung die Funktion auferlegt, die Unmöglichkeit aller Mitteilung zu erweisen. (ibid.:156)

At least two advocates of Kobs' theses, however, do review his work and, in part, both dispute some of his findings. Steinmetz (1977), for example, maintains that Kobs' analysis of *Die Bäume* is excessively stringent and his use of the term 'paradox' inappropriate (op.cit.:86ff.). Nevertheless, after examining the nature of Kafka's literary reception and what he regards as characteristic structural features of the author's texts, he, too, is led to the contention: "Die Interpretation Kafkascher Texte kann nicht weiter vordringen als bis zur Deskription ihrer inneren Struktur, in der alle gängigen Deutungskategorien annihiliert werden" (ibid.:81). Similarly, Corngold criticises Kobs' notion of 'the pure expression' (cf. Kobs, 1970: 94ff., 411ff.; s.a. Binder, 1976:209ff.). maintaining that it jeopardises the "absoluteness of congruence as a narrative principle" (Corngold, 1977:63) and logically requires "a narrator inscribed within the text", one who is "not identical with 'Kafka the writer', the author of the entire oeuvre" (loc.cit.). Despite this objection, however, he then proceeds to argue that "the felt presence of a narrator is no guarantee of the truth" (loc.cit.) and that the narrator of *Der Verschollene*, like Karl Roßmann, "is not wholly reliable" (loc.cit.). Consequently, his views eventually coincide with Kobs' when he deduces that:

it is impossible to decide authoritatively whether at any given moment the language of *Der Verschollene* is to be read literally, as accurately presenting Karl's own erroneous grasp of the world; or figuratively, as profferring Karl's experience as pure expression, as a gesture whose truth undoes the manipulative, 'ironically distancing' perspective of the narrator. This zone of indetermination in Kafka, which Kobs (if inadvertently) leads us to discover, appears to be the ultimate field of Kafka's paradox. (ibid.: 64)

Between those studies supportive of Kobs and those that clearly oppose him, there stands one detailed discussion of *Einsinnigkeit* which, even in the perplexing world of Kafka scholarship, is so conspicuous for its illogicality that it warrants special mention. The work in question is that by Szanto (1972). Totally disregarding the theories of Kobs and Walser, not to mention the various critical responses to them, Szanto fully endorses Beißner's notion of *Einsinnigkeit*, but relabels it "narrative consciousness" (op.cit.:6), since he believes that it is the protagonists' consciousness which "narrates the stories and controls their point of view" (ibid.:9). As a consequence, he maintains, "each novel is essentially concerned with process rather than established fact. The novel becomes not a product but a medium, not the writing about something, but the process of something being transmitted; the process becomes the created object" (loc.cit.). Thus the actual text of Kafka's works "becomes the end in itself (...) It leads backwards to the narrating consciousness instead of forward to environment described. It is the written word with which the reader becomes involved, he need no longer look to the formulated message it transmits" (loc.cit.).

None of these arguments is, of course, entirely new. On the contrary, all of them bear a close resemblance to views already propounded by Walser, Fietz, Schillemeit and Kobs, as becomes even more apparent when Szanto later asserts that a corollary of narrative consciousness is "the impossibility of a phrase-by-phrase, analytic, interpretative explanation" (ibid.:42). Yet, in manifest contradiction of these theoretical pronouncements, the same commentator has no hesitation whatever in describing Kafka's works as "stories of unsuccessful, incompleted quests" (ibid.:9) or in declaring Kafka's anonymous country doctor and Georg Bendemann of *Das Urteil* to be thoroughly "self—centred" characters (ibid.:50, 67). And the ostensible justification for this obvious inconsistency is that, in Kafka's texts, "each word present has its purpose, each word can be explained without interpretation" (ibid.:45). However, by what ingenious process the words of a literary composition or their purpose can be 'explained' without being 'interpreted' regrettably remains an undivulged secret. Nevertheless, from the so-called explanations just quoted, it would not seem unfair to assume that the stated distinction is just as arbitrary and irrational in its suppositions as the majority of Szanto's study, and that the effect of both is less likely to be clarification than further, quite unnecessary confusion.

Fortunately, the same cannot be said about those commentaries which unequivocally oppose Kobs' views, for even the most inadequate of them is still, for the greater part, logically consistent. Among such critiques, by far the most exhaustive is Beicken's doctoral dissertation (1971). Recognising that Kobs' arguments depend primarily on his interpretation of the relationship between narrator and *Perspektivgestalt*, Beicken first sets out to prove that the former has not been reduced to the level of a 'mere recorder' and that the question of congruence is more complex than is generally acknowledged. Initially, therefore, he undertakes a lengthy review of literature about the nature of the narrator and, preferring the functional theses of Hamburger (1957) to definitions in terms of person, he concludes that the narrator is to be construed as "eine Teilerscheinung des erzählenden Autors" (Beicken, 1971: 21f.), "eine funktionale und synthetische Größe (...), die aus den Erzählakten aufgeschlüsselt werden muß" (op.cit.:59), an "erzählerische Instanz oder Intelligenz" (ibid.:66). As he later summarises:

Es wäre verfehlt, aus dem funktionalisierten Erzählvorgang, der durch den subjektiven Bewußtseinsraum der Perspektivgestalt bestimmt ist, auf einen unabhängigen und distanzierten Erzähler zu schließen. Kafka tritt 'als Erzähler nicht selbst auf', sondern der Dichter hat sein erzählerisches Wirken ganz in die dargestellte Welt hineinverwebt.(ibid.:100)

Throughout most of his study, therefore, Beicken follows the example of Hamburger (1957:46) in employing the obviously active term 'narrating author' instead of 'narrator'. And since the former cannot, by definition, be identified with any one of his characters,

58

the relationship between 'narrator' and *Perspektivgestalt* cannot be one of virtual identity, as Kobs' notion of congruence implies.

This form of argument is given added weight by Beicken's early and very important distinction between *Perspektive* and *Sehweise*:

> In dem allgemeineren Begriff der Erzählperspektive kommen zwei verschiedene Sachverhalte ungeschieden zusammen. Es handelt sich um den Standort im Sinne des wahrnehmungsmäßigen Erfassens der dargestellten Welt, von dem der Standpunkt der Wertung und Deutung getrennt werden müßte. Beide Standpunkte begründen zwei verschiedene Bezugsfelder. (ibid.:2)

Perspektive he limits to the perceptual of these two viewpoints, and *Sehweise* to the evaluative.

On the basis of this distinction, Beicken is then able to refine the notion of *Einsinnigkeit* still further, maintaining that, although the 'narrating author' may restrict his *Perspektive* to that of his protagonist, it does not necessarily follow that he therefore also identifies with the latter's *Sehweise*. On the contrary, there is a whole range of indirect means by which he may clearly create his own *Sehweise* alongside and in opposition to that of his *Perspektivgestalt*:

> Tonfall, Sprechhaltung, Wortwahl, Emphase oder Untertreibung sind Mittel der erzählerischen Redeweise und Rhetorik, die in der sprachlichen Gestaltung dem erzählenden Autor Wege schaffen, sich gegenüber seinen Figuren wertend, distanzierend und deutend zu verhalten. Dieses Verhalten ist ohne Zweifel auf den erzählenden Autor, auf seine erzählerischen Absichten und Wirkungen zurückzuführen. (ibid.:7)

What Beicken is discussing here is, of course, that extremely important narrative technique noted in a few earlier studies, namely, the use of indirect or implicit commentary. And towards the end of his analysis, substituting 'das erzählende Subjekt' for 'the narrating author', he provides a considerably more comprehensive list of the elements by which such commentary may be created:

> Es handelt sich beim erzählenden Subjekt um eine synthetische Größe, die in der Gesamtheit der Erzählakte greifbar wird, also im Erzählaufbau, in den Eigenarten der Erzählkomposition und in der sprachlichen Gestaltung, die in den Wertbestimmungen der Darstellung einen besonderen Wirkungs-

bereich für das erzählende Subjekt schafft. Die Darstellung der erzählten Welt umfaßt immer eine Auswahl und Zusammenstellung von Wirklichkeitsmomenten. In diesem Gestaltungsprozeß macht sich das urteilende Sehvermögen des Autors, seine besondere Sehweise geltend. (ibid.:496f.)

In his more recent statements, Beicken (1977; 1978; 1979) associates this form of rhetoric with Kafka's term "Tat-Beobachtung" (*Tb* 563) and contrasts it with the notions "Berechnung" and "Kunstaufwand" (*Tb* 448f.), which he uses to denote Kafka's opposite technique of trying to make the reader identify with the protagonist.

Having thus established the possibility of covert authorial commentary in Kafka's works, Beicken is also in a position to reinterpret the final main concern of Kobs' deliberations, that is, the protagonist's factual inconsistencies and his degree of reliability. Kobs, it will be recalled, had attributed the former to the protagonist's flawed consciousness, projected on to the 'external world' (cf. Kobs, 1970:33, 349f.), and had regarded them as both incontrovertible and unverifiable. Beicken, on the other hand, agrees with Sokel (1964; 1965; 1976; 1976b; 1980) and Henel (1967) in maintaining that their source is not simply perceptual or cognitive, but rather psychic:

Wenn die Außenwelt als Bewußtseinsphänomen zu begreifen ist, dann nimmt diese Projektion des Innern auch die Probleme der Psyche auf (...). Die Prinzipien der Unstimmigkeit und Widersprüchlichkeit lassen sich nur dann schlüssig erklären, wenn psychische Momente als Störfaktoren des subjektiven Bewußtseins auftreten und die Bewußtseinstätigkeit steuern. (ibid.:141)

Furthermore, since it is possible to assess the protagonist's *Sehweise* by comparison with the author-narrator's, it is also possible to isolate and define each work's "Wirklichkeitsmomente in ihrer überformten Gestalt" (ibid.:142), even if this does not yield "ein objektives Bild der Außenwelt im Sinne einer wahren Realität" (loc.cit.).

Although H. Kraft (1972) would tend to agree with Beicken about this last point, arguing that the world confronting the protagonist is "meist nur strukturell vorhanden: als Negierung des Realität ermangelnden Wirklichen, als Zerstörung der Illusion; sie hat selber noch keinen positiven Inhalt" (op.cit.:42), he nevertheless rejects the idea that it is merely the protagonist's mental projection, whether psychic or otherwise:

Bedeutung (für den Leser) gewinnt diese Dichtung, weil die dargestellte Innerlichkeit nicht subjektive (*individuelle*) *Innerlichkeit* (des Autors) *abbildet*, sondern weil sie *allgemeine Wirklichkeit deutet*. (...) Der 'Solipsismus' ist 'nur scheinbar; denn die intensive Gegenwelt entspricht einer extensiven, einer gegebenen, gefürchteten, in satirischer Aggression, in Deutungswut und Selbstdemütigung anerkannten Wirklichkeit'". (ibid.:22f.; cf. Fischer, 1962: 548)

For the rest, however, Kraft strongly supports Beicken's opposition to Kobs, devoting the major part of his study to a detailed consideration of the specific means Kafka employs in order to distance the reader, question the protagonist's view of things and implicitly establish a *Sehweise* superior to that of the *Perspektivgestalt*. Among the more important factors he discusses are the clash between style and content (ibid.:21), discrepancies between the reader's general empirical knowledge and the central character's version of it (ibid.:30ff.), comic effects (ibid.:33ff.), the juxtaposition of levels of reality (ibid.:39ff.), animals as characters or narrator-agents (ibid.:62f.), and irony (ibid.:67). Thus, while affirming Beißner's notion of *Einsinnigkeit*, Kraft, like Beicken, is still not prepared to accept Kobs' belief that this technique necessarily implies works which are 'subjectively hermetic'. Nor does he subscribe to the view that *Einsinnigkeit* characterises all of Kafka's works (ibid.:45,58). In this last respect, he echoes the opinion not only of Kobs (1970:25) and Beicken (1971:473f., 477), but also of virtually every major commentator on the subject since Hillmann (1964) and Sokel (1964), including Binder, whose more recent studies either mention narrative perspective only in passing (Binder, 1976) or merely repeat his arguments of 1966 (Binder, 1979b:62ff.).

Two of the small, but very significant minority who find no need to distinguish between works by Kafka which do or do not give evidence of *Einsinnigkeit* are Beutner (1973) and Sheppard (1973; 1977). And their reason for omitting such distinctions is, quite simply, that they consider Beißner's theory and its subsequent elaborations to be deficient. In particular, they disagree with the assertion that, in Kafka's novels, there is no perceptible narrator above or beyond the consciousness of the 'hero'. Beutner, for example, maintains that such a narrator is always evident, especially in the narrative's account of the central character's gestures, feelings and motives (op. cit.:24). Indeed, for her, the existence of a perspective superior to that of the protagonist is a fundamental element of Kafka's technique in all three of his novels:

> Zwar konstituiert nur das von der Figur Wahrgenommene die Erscheinungsweise der erzählten Welt, zum anderen aber wird das Wahrgenommene wiederum zu einer Wiederspiegelung der inneren Gestimmtheit des Wahrnehmenden. Der Wahrnehmende und das Wahrgenommene stehen bei Kafka in unlösbarer Wechselbeziehung, bestimmt von einer übergeordneten, nicht an den Wahrnehmenden gebundenen Perspektive. (loc.cit.)

Furthermore, this superior perspective is to be attributed to an intellectually advantaged narrator: "eine über K. hinausgehende Perspektive (...) findet sich in allen drei Romanen auch dann, wenn Gedanken und Überlegungen der Helden ohne besondere Kennzeichnung unmittelbar genannt werden. Es ist also kein Erzähler da, der uns dergleichen referiert, sondern ein Erzähler, der alles das einfach weiß" (ibid.:26).

In a similar fashion, Sheppard (1973), after referring to certain breaks in perspective already noted by Leopold and Kudszus, as well as "a small number of episodes which are reported 'above K.'s head'" (op.cit.:26), soon reaches the conclusion that "just because the narrator of *Das Schloß* does not intervene directly 'interpreting, teaching, reflecting', it does not follow that he is necessarily a *Deus Absconditus*" (ibid.:29). Rather, he is more accurately to be construed as "a captive of the world which he has created. At key points he reveals himself as directly as he dare, but more typically he exists within that world as a unifying substance or nameless, shaping presence who provides the reader with a subliminal sense that K., appearances to the contrary, is himself under judgement" (loc.cit.). Moreover, if a narrator, "though not obvious, is nevertheless present" in *Das Schloß*, in *Der Prozeß* he is "more tangibly" so (Sheppard, 1977:398).

Consistent with his understanding of the narrator, Sheppard also recognises the important principle of indirect commentary and, through his excellent analysis of *Das Schloß* (Sheppard, 1973), provides the most comprehensive account so far of the means Kafka employs to this end. However, because "the patterns generated" within the novel "have the effect of distancing the reader from K.'s assessment of any given situation, of drawing attention to other possibilities of interpretation and of arousing the suspicion that the world external to K. has a secret life of its own" (op.cit.:34), Sheppard describes these means as "alienation-devices" (loc.cit.) and divides them into eight broad types: "parallelisms, discrepancies, leitmotivs, changes of register, reflection, indirect narrational comment, direct comment on K. by others and breaks in narrative perspective" (ibid.:35). The one aspect of this argument that needs to be questioned here is what Sheppard calls 'indirect narrational comment', for if one examines the passages he quotes to substantiate this classification (ibid.:117f.), it becomes evident that, far from being indirect, they actually constitute unmistakably direct, albeit unobtrusive commentary, as the use of 'undankbar' in the following sentence demonstrates: "K. aber, undankbar, machte sich von Olga los und nahm den Wirt beiseite" (ibid.:117). The only person who can possibly be thinking and uttering the word 'undankbar' in this context is the impersonalised narrator, and since he utters it quite directly, unmediated by another, there can be no justification for regarding it as anything but direct, evaluative commentary, however skilfully it may be concealed in the text (s.a. Sheppard, 1979).

By comparison with other studies opposed to Kobs' views on *Einsinnigkeit*, the last two commentaries that need to be mentioned in this survey are not only less original, but also much less convincing. Nevertheless, they do have the merit of serving to illustrate the extremes towards which scholars have been attracted in their attempt to break the vicious interpretative circles postulated by Walser, Fietz, Schillemeit and Kobs. In essence, Walther's contribution (1977) to this debate is to reaffirm Beißner's later version of *Einsinnigkeit* by deducing from the narrative point of view that the contents of *Das Schloß*, for example, are to be explained in terms of dreams: "Wir fahren deshalb am besten, wenn wir alles, was im Roman passiert, als traumhafte Imagination Kafkas auffassen" (op.cit.:10); "Alle der Hauptperson begegnenden Geschehnisse sind, wie das auch in Träumen der Fall ist, funktional auf diese bezogen" (ibid.:11). Unlike Beißner, however, he grants the reader a certain superiority to the protagonist's viewpoint: "Wir sehen also alles mit K.s Augen, können aber Widersprüchlichkeiten, die er nicht reflektiert, in unsere Beurteilung des Geschehens einbeziehen und sind insofern der Perspektivgestalt überlegen" (loc.cit.). Furthermore, following the example of Sokel, Henel and Beicken, he construes the confrontation between K. and the allegedly oneiric world of the castle as a form of "Ich-Spaltung, in der Weise, daß ein bewußterer, mehr an der Oberfläche liegender Teil, eben K., wie er im Roman als handelnde Person auftritt, mit einem bisher weitgehend unbewußt gebliebenen Teil, verkörpert in der Dorf- und Schloßwelt, konfrontiert wird" (ibid.: 20). Finally, he, too, feels it necessary to distinguish between 'dreamlike' works, which are characterised by *Einsinnigkeit*, and others that display an 'objective' form of presentation, "sei es in realistischer oder Fabelmanier" (loc.cit.).

In stark contrast to Walther's eclectic reassertion of *Einsinnigkeit* as consistent with interpretation, Steffan (1979) will have no truck with the notion in any of its formulations, orthodox, radical or revised: "Die 'Einsinnigkeit' erweist sich weder in totaler Ausweitung noch in eingeschränkter Form als richtig. Sie ist nicht das Prinzip, das die Eigenart des Kafkaschen Erzählens erklären würde" (op.cit.:29). Going still further, he also repudiates, in its entirety, the narrative theory on which he considers Beißner, his supporters, modifiers and opponents have all based their arguments, namely, the assumption of the "Mittelbarkeit der Darstellung im Roman" (Stanzel, 1955:4). For, according to Steffan, mediacy of this kind "bedeutet die Anwesenheit eines persönlichen Erzählers im Roman, der die dargestellte Welt vermittelt" (op.cit.:30), and this he regards as impossible, "denn wie kann die fiktionale Welt von etwas vermittelt werden, das selbst in den Bereich der Fiktion gehört. Der Erzähler bzw. der entsprechende Personalindikator kommt ja in Sätzen vor, die den Text mitkonstituieren" (loc.cit.).

One very obvious difficulty raised by such statements is, of course, the task of reconciling them with the enormous number of frequently highly personalised narrators to be encountered in virtually every period of literary history. Well aware of this difficulty, Steffan returns to the source of his radical pronouncements and, in ostensible refutation of conventional wisdom, quotes the following passage from Leistner (1975):

Diese andere Beziehung des 'ich' zu Ich, die sich aus der Möglichkeit sprach-
lich handelnder Menschen ergibt, sich zum Erzählen wessen immer *aller* in
der jeweiligen Sprache vorkommenden Nominatoren, z.B. des 'ich' bedienen
zu dürfen, hat nun für die, die mit ihm erzählen, zur Folge, daß sie mit dem
je erzählten 'ich' alles, bis auf die einzige Ausnahme, den zum 'ich'-Sagen
existentiell befähigten und benötigten Menschen, personalindizieren *können*, wenn sie es eben wollen, wie für die, die icherzählte Texte verstehen,
daraus folgt, daß sie mit den Marken 'ich' alles, nur eben nicht Menschen,
darum also auch weder sich selbst, noch den Verfasser des icherzählten Tex-
tes personalindiziert sehen/verstehen *können*. (op.cit.:399)

For all their opacity, however, these elusive assertions prove nothing
of any substance about the nature of human communication or of
literary narration. On the contrary, if what Leistner asserts were
correct, then no-one employing the pronoun 'I' could ever give an
account, spoken or written, of something he had done, even an hour
beforehand, and still unequivocally indicate himself when using the
term 'I'. In other words, if Leistner's remarks were valid, then the
universally accepted pronoun of self-identification would be summarily transformed into some alter-referential or purely fictional
indicator, and one of the most fundamental assumptions of all
human communication, including legal evidence, would be arbitrarily
and totally discarded, with inevitably chaotic results. As a consequence, when Steffan, basing himself on such absurd propositions,
draws the inference that "Konstruktionen eines Ich-, Er- oder aukto-
rialen Erzählers" are both superfluous and inadmissible, because the
author is "der einzige Erzähler" (op.cit.:32), his argument is deserving of no more credence than that of his acknowledged source.[10]

Since Beißner first published his theory, then, thirty years have
now elapsed and, as the foregoing review will have indicated, during
that time the debate about *Einsinnigkeit* has been virtually constant
and undeniably extensive. Yet, to judge by the results achieved so
far, it is clear that, despite its professed aim of philological rigour,
this approach to Kafka's work has proven to be scarcely any more
fruitful than the admittedly arbitrary, interpretative methods it
sought to displace. Indeed, in some very important instances, its
conclusions have been practically identical with those of its rivals
and, in a few others, they have been even more extreme. This is not

to deny, of course, that certain individual scholars have done a great deal to clarify the matter of Kafka's rhetoric and its implications for interpretation. Beicken, H. Kraft and Sheppard are three obvious cases in point. However, if one were pressed to define the consensus of opinion among the many who have now written about Kafka's narrative technique, it is doubtful whether one could go beyond the two vague statements that some of the author's works exhibit *Einsinnigkeit* while others do not, and that the relationship of technique to meaning in his works remains uncertain.

Given the self-evident validity of the principle that fiction, like all art, should be analysed and interpreted by methods appropriate to its intrinsic nature, it might well be asked how so much debate about the rhetoric of Kafka's oeuvre could possibly have produced such meagre results. And to find the most likely answer, one need look no farther than to the pioneering statements of Beißner. For there one discovers that the narrator is variously characterised as being distinct from the author (1952:35; 1958:12,15), yet identical with him (1952:28,36) and with the central character (1952:29,34; 1958:12) as well as the narrative (1952:34), while at the same time not existent at all, because the action narrates itself (1952:32,35). From such utter confusion, the inference is inescapable that, before the theory of *Einsinnigkeit* can be properly assessed, there exists a fundamental need to define precisely what a narrator is or is not. Consequently, an attempt will now be made to satisfy this need.

With the exception of Beißner (1952:32,35) and Walser (1961: 22), whose views defy all reason, narrative theorists are unanimous in affirming the axiom that every act of narration logically presupposes a narrator or, in the words of Kayser (1948:351), that the narrator is the "conditio sine qua non aller epischen Literatur". The most basic matter at issue about this entity or agent is, therefore, not whether it may or may not exist, but rather whether, in literature, it should be construed as fictional. And, according to the vast majority of scholars, the answer to this question is totally beyond doubt, so that from Friedemann (1910:26) and Petsch (1934:111) to Chatman (1978:248) and Genette (1980:123) one finds repeated acceptance of the principle that the narrator is "immer eine gedichtete, eine fiktive Gestalt" (Kayser, 1954:17). Yet, for a very small number of

scholars, such a principle is completely mistaken. Apart from Leistner and Steffan, this group also includes Hamburger (1953:347ff.;
1957:76ff.) and Beicken (1971:17). However, since Hamburger's
theories have already been conclusively refuted by Stanzel (1959)
and the demonstrably fallacious reasoning of Leistner and Steffan
has been analysed earlier in this discussion, the only argument that
remains to be considered is that of Beicken.

Referring to Kayser's definition of the narrator as an invented,
fictional figure, "eine Rolle, die der Autor erfindet und einnimmt"
(Kayser, 1957:451), Beicken (loc.cit.) maintains that there is an
insuperable difficulty in this notion: "Die Schwierigkeit liegt darin,
daß man fragen muß, wie der Erzähler sowohl fingiert und gleichzeitig dem Fiktiven überlegen und übergeordnet sein kann". In posing
such a question, however, he is suggesting difficulties where none
exists. For the principal, though not always the only sense in which
a narrator may be said to be "dem Fiktiven überlegen und übergeordnet" resides in the fact that he alone tells the whole of a story. To
construe the narrator as being intrinsically non-fictional is, therefore,
to assume not only that fictional characters do not have the ability
to narrate, but also that they do not have the power of human speech,
because to possess the latter is necessarily to have the potential for
the former. And since it is manifestly obvious that fictional characters
may be and generally are endowed with the power of human speech,
it must logically follow that they are also capable of narrating, without in any way jeopardising, let alone forfeiting their fictional status.
On the contrary, insofar as the narrator of a literary work actually
performs his special function, he simultaneously confirms his fictionality, for the simple reason that, as voice or transmitter, he
constitutes the immediate precondition of the narrative's existence,
so that he and it are ontologically interdependent. And because the
narrative, as literary creation, is fictional, its narrator must be as well
(cf. Stanzel, 1955:4f., 24f., 38; Kayser, 1956:230; Seidler, 1959:
461,473; Booth, 1961:149ff.).

Since all narrators ipso facto possess the power of human speech,
together with at least all the faculties which that gift implies, it must
also be logically inferred that they are personal as well. Yet, although
this notion, too, is accepted by the vast majority of scholars,[11] it is

just as firmly rejected by a significant few, and not merely the four dissenters already mentioned, but also by Tillotson (1959), who calls the narrator "a method rather than a person" (op.cit.:22), and by Langguth (1968), who describes Kafka's narrators as "merely a neutral grammatical source" (op.cit.:55). In denying that narrators are inherently personal, however, all of these scholars, except Langguth, plainly contradict themselves, in that each of them repeatedly identifies the narrator with the author, and if he is not to be understood as personal, it is difficult to imagine who is. Langguth's error, on the other hand, consists in the quite untenable assumption that something other than a person can narrate. For no matter what form of creature an author may choose to adopt as his narrator, he must always endow it with the capacity for human thought and speech before it can tell a story at all, and as soon as he does that, he transforms it into a person. Consequently, no narrator can be a 'neutral grammatical source'. Rather, as Moffet/McElheny (1966:568) have explained: "*Every* story is first-person, whether the person identifies himself or not", and their point is strongly supported by Genette (1980) when he refers to "the element of the narrative situation that is in fact invariant — to wit, the presence (explicit or implicit) of the 'person' of the narrator. This presence is invariant because the narrator can be in his narrative (like every subject of an enunciating in his enunciated statement) *only* in the 'first person'" (op.cit.:243f.). Similarly, "insofar as the narrator can at any instant intervene *as such* in the narrative, every narrating is, by definition, to all intents and purposes presented in the first person" (ibid.:244).

Applied to the theory of *Einsinnigkeit*, the implications of these statements are extremely far-reaching. To begin with, they invalidate all of the following, specific propositions about Kafka's rhetoric which were encountered in the preceding survey: that the narrator is always to be identified with his central character (Beißner; Szanto) or with what is narrated (Beißner); that the world of the narrative is independent of the narrator (Walser); that parts of a narrative can be totally neutral in perspective (Philippi; Langguth); and that the narrator can be reduced to the function of a mere recording instrument (Kobs), a notion also necessarily assumed by those who interpret the world confronting Kafka's protagonists as the implied creation

68

of the latter's oneiric, cognitively flawed or neurotic self-projections (Beißner; Kobs; Henel; Sokel; Beicken; Rolleston; Walther; s.a. Greenberg, 1965:10; Neumann, 1968:722; Elm, 1976:486). More generally, however, the views of Moffet/McElheny and Genette tend to make the term *Einsinnigkeit* quite useless as a defining characteristic of any fiction, whether Kafka's or not. For, if all narrators are first-person, then so is all narration, so that every narrative whatever becomes *einsinnig*, at least in the sense that, ultimately, the whole of each has been filtered through and transmitted by the consciousness of only one person, namely, *the* narrator.

To accept that, logically speaking, every narrator must be construed as first-person is, therefore, to acknowledge the need not only for a more precise concept than *Einsinnigkeit*, but also for a valid alternative to the traditional distinction between first-person and third-person narration. Approaching the second of these matters by way of the long-standing debate about telling and showing, scene and summary, Booth (1961:151ff.) advocates the adoption of the terms 'dramatised' and 'undramatised'. However, because of their inevitable and inappropriate theatrical associations, as well as a certain, inherent ambiguity later admitted by Booth (op.cit.:161ff.) and, above all, their failure to indicate directly the crucial notion of person, these terms are really not sufficiently exact to be of use.

A more adequate solution to the problem is suggested, instead, by another of the issues raised by Beicken (1971). Noting that Kayser (1954:29) defines the technique of *Madame Bovary* as impersonalised narration, but still insists that a personal narrator is present in the novel, Beicken is moved to enquire: "Wie kann ein Erzählen, das durch den bewußt angestrebten Erzählerschwund gekennzeichnet ist, unter dem Begriff der fiktiven Erzählergestalt subsumiert werden (...)?" (op.cit.:17). The answer to this question lies, of course, in the now commonplace distinction between person and personality. For it is to the latter that the word 'impersonal' refers and not the former, as may be gleaned from any comprehensive dictionary of current English, German, French or Italian, and probably a large number of other living languages as well. Thus, to describe a person, his manner or his mode of expression as impersonal is to denote that he or it is lacking in personality or personal reference; it is not, under any circumstances, to signify that he or it has disappeared or ceased to exist. Consequently, there is no contradiction whatever in Kayser's statements. On the contrary, they so accurately delineate two of the narrator's most basic features that, combined with the category 'personalised', they provide a thoroughly convincing, alternative framework within which all further discussion of the narrator in this study can securely proceed. In other words, from this point onwards, it will be taken for granted not only that all narrators are alike in being the necessary, immediate precondition of a narrative and, therefore, fictional as well as logically first-person, but also that they may differ fundamentally in the extent to which they are personalised or impersonalised, the absolutely minimum requirement for the former quality normally being that the narrator should actually identify himself with the pronoun 'I' or 'we'.[12]

Since it has already been established that literary narrators are inherently fictional, it may seem unnecessary to conclude this analysis of their essential nature by seriously discussing those frequently encountered claims or tacit assuptions that they are nevertheless to be identified with their authors. After all, authors can never be fictional. Unfortunately, however, the matter is not quite so simple, as the following remarks by Brod (1954) clearly suggest: "Ich habe es immer wieder erlebt, daß Verehrer Kafkas, die ihn nur aus seinen Büchern kennen, ein ganz falsches Bild von ihm haben. Sie glauben, er müsse auch im Umgang traurig, ja verzweifelt gewirkt haben. Das Gegenteil ist der Fall. Es wurde einem wohl in seiner Nähe" (op.cit.:44).

Although Brod's use of the term 'false' in this passage should certainly be disputed, particularly when one considers his own interpreted image of Kafka, the point that he is making is nevertheless of considerable importance, because it corresponds to a distinction which literary theorists have been drawing for more than a century. According to Tillotson (1959:22), a certain Dowden felt the need to contrast George Eliot's "historical self" with "that second self who writes her books, and lives and speaks through them" as early as 1877. And since that time it has by no means been uncommon

70

to find others differentiating in the same manner between the historical person and the "poetica personalità" (Croce, 1936, in Kayser, 1948:176), "the whole man" and "the writing self" (Liddell, 1947: 53), "die menschliche Persönlichkeit" and "die schaffende, künstlerische Persönlichkeit" (Kayser, 1948:288), "the novelist" and "the official scribe" (West, 1957, in Booth, 1961:71), "the real man" and "the implied author" (Booth, 1961:151), "die bürgerlich-biographische Persönlichkeit" and "die dichterische Persönlichkeit" (Walser, 1961:11), "the empirical personality" and "the literary personality" (Corngold, 1977:68), or "the real author" and "the implied author" (Chatman, 1978:148). Exactly what is meant by these distinctions has been explained in most detail by Booth (1961):

> Even the novel in which no narrator is dramatised creates an implicit picture of an author who stands behind the scenes, whether as stage manager, as puppeteer, or as an indifferent God, silently paring his fingernails. This implied author is always distinct from the 'real man' – whatever we may take him to be – who creates a superior version of himself, 'a second self', as he creates his work. (op.cit.:151)

Earlier in his study, he also makes the comment:

> Our sense of the implied author includes not only the extractable meanings but also the moral and emotional content of each bit of action and suffering of all of the characters. It includes, in short, the intuitive apprehension of a completed artistic whole; the chief value to which *this* implied author is committed, regardless of what party his creator belongs to in real life, is that which is expressed by the total form. (ibid.:73f.)

In recognising and attempting to remove so much basic confusion about the implications of the term 'author', Booth and other like-minded scholars have unquestionably made a major contribution to critical theory, and it is strongly to be regretted that the many biographical allegoretes of Kafka's works remain apparently unaware of the fact. Nevertheless, to acknowledge the validity of Booth's and related distinctions is not necessarily to accept the need for the term 'implied author' or any of the other proposed alternatives. On the contrary, at least three major objections can be raised to the introduction of such concepts. In the first place, if critics are to talk about implied authors, then logically they will also have to talk about implied poets, implied dramatists, implied painters, etc., and it is extremely difficult, indeed, to imagine such cumbersome expressions becoming accepted usage in any language. Furthermore, because, strictly speaking, the term 'author' has validity only in reference to something actually created, the epithet 'implied' is superfluous. In other words, the notion of author is primarily and necessarily an inference from the existence of a particular example or body of art, so that the addition of 'implied' to the notion is actually tautologous. Finally, unless it is to be assumed that all artists are total schizophrenics (and even Freud did not go that far), there can never be a complete disjuncture between 'the real man' and 'the implied author', so that to insist on the rigorous separation of the two is artificial. The really crucial point, then, about the meaning and use of the term 'author' is not that its biographical dimension should be excluded, but that critical discussion should always and emphatically proceed from the principle that the person in question is first and foremost the image one gains of him from his work, for without a clear, sensitive and comprehensive awareness of that image, the evidence of biographical research can very easily become what Liddell (1947:53) has aptly called "irrelevant gossip". Provided this fundamental principle is strictly observed, there will be no need to invent or apply terms like 'the implied author'.

Nor, it must now be conceded, will it be possible to distinguish between author and narrator simply on the basis of fictionality, since the author "as an ideal, literary, created version of the real man" (Booth, 1961:75) is, himself, fictional. This is not to say, however, that author and narrator are or ever can be totally identical. For, even apart from the author's additional, empirically actual dimension, he still remains "the principle that invented the narrator, along with everything else in the narrative" (Chatman, 1978:148), and "the narrating situation of a fictional account is *never* reduced to its situation of writing" (Genette, 1980:214). Nevertheless, there will be occasions when the differences between the two, at least in terms of literary image and values, will be minimal, if not nonexistent, and the determinant of these occasions will be the extent or degree to which the narrator is impersonalised. As Booth (1961) overstates

72

the matter: "In so far as a novel does not refer directly to this (implied) author, there will be no distinction between him and the implied, undramatised narrator (...)" (op.cit.:151).

In summary, then, the narrator of a literary work is always to be construed as fictional; as first-person, but with the potential to vary considerably in his degree of personalisation or impersonalisation; and as distinct from the author in lacking any empirically actual dimension and in directly transmitting or being the voice of the entire work. Although it has been mentioned several times before, the one idea in this definition which may need to be elaborated further is the last, namely, that a narrator transmits the whole of his narrative or, in other words, that every complete narrative has but one narrator. Many will, of course, dispute this notion, possibly pointing out, for example, that in Storm's *Der Schimmelreiter* there are obviously three narrators (the anonymous magazine-reader of the first paragraph, the traveller and the schoolmaster) or that in Uwe Johnson's *Mutmaßungen über Jakob* there are four (the impersonalised 'editor', Rohlfs, Jonas and Gesine). In doing so, however, they will all miss the point. For while it is true that each of these figures narrates, in the sense of relating one or more series of events, only one of them transmits the whole of *Der Schimmelreiter*, namely, the anonymous magazine-reader, and only one of them transmits the whole of the *Mutmaßungen*, namely, the impersonalised 'editor'. Without these two figures, neither of the works in question would ever have come into existence in its present form, since it is these two figures and they alone who are the immediate precondition of the other characters' fictional existence, including those few that also narrate. Whether one designates these other narrating characters 'sub-narrators' or chooses an entirely different term, the decisive point remains that there can be but one narrator of a whole work, namely, the narrator. To abandon this principle is inevitably to cause confusion, if not chaos, as is evident from some of the unfortunate statements by Booth (1961), who would turn not only "third-person centres of consciousness, through whom authors have filtered their narratives" (op.cit.:153) into narrators, but also "every speech, every gesture", for "most works contain disguised narrators who are used to tell the audience what it needs to know, while seeming merely to

73

act out their roles" (ibid.:152). It is small wonder that such misleading usage should have attracted the strictures of Genette (1980: 188).

Besides creating the need for a thorough review and redefinition of the notion 'narrator', Beißner's theory of *Einsinnigkeit* has also and necessarily raised the vexed question of narrative perspective or point of view, a concept "whose plurisignification must give pause to anyone who wishes to use it in precise discussion" (Chatman, 1978:151). According to Lubbock (1921:151), point of view is concerned with "the relation in which the narrator stands to the story", but Kayser (1948:204) extends it to mean "das Verhältnis des Erzählers zum Publikum und zum Geschehen", whereas Booth (1961:155) evidently regards it as pertaining to "an implied dialogue among author, narrator, the other characters, and the reader". Similarly, some scholars would limit the concept essentially to the issue of perceptual perspective, 'focus', 'vision', or 'focalisation' (Brooks/ Warren, 1943:589; Pouillon, 1946:72ff.; Binder, 1966:188ff.; 1979b: 62ff.: Genette, 1980:186), while others would place more emphasis on the narrator's degree of omniscience and personalisation (Lubbock, 1921; Stanzel, 1955), and yet a third group would insist upon an evaluative dimension as well (Friedmann, 1955:123ff.; Booth, 1961:155ff.; Beicken, 1971:1; Chatman, 1978:151f.).

The basic fault with almost all of these theories and their various typologies, however, is not that they fail to distinguish "between 'point of view' and narrative voice" (Chatman, 1978:153) or between "the focal character" as an element of "mood" and "the narrator" as "voice" (Genette, 1980:188), but rather that they are too restricted in their understanding of the term 'point of view' and, therefore, in their choice of distinguishing criteria. One need only reflect for a while on non-fictional communication to realise that one person's expression of his point of view and another person's assessment of it are determined by far more than matters of optical range, cognitive limits, personal or impersonal style and intellectual values. Both may also be strongly influenced, for example, by differences in physique (e.g. deformity, colour of skin), in temperament, in kinds and levels of taste, in vocabulary or linguistic register, and so on. And since this is the case in actual human communication,

74

it is bound to be so in narrative fiction as well. For, no matter how 'non-representational' or 'objective' the latter may become, insofar as it communicates at all, it will employ human speech and, therefore, an essentially human, first-person narrator, from whom point of view, in the sense just explained, is inseparable, however carefully it may be disguised.

Assuming, then, as all narrative theory does, that in considering fictional point of view, one is basically concerned with the manner in which a work is transmitted from author to reader, there are always four factors involved: the author, the narrator, the narrative and the reader. However, as the immediate determinant of what is transmitted, the most important of these is obviously the narrator, whose nature may comprise any number of properties, from the human to the quasi-human (e.g. narrating animals) and the extra-human (e.g. immediate knowledge of other people's thoughts; clair-audience, etc. in Grass's narrating dwarf), every one of which will in some way affect the manner and therefore the content of his narrative. Consequently, as already indicated, discussion of point of view cannot be limited simply to the analysis of such issues as the narrator's visual, cognitive or evaluative perspective, however significant each of these may be. Rather, it must endeavour to define all or at least the most important of the narrator's characteristics that condition the necessarily interrelated method and message of his narration, thus establishing his relationship to the author, the narrative and the reader. In other words, confirming the implications of Booth's typology, but modifying some of its terminology (Booth, 1961:149ff.), statements about point of view should more properly be concerned with the extent to which the narrator is personalised or impersonalised, advantaged or disadvantaged,[13] involved or distanced,[14] commentative or reticent, self-aware or unself-aware,[15] and reliable or unreliable.[16] Because these categories, as qualitative polarities, are naturally capable of gradation ('slightly personalised', 'highly personalised', etc.) and, unlike Booth's associated concepts, may refer to any fundamental dimension of human nature, be it physical, emotional, intellectual, moral, aesthetic, spiritual or social, they not only allow more adequately for the virtually infinite variety of narrators and points of view; they also conform more closely to what must surely be the sole, valid purpose in examining point of view, namely, the attempt to relate narrative means to narrative effects (cf. ibid.:158). Furthermore, since any of the possible combinations and permutations of these qualities will inevitably regulate the type of voice the reader hears at any given moment in a narrative, including the amount and kind of scene or summary (ibid.: 154f., chaps. 1,2), those scholars who insist on distinguishing between point of view and narrative voice are misguided.

Integral to the theory of *Einsinnigkeit*, however, are not only erroneous notions about the nature of the narrator and, by implication, point of view. From the beginning, Beißner also propounded a demonstrably false view of narrative commentary. Thus, in 1952, he asserted: "Kafka läßt dem Erzähler keinen Raum neben oder über den Gestalten, keinen Abstand von dem Vorgang. Es gibt darum bei ihm keine Reflexion über die Gestalten und über deren Handlungen und Gedanken" (op.cit.:35). And in all of his subsequent monographs on Kafka, he never once attempted to modify or abandon this claim (Beißner, 1958:13,25; 1963:7; 1972:34,35). Yet, of the fourteen texts comprising the *Landarzt* collection, no fewer than twelve contain direct commentary of the type he describes, while three of them (*Ein Besuch im Bergwerk*; *Die Sorge des Hausvaters*; *Elf Söhne*) consist, to a large extent, of nothing else. Indeed, the only pieces that actually lack such commentary are those where everything, apart from a very brief and factual, introductory phase, is either stated by a non-narrating character (*Das nächste Dorf*) or mediated through his subconscious (*Ein Traum*).

To recognise the fallacy of Beißner's statement, which numerous other scholars have uncritically repeated, one need only examine the two longest and most personalised narratives of the collection: *Ein Landarzt* and *Ein Bericht für eine Akademie*. In the former, the totally involved narrator nevertheless comments directly and evaluatively on at least all of the following subjects: the gods (*Se* 125), his patient's family, himself, communicating with people (*Se* 126), the neighing of his horses, his patient's condition, the people in his district (*Se* 127), his patient's wound and the human estate, his successor, his era, his patients' nature, their treatment of him, and the answering of the nightbell (*Se* 128). Similarly, in his autobiographical report, the more distanced, human-simian narrator of the second work provides both his fictional listeners and the actual reader with his explicit views on a whole range of topics: his progress and attainments (*Se* 147), the nature of all earthly creatures, his theatrical standing, his name, newspaper reporters (*Se* 148), truth and the high-minded (*Se* 149), his own narration (*Se* 149f.), freedom (*Se* 150), the ship's crew (*Se* 150,152), promises and their fulfilment (*Se* 151f.), his fate, imitating human beings (*Se* 153), learning, his educative progress, the notion of *Ausweg*, his development, his chimpanzee mate (*Se* 154), his present level of achievement (*Se* 154f.) and other people's opinion of it (*Se* 155). By comparison with these two stories and the trio of works already mentioned, the remaining personalised texts containing direct commentary (*Der neue Advokat*; *Ein altes Blatt*; *Schakale und Araber*) differ only in the extent and topical range of their explicit judgements, the most reticent narrator being the traveller in *Schakale und Araber*, who limits himself to a tentative assessment of the conflict between the story's two opposed groups (*Se* 133), a brief remark about the innate reserve of Arabs (*Se* 135), and a highly emotive description of the jackals as they consume a dead camel (*Se* 135).

Among the impersonalised works, on the other hand, direct commentary is, as one might expect, usually less common and far less obtrusive. Nevertheless, in *Auf der Galerie*, for example, it is still clearly present in every evaluative statement the disembodied speaker utters about each of the participants, especially the actual ringmaster and his attitude towards the equestrienne, in the second paragraph: "der Direktor, hingebungsvoll ihre Augen suchend, in Tierhaltung ihr entgegenatmet; vorsorglich sie auf den Apfelschimmel hebt, als wäre sie eine über alles geliebte Enkelin (...); die Sprünge der Reiterin scharfen Blickes verfolgt; ihre Kunstfertigkeit kaum begreifen kann" and, at the end of her performance, "keine Huldigung des Publikums für genügend erachtet" (*Se* 129). Exactly the same kind of technique is also to be encountered in *Eine kaiserliche Botschaft*, where the impersonalised narrator is even more overtly commentative. For not only does he open his account with a reference to the imperial subject as "dem jämmerlichen Untertanen, dem winzig vor der kaiserlichen Sonne in die fernste Ferne geflüchteten Schatten"

(*Se* 138), he also breaks another of Beißner's ostensible and widely accepted rules (s. Beißner, 1952:32) by frequently anticipating the outcome of the action (*Se* 138f.), a characteristic shared, to a lesser extent, by those other direct commentators: the country doctor, the cobbler of *Ein altes Blatt* and the worried family man, all of whom end their utterances with observations about the future and, like the narrator of the imperial message, always in negative, even desolate terms.

The last two pieces that need to be considered in this context present such a sharp contrast that, in almost every respect, they constitute the virtual extremes of Kafka's impersonalised narrative practice in the *Landarzt* collection, and their use of direct commentary is no exception. The works in question are, of course, *Vor dem Gesetz* and *Ein Brudermord*, the one a model of subtlety in its control of narrative techniques and effects, the other a striking example of self-indulgence and confusion. Thus, although the highly impersonalised and intellectually advantaged or 'omniscient' narrators of both works employ direct commentary of the kind already mentioned, in the former it is restricted to a description of the doorkeeper's enquiries as "teilnahmslose Fragen, wie sie große Herren stellen" (*Se* 132) and a remark so matter-of-fact that it has generally gone unnoticed as commentary at all, namely, that "das Tor zum Gesetz offensteht wie immer" (*Se* 131). The crucial words here are, of course, the last two, since they contradict the doorkeeper's final, bellowed declaration that he is going to shut the door. Thus they assume enormous importance in a complete interpretation of the work. So, too, do the direct comments of the narrator in *Ein Brudermord*, the glaring difference being that, in this case, they are cheaply emotive and ultimately contradictory. When the murderer, for example, notices the flash of his dagger in the moonlight, the narrator remarks: "nicht genug für Schmar" (*Se* 144), and continues to paint a picture of a totally antipathetic, bloodthirsty killer. He also does his utmost to make the reader disapprove of an eye-witness to the murder: "Warum duldete das alles der Private Pallas, der in der Nähe aus seinem Fenster im zweiten Stockwerk alles beobachtete? Ergründe die Menschennatur!" (*Se* 144). The approaching, unsuspecting victim, on the other hand, is portrayed with almost

78

excessive pathos, so that when he gazes up at the dark-blue and gold of the night sky, the narrator observes: "Unwissend blickt er es an, unwissend streicht er das Haar unter dem gelüpften Hut; nichts rückt dort oben zusammen, um ihm die allernächste Zukunft anzuzeigen; alles bleibt an seinem unsinnigen, unerforschlichen Platz" (Se 145). Yet, after this innocent, diligent, law-abiding citizen and husband has just been stabbed twice in the throat and once in the stomach by a friend, the very same narrator callously remarks: "Wasserratten, aufgeschlitzt, geben einen ähnlichen Laut von sich wie Wese" (Se 145). As a later, detailed analysis of the whole story will confirm, this is the rhetoric of turbid sensationalism.

If the views of Beißner and many other Kafka scholars are deficient in their failure to recognise direct narrative commentary, they are even more so in their apparent ignorance of the numerous indirect forms such commentary may assume. However, since the latter have been considered at some length in the earlier sections of this discussion (s.a. Lubbock, 1921:67f.; Petsch, 1934:113f.; Kayser, 1954:28), further elaboration becomes superfluous. Consequently, the point has now been reached where all the notions central to the theory of *Einsinnigkeit* have been closely examined and, when necessary, revised, so that an attempt can finally be made to define more precisely the real nature of the technique which Beißner and so many others have debated for so long. And because *Das Urteil* (Sept. 1912), apart from being relatively brief, is also generally acknowledged as the first work in which Kafka actually employed this technique, it will be taken as a typical example.

In terms of the categories already proposed, the fundamental and most obvious characteristic of this story's narrator is his high degree of impersonalisation, the fact that he is known to the reader almost exclusively by implication, as an anonymous voice relating a certain set of circumstances and events in a particular manner. Consistent with this attitude, he is also totally unself-aware, never once drawing attention to or discussing himself in any of his dimensions, least of all his role as narrator. Furthermore, he is extremely advantaged, being endowed with the power of direct access to another's thoughts and emotions or what Booth (1961:163) calls "inside views". Because he is constituted of these three basic qualities, the differences between him and the image the reader gains of the work's author will be minimal, so that he must also be construed as highly reliable, that is, as conforming most closely to the author's implied norms in the text (cf. Booth, 1961:158ff., chaps. 7,8; Chatman, 1978:149).

Despite his capacity for inside views, however, this narrator's advantage is strictly limited, being applied solely to the mind of the story's central character, Georg Bendemann, although it must be conceded that, in the following passage, the phrase: "wie er erwartet hatte", lacking any such adverb as 'offenbar' or 'vermutlich', could be interpreted as the narrator's direct insight into the father's mind as well: "Der Vater beugte sich vor, fiel aber nicht. Da Georg sich nicht näherte, wie er erwartet hatte, erhob er sich wieder" (*Se* 31). Besides being rigorously concentrated in this way, the narrator's psychological advantage is also not continuously exploited, so that parts of the story are not transmitted through the immediate, personal consciousness of the 'hero' at all. In the opening paragraph, for example, the narrator is clearly at a distance from his central character, setting the scene and portraying Georg from without, as is evident from his use of the phrase "in spielerischer Langsamkeit" (*Se* 23), an expression which cannot possibly be interpreted as having passed through Georg's mind at the time he was sealing the letter. Similar instances of distanced narration are provided by the summary beginning "Im Laufe dieser drei Jahre" (*Se* 24), the dramatically presented flashback to a conversation between Georg and his fiancée (*Se* 25), the bridging passage from "Mit diesem Brief in der Hand" to "das Zimmer seines Vaters, in dem er schon seit Monaten nicht gewesen war" (*Se* 26), another flashback, about his decision never to be taken by surprise (*Se* 30), the depiction of the maid's reaction *after* Georg has rushed past her (*Se* 32), and the very last sentence with its reference to phenomena of which Georg can scarcely any longer be aware (*Se* 32).

Nevertheless, for the greater part, the narrator of *Das Urteil* transmits his story through or from the standpoint of his central character's consciousness, relating only what that figure could be construed as actually perceiving, thinking or feeling at any given moment in the fiction. Necessarily, therefore, he shows a high degree of intellectual and emotional involvement in what he is narrating, a fact he sometimes emphasises (*Se* 23,26,29) by employing *erlebte Rede* or 'narrated monologue'.[17] And the combined effect of these interrelated, narrative features is to make the reader identify with Georg as well, even to the extent of uncritically accepting his whole evaluation of the work's contents and thus of condemning all that his father represents, an attitude unmistakably implicit in the many Oedipal and similar interpretations of the text (cf. Beicken, 1974: 241ff.). Yet, quite apart from the distanced passages just mentioned, the narrator, in league with the author, also adopts other subtle means of counteracting this unquestioning empathy. One is to make the confrontation between Georg and his father considerably longer than the opening section of the work and to present it in a generally scenic manner, so that inside views of the protagonist become increasingly fewer and briefer, while direct speech, of which the father has the lion's share, becomes the dominant method of narrative communication, thus lending added weight to an outlook opposed to Georg's.

Another means of creating distance between the reader and the central character is the narrator's use of unobtrusive, direct commentary, most of which is directed against Georg, at least in the sense of undermining the initial impression he creates of complete self-confidence and moral certainty. Thus, very soon after his father has opened their conversation, he begins to lose track of things, speaking "wie im Nachhang zu dem Früheren" (*Se* 27) and following his father's movements "ganz verloren" (*Se* 27). A short while later, he is described as "verlegen" (*Se* 28) and, before long, feels impelled to make a decision "kurz mit aller Bestimmtheit" (*Se* 29), although the narrator clearly doubts the efficacy of his decision: "Es schien ja fast, wenn man genauer zusah, daß die Pflege, die dort dem Vater bereitet werden sollte, zu spät kommen könnte" (*Se* 29).[18] As his self-assurance continues to wane, he tries to jog his father's memory by childishly nodding at him "aufmunternd" (*Se* 29), he rushes about "fast zerstreut" (*Se* 30), and remembers a personal resolve, only to forget it immediately, "wie man einen kurzen Faden durch ein Nadelöhr zieht" (*Se* 30). From then on, thoughts simply whizz through his mind, "denn immerfort vergaß er alles" (*Se* 31), and the process of psychological disintegration gathers such pace that finally he implicitly admits his alleged guilt, is condemned to death by drowning, and straightway hurtles from the room to carry out the sentence. It is only at this point that the direct commentary becomes positive: "Schon hielt er das Geländer fest, wie ein Hungriger die Nahrung. Er schwang sich über, als der ausgezeichnete Turner, der er in seinen Jugendjahren zum Stolz seiner Eltern gewesen war" (Se 32). But it is too late, for what had previously been positive now serves only to confirm the negative.

The final, most important method by which narrator and author conspire to distance themselves and the reader from Georg consists in that indirect commentary deriving from the work's very structure. Here, as in *Die Verwandlung*, *Der Verschollene*, *Der Prozeß* and *Das Schloß*, this effect is produced essentially by so shaping the course of events that they profoundly challenge the protagonist's version of reality and should cause the reader to do the same. In other words, like Milena Jesenskà-Polak when Kafka promised to send her his now famous letter to his father (*Hv* 162-223), through the total form of *Das Urteil* the reader, too, is tacitly warned: "Und verstehe beim Lesen alle advokatorischen Kniffe" (*Bm* 80),[19] that skill at which so many of Kafka's eminently plausible, non-narrating 'heroes' are so extremely adept. Among the scores of commentators on this story (cf. Beicken, 1974:241ff.; A. Flores, 1976:168ff.; A. Flores, 1976a), the only one to explicitly recognise this principle is Stern (1976a), who refers to "the extraordinary narrative triumph that is achieved here, where the words on the page are assembled ostensibly to assert proposition A but in reality — and I do not mean any obscure, hidden reality, but the narrative reality conveyed through the text — but in reality assert *non* A" (op.cit.:124). Since Stern's outstanding interpretation and evaluation then provide a detailed account of this subtle technique and its implications for the entire work, it will be illustrated here by only one example, a case he actually does not mention.

Before Georg's father condemns him to death, one of the accusations he levels against him is that he has "unserer Mutter Andenken geschändet" (*Se* 30). Yet, at a very early stage in the text, the narrator, employing an inside view and discussing Georg's friend in Russia, creates the very opposite impression when he relates:

Von dem Todesfall von Georgs Mutter, der vor etwa zwei Jahren erfolgt war und seit welchem Georg mit seinem alten Vater in gemeinsamer Wirtschaft lebte, hatte der Freund wohl noch erfahren und sein Beileid in einem Brief mit einer Trockenheit ausgedrückt, die ihren Grund nur darin haben konnte, daß die Trauer über ein solches Ereignis in der Fremde ganz unvorstellbar wird. (*Se* 24)

Obviously there is a clash here between two opposed assessments of the same reality. Shortly afterwards, however, the reader is told that, since his friend's return to Russia, more than three years earlier, Georg has been at pains to keep from him any news that might disturb the image he retains of his hometown (*Se* 24f.). Consequently, he has limited himself to writing letters about "bedeutungslose Vorfälle" (*Se* 25). But since Georg's secretiveness is futile unless it presupposes that he, alone, has remainded his friend's correspondent at home, it becomes evident that, despite the hedging "wohl noch" of the text, the friend must actually have heard from Georg, himself, about his mother's death. And because the latter occurred only about two years previously, it, too, must be included among those incidents that Georg explicitly regards as "bedeutungslos", so that his implied claims of profound grief at his mother's death are, in reality, a sham. In this indirect way, the text repeatedly establishes the central character's unreliability beneath his façade of amiable plausibility, though whether this justifies the father's sentence of death is quite another matter.

Briefly, then, the narrative method inadequately defined as *Einsinnigkeit* consists in the highly impersonalised, unself-aware, yet reliable narration of a story, in which the narrator's extremely advantaged inside views are generally very detailed, but remain limited to the mind of his central character, who may be and, in Kafka's case, always is emotionally, intellectually and morally unreliable. Contrary to the assumptions of most scholars, however, this does not imply that stories told in such a manner may consist only of what the protagonist could be regarded as having actually perceived, thought or felt, consciously and subconsciously, at any particular moment in the narrative. Rather, as the analysis of *Das Urteil* should have demonstrated, the method in question is considerably more flexible, affording the narrator a whole range of means by which he may distance himself, to varying degrees, from the immediate awareness of his central character. Apart from indirect commentary through structure, context within a collection, recurring motifs, symbols and the like, these may include summary, flashbacks, previews (cf. opening of *Der Prozeß*), the mention of phenomena clearly beyond the range of the central character's mind (cf. ending of *Die Verwandlung*), unobtrusive direct commentary and, in some instances, even brief remarks by the narrator in his own person, a practice to be observed not only in the novels of Henry James, "the old intruder" (cf. Booth, 1961:58f.), but also in the last few pages of Uwe Johnson's *Eine Reise wegwohin, 1960*. As Kudszus (1964:193) has quite rightly observed, the use of this narrative method also seems invariably to entail a degree of ambiguity, in the sense that the thoughts of figures other than the protagonist may be directly presented as well, but without being unequivocally attributable either to the knowledge of the impersonalised, advantaged narrator or to the unsignalled inference or supposition of the central character. In addition to the example already quoted from *Das Urteil*, a considerable number of others have been noted in all three of Kafka's novels, though they have generally been misinterpreted as breaks in perspective (e.g. Leopold, 1963; Sheppard, 1973), *Versehen* and *Verfehlungen* (e.g. Walser, 1961:32), or they have simply been assigned, usually somewhat arbitrarily, to the protagonist (e.g. Beißner; Kobs). That such ambiguity is not to be resolved in these ways, that it is evidently intrinsic to the method under discussion and far from being peculiar to Kafka, may be illustrated by a short extract from Henry James' *What Maisie Knew* (1897). At the very beginning of Chapter 3, Maisie is loudly told by her mother that she must learn to keep her thoughts to herself. The text then continues:

> This was exactly what Maisie had already learned, and the accomplishment was just the source of her mother's irritation. It was of a horrid little critical system, a tendency in her silence, to judge her elders, that this lady suspected her, liking as she did, for her own part, a child to be simple and confiding.

From every stylistic feature of this passage, it is obvious that the voice uttering these words cannot possibly belong to six-year-old Maisie. What is not clear, however, and what cannot be immediately clarified is whether this voice is expressing its own direct insight into Ida Farange's mind or Maisie's implied version of it, since every idea in the extract could be paraphrased into the language of a very perceptive and sensitive child like Maisie. As a consequence, for want of evidence to the contrary, the reader is left with no valid alternative to the assumption that both interpretations must apply (cf. Kudszus, 1964:205).[20] Had this fact been more widely acknowledged by Kafka scholars, most of the debate about *Einsinnigkeit* would never have arisen. Indeed, as a description of narrative perspective, the term might never have been coined.

Nor need it have been. For the technique at issue had been consistently and more accurately described by Henry James in his critical prefaces, the first of which appeared in 1907 (cf. Blackmur, 1934), and since that time his terms (third-person) 'centre of consciousness' or 'reflector' have become so firmly established in the vocabulary of narrative theory that they will be used in the remainder of this study as well, although the term 'reflector' will be preferred, since it does not exclude the element of the subconscious or unconscious, so important, for example, in *Ein Traum* and *Auf der Galerie*. Moreover, before Kafka had composed a single extant work, James had already brought this technique to a level of extreme refinement in a long series of short stories and novels, while other writers to follow his example include James Joyce, Virginia Woolf, Graham Greene, François Mauriac, Jean-Paul Sartre, Albert Camus, Robert Musil, Thomas Mann and Uwe Johnson. To call such a technique "Kafkas einzigartige und neue Errungenschaft" (Beicken, 1971:498) or to claim that "Kafka was the first to succeed with the possibilities of narrative consciousness" (Szanto, 1972:7) and that "his narrative technique was unique" (ibid.:42) is therefore, at the very least, to be mistaken.

Before this discussion of *Einsinnigkeit* can be concluded, however, there is one further, extremely basic issue that needs to be examined, namely, the almost universal assumption that Kafka's fiction is to be regarded as invariably narrative. Among the vast majority of scholars, including virtually everyone who has attempted to analyse the rhetoric of his works, this matter has simply been taken for granted. But a significant few have thought otherwise.

85

Rohner (1950), for example, maintains of Kafka, "daß er zum großen Teil überhaupt nicht erzählt, sondern die Problematik seiner Gegenstände erörtert" (op.cit.:54); Fürst (1956) is convinced: "Kafka erzählt nicht Geschichten, immer macht er Forschungen" (op.cit.: 50); Wiese (1962) refers to *Die Verwandlung* as "mehr Analyse als Erzählung" (op.cit.:325); Krusche (1974) remarks about the novels: "nicht das, was geschieht, steht im Vordergrund des Erzählinteresses, sondern die verschiedenen Deutungen, die das Geschehen durch die Personen der Handlung erfährt" (op.cit.:53); and similar views are to be found in studies by Martini (1954:319f.), Leopold (1959: 59ff.), Hasselblatt (1964:59), Flach (1967:129ff.), M. Greenberg (1968:146), Fingerhut (1969:117) and Kobs (1970:25,33).[21]

Implicit in all of these dissenting statements and the supposition they are opposing is, of course, a theory about the nature of narration. Yet, apart from Flach, who esoterically construes as non-narrative any text which "keinen intentionalitätsbestimmenden Satz enthält" (Flach, 1967:129ff.), no other scholar broaches the subject at all, despite its self-evident and crucial relevance. Before the issue can be pursued any further, therefore, an attempt must obviously be made to provide what so many others have omitted. Summarising the arguments of Müller (1947:10; 1950:5) and Lämmert (1955: 20f.), Seidler (1959) defines the essence of narration thus:

> Die Ursituation des Erzählens besteht im Berichten. (...) Eine Welt von Begebenheiten ist gleichsam die Energiequelle, sie wird im Sprechen aufgebaut und zu einer Handlung zusammengezogen. Die Grundform lautet — so hat schon Herder erkannt — 'es ward'. Aber sofort muß man diesem 'Es ward' noch hinzufügen: 'und dann'. Damit ist das ideale Grundgerüst alles Erzählens festgelegt. (op.cit.:456; s.a. Petsch, 1934:61; Kayser, 1948:349ff.)

If one accepts these well-founded, eminently reasonable distinguishing criteria and applies them to the forty-four works Kafka published in his own lifetime, the astonishing fact to emerge is that approximately two-thirds of his output consists of texts which are clearly non-narrative. The dividing-line is, admittedly, not always easy to draw. Nevertheless, of the fourteen pieces constituting the *Landarzt* collection, six can certainly be classified as non-narrative (*Der neue Advokat; Auf der Galerie; Ein altes Blatt; Das nächste Dorf; Die Sor-*

ge des Hausvaters; Elf Söhne), while two others (*Ein Besuch im Berg-werk; Ein Bericht für eine Akademie*) may be regarded as borderline cases, for although their basic structure derives from an interconnected series of events, this is so overlaid with description and commentary that one can scarcely regard incidents as providing their primary "Energiequelle".

The significance underlying this preponderance of non-narratives is suggested by Wellek/Warren's observation that narrative fiction "or, better, a term like 'story', calls our attention to time, and a sequence in time" (Wellek/Warren, 1942:222). In other words, Kafka's unmistakable preference for non-narrative composition is a corollary of his attitude to time. Many scholars have commented on this latter aspect of his ouevre, stressing its constantly present, static or iterative quality.[22] However, Martini (1954) and Leopold (1959) are alone in directly relating it to the matter of narrative essence, though even they are still not prepared to infer that some of Kafka's fiction is actually non-narrative. Furthermore, because so relatively few scholars have concerned themselves with the present collection, there has also been a general failure to recognise that Kafka does have a temporal perspective, an awareness of the present in terms of the past and the future, but that the past is always presented as an irrevocably lost positive, while the future becomes simply an extension of the present's fundamental negativity, culminating inevitably in utter failure, ruin, death or total oblivion (cf. *Josefine die Sängerin*). Thus the distinctive characteristic of time in Kafka's total literary world-view is not so much "stehender Sturmlauf" (*Tb* 169) or "immerwährender Augenblick" (Ramm, 1971:47ff.; cf. *Hv* 39f.), but rather its radically disjunctive or inorganic quality, and this, as later discussion of *Das nächste Dorf* will attempt to show, has crucial implications for the notion of identity as well (cf. Martini, 1954:319f.). Moreover, questions of "Schaffensprozeß" apart (Binder, 1971; 1976a; Hillmann, 1979), it may also serve to explain why twenty-seven of the forty-four works Kafka, himself, had published do not extend beyond two printed pages, while only nine exceed five pages, a surely not insignificant fact, but one which has been totally ignored in favour of empty speculation about intrinsic fragmentariness (cf. Binder, 1979b:67ff.).

Assuming, then, that much of Kafka's fiction is not narrative, one is immediately faced with a problem of nomenclature, since the terms 'non-narrative' and 'non-narrator' are both too imprecise and too negative to be at all adequate. As possible alternatives, Leopold (1959:59f.) has proposed 'report' and Krusche (1974:21) 'Reflexionen' or 'Betrachtungen'. However, since the former does not exclude the concept of narration and both the latter imply an attitude of composure generally quite foreign to the works concerned, a more satisfying solution is to be derived from the following remarks by Lämmert (1955): "Die Formel 'es war einmal' drückt noch keinerlei Geschehens-Intention aus; sie kann deshalb nur als das Urschema erzählerischer *Exposition* gelten, als das Einlaßtor in die fiktive Welt, die erst dann erzählerisch gestaltet wird, wenn aus dem zuständlichen 'es war' ein 'es ward' oder 'es geschah' sich entbindet" (op.cit.:21). What Lämmert is describing here as 'exposition' corresponds precisely to the type of enunciation in all of Kafka's non-narrative fiction. Consequenty, although it logically requires the less than euphonious term 'expositor', both will be employed as alternatives to 'narrative' and 'narrator', respectively, in the remainder of this study, while later analysis of point of view will naturally refer to expositors as well, since they are just as subject to the qualitative polarities already mentioned as are narrators. *Einsinnigkeit*, on the other hand, and all the erroneous notions associated with it, will now be taken as disproven and, therefore, of no further use.

Paradoxie

The last concept to be examined in this survey also gained currency during the 1950's, since which time it has become as prominent among Kafka studies as the word 'parable'. Like the latter, it, too, owes its widespread adoption to the commentaries of Politzer, who, in one of the earliest reviews of Kafka research (s.a. Ackermann, 1950), firmly asserted: "Das charakteristische Stilmerkmal von Franz Kafkas Werk ist das Paradox. (...) Wo immer und von welchem Standpunkt auch man Kafkas Werk anrührt, man wird immer einem Paradox begegnen" (Politzer, 1950:214). And although, in his later, far more comprehensive analyses, Politzer (1962; 1965; 1973a) broadened his views considerably, he has never ceased to regard the paradox as being of central importance to Kafka's fiction and its interpretation.

Through his popularisation of this notion, however, Politzer has created extensive confusion as well, because his own use of the term is so loose that numerous others have been led to follow his example. As Kobs (1970) has rightly observed:

> Für Politzer gilt jede befremdende Wendung, jede Unstimmigkeit, jeder Widerspruch schon als ein Paradox; für paradox hält er es zum Beispiel, wenn ein Schutzmann statt einer Auskunft eine abweisende Antwort gibt, paradox erscheint ihm sogar die Redeweise von einer 'gesteigerten Erlösung', wie sie sich am Ende der Erzählung *Josefine, die Sängerin* findet. (op.cit.:12)

In common parlance, it is true, 'paradox' may be and often is employed in this imprecise manner. But, from the Stoics onwards, its exact meaning has always been, in essence, 'a seeming contradiction', a fact which has recently been confirmed by such Kafka scholars as Sandbank (1967), Neumann (1968:704,730), Fingerhut (1969:299) and Steinmetz (1977:87f.). Neumann, for example, after reviewing acknowledged standard works on the subject by Heiss, Schilder, Friedrich and Schröer, reaches the conclusion:

> daß von der Antike bis zu Kierkegaards 'schlechthinnigem Paradox' in den 'Philosophischen Brocken' (Düsseldorf-Köln, 1960, S. 34ff.) das Paradox als scheinbar Widersinniges, als 'ganz Unwahrscheinliches' (a.a.O.S.49), als eine der allgemeinen Meinung widersprechende Aussage betrachtet wird, die sich bei genauerem Nachdenken als entweder richtig, oder doch für einen bestimmten Zusammenhang (etwa die in sich widersprüchliche Tatsache der Erbsünde) als sinnvoll erweist. (op.cit.:704)

Yet, despite their recognition of this current, traditional meaning and their repudiation of the very frequent, inaccurate usage encouraged, if not initiated by Politzer, two very influential scholars have argued that Kafka has produced a new, individual form of paradox which constitutes the basic feature of all his works. The first of these is Neumann (1968), who claims that Kafka's mode of thinking and writing defies the conventional laws of logic and rhetoric in that it creates a "gleitendes Paradox". What he means by this term, he first illustrates by analysing the following two aphoristic statements from Kafka's notebooks: "Wer sucht, findet nicht, aber wer nicht sucht, wird gefunden" (*Hv* 94) and "Ein Käfig ging einen Vogel suchen" (*Hv* 41,82). Then he provides this general explanation:

> Kafkas Paradoxa leben nicht aus einer Verkehrung des Normalen, sie basieren selbst schon auf einem Widerspruch. Sie lenken nicht auf eine Synthese des Widersprüchlichen hin, wie das traditionelle Paradox, sondern von jeder erwarteten Stimmigkeit ab; jede Auflösung ist bloß eine Reduktion auf neuerlich und viel ursprünglicher Unbegreifliches. Dadurch wird jedoch die Beziehung zwischen Vogel und Käfig, zwischen Suchen und Finden nicht aufgehoben; sie bleibt bloß unbestimmt, ist weder auf einen glatten Widerspruch, noch auf vorschnelle Harmonisierung und Ausgleichung festzulegen. Kafkas 'Umkehrung' ist also nicht die des 'klassischen' Paradoxes; sie erscheint vielmehr stets verbunden mit einer 'Ablenkung' von konventionellen Denkbahnen und erzielt dabei zwei entscheidende Wirkungen: Einerseits treten durch sie zwei Pole — im vorliegenden Beispiel Suchen und Finden, Vogel und Käfig — in einen ebenso entschiedenen wie befremdlichen Bezug; und gerade auf diesen Bezug scheint es Kafka anzukommen. Andererseits läßt sich dieser Bezug auf keine der üblichen Denkverknüpfungen reduzieren. (op.cit.:706)

Although there are many objections which might be raised to Neumann's definition and its subsequent elaboration, the most obvious and basic point to be made is that, if the phenomena he is discussing are to be described as paradoxical in any sense, then they must necessarily partake of the essence of the paradox, that is, they must consist of a contradiction which is later resolved and thus proves to have been only apparent, as is the case in the following line from Paul Fleming's *Gedanken über der Zeit*:

"Ach daß doch jene Zeit, die ohne Zeit ist, käme (...)." However, since in Neumann's own explanation it is openly conceded that the stylistic features he is discussing do not, in his opinion, conform to these criteria, there is no justification for regarding any of them as a paradox, 'gleitend' or otherwise. Indeed, it is difficult to imagine how a paradox could ever be aptly described as 'gleitend' and still remain true to its essential nature.

To reject Neumann's term, however, is not to deny that much of Kafka's prose exhibits some of the characteristics he mentions. No-one would seriously question, for example, that the author deliberately aims to challenge conventional ways of thinking or that, to this end, he may employ "semantische Verschiebung" (ibid.:722ff.), "Zitatentstellung" (ibid.:726ff.), "entfremdete Metaphern" (ibid.:728ff.) and even banal pictures which still manage to assume enormous significance, like that of the fur-clad woman in *Die Verwandlung*. On the other hand, one would certainly have to dispute the assertion that "Stilgesetze der kafkaschen Prosa überhaupt" (ibid.:733) can be derived, very largely, from a selection of the author's most enigmatic aphorisms and that the "beliebige Reproduzierbarkeit" of a picture therefore renders it "trivial" (ibid.:736). Nevertheless, what remains of paramount importance is that the devices analysed by Neumann in no way exhaust the range of Kafka's rhetoric, and that they do not constitute paradoxes of a radically novel kind. On the contrary, they do not necessarily constitute paradoxes at all. To insist on this point is all the more essential because, as Henel (1964:247) has already indicated and the later interpretations of this study will confirm, Kafka's literary world-view is undoubtedly and fundamentally paradoxical, not as the expression of some drifting antinomies, but in the very precise sense accepted since the Stoics. Had Neumann, like Kafka (cf. *Br* 20; Pasley, 1966; Walther, 1977), been more familiar with the writings of neo-Platonist, Christian mystics, he, too, might have recognised this fact. For one of the statements he quotes, namely, "Wer sucht, findet nicht, aber wer nicht sucht, wird gefunden" is either an empirical hyperbole or a close paraphrase of Angelus Silesius' paradoxical couplet entitled: "Gott findet man mit nicht-suchen" in *Der cherubinische Wandersmann* I, 171 (s.a. *Hv* 124).

Towards the end of his article, Neumann explains that the aim of his "Arbeit" has been to show, "wie man nicht denken darf, wenn man Kafkas Texte nicht verfehlen will; und sie versucht, in die Kafkasche Denkbewegung — die im Grunde eher eine Schreibbewegung ist — einzuführen; sie kann nicht Resultate formulieren, sondern nur den Nachvollzug kafkascher Denkbewegungen erleichtern" (op.cit.: 732). Thus, two years before the appearance of Kobs' study (1970), he anticipated not only the ultimate conclusion of the latter's commentary, but also one of its central concepts. For, as noted in the discussion of *Einsinnigkeit*, Kobs, too, believes that the interpretation of Kafka's work cannot proceed beyond formal description, and that this is due to the creation of a special kind of paradox:

> Drei Monate sind es, die ein Paradox von dieser Art bestimmen. Die Teile müssen in einem streng logischen Zusammenhang stehen, müssen für sich und in ihrem Verhältnis rational überprüfbar sein. Sie müssen am Ende überraschend umschlagen: die Argumentationskette muß zu ihrem Ausgangspunkt zurückkehren und sich so zu einem Zirkel verschließen. Dieser Zirkel ist das wesentliche Strukturmoment des Paradoxes. (...) Als drittes aber gehört zu einem Kafkaischen Paradox der Zwang, sich immer wieder auf diesen Zirkel einzulassen, ihn stets neu zu durchdenken; denn das Bewußtsein kann sich nicht damit zufriedengeben, daß eine Folge von logisch aufeinander bezogenen Einzelsätzen insgesamt keinen positiven Sinn ergeben will. (Kobs, 1970:12f.)

According to Steinmetz (1977:87f.), Kobs' notion of a paradox is based on Kierkegaard's original understanding of the term as "eines als radikal erfahrenen Widerspruchs" (op.cit.:87), an idea he later abandoned because he wanted "durch das Paradox 'Platz schaffen, daß Gott kommen kann' (...)" (loc.cit.). Whether this is true or not, the obvious fact remains that the phenomenon Kobs is describing does not conform to the essential criteria of the paradox in its traditional, exact and still generally accepted definition. Rather, it would seem to correspond more closely to a vicious circle, in the same way that most of the allegedly 'gleitenden Paradoxa' mentioned by Neumann are actually what others would more aptly regard as riddles or enigmas. In any case, despite their justified criticism of Politzer, neither of these two scholars can be said to have employed the term with much more precision than their predecessor or to have elucidated its crucial significance in Kafka's literary world-view. What they have achieved, however, is to assist in establishing that increasingly popular dogma which asserts that Kafka's works are ultimately and intrinsically resistant to interpretation, that they may be structurally described, even 'explained' (Szanto), but never explicated. Already it has been shown that, in respect of narrative perspective or point of view, such an argument is simply not valid. Now an attempt will have to be made to assess the same contention on the level of verbal logic as well. And since Kobs' analysis of the brief exposition *Die*

Bäume has come to be regarded as definitive proof of this claim, it will be examined as a test-case.

Although first written probably late in 1904[23] as part of Kafka's incomplete work, *Beschreibung eines Kampfes* (s. *BkII* 122,123), the text now known as *Die Bäume* was later removed from its original context, stylistically revised, and initially published by Kafka in a collection of eight pieces called *Betrachtung* (1908), then as one of five pieces designated *Betrachtungen* (1910), and finally in its present form, reproduced below, as the second last of eighteen pieces collectively entitled *Betrachtung* (Dec. 1912; cf. *Bf* 175; Binder, 1975:56, 116ff.; A. Flores, 1976:3f.).

Die Bäume

Denn wir sind wie Baumstämme im Schnee. Scheinbar liegen sie glatt auf, und mit kleinem Anstoß sollte man sie wegschieben können. Nein, das kann man nicht, denn sie sind fest mit dem Boden verbunden. Aber sieh, sogar das ist nur scheinbar. (*Se* 19)

In order of priority, the first issue raised by Kobs is the meaning of 'scheinbar' in the second sentence. As he understands it, this adverb must be construed in the same sense as the 'nur scheinbar' of the last sentence (Kobs, 1970:9). Steinmetz (1977), on the other hand, regards such a proposition as "unnötig stringent" and suggests that the word should be taken "in der neutraleren Bedeutung von 'es sieht so aus', 'es hat den Anschein', 'es scheint' (...)" (op.cit.:89). However, from Kafka's usage elsewhere, it is evident that he employs the term 'scheinbar' very carefully, in its strict sense, as the following extract from *Forschungen eines Hundes* should serve to demonstrate: "den anderen (Hunden) scheint im Schweigen wohl zu sein, zwar hat es nur diesen Anschein, so wie bei den Musikhunden, die scheinbar ruhig musizierten, in Wirklichkeit aber sehr aufgeregt waren (...)" (*Se* 339). Kobs' interpretation of 'scheinbar' is, therefore, to be affirmed.

Concerning the same sentence, Kobs then maintains that 'scheinbar' can only apply to the first half, because the modal construction 'man sollte ... können' does not permit "die zusätzliche Modalbestimmung durch das Adverb 'scheinbar', sondern nur die durch das Wort 'eigentlich'" (op.cit.:9). But Fingerhut (1972) disagrees, contending:

"so transformiert er ein nichtausformuliertes 'scheinbar' in ein 'eigentlich' (...)" (op.cit.:393). Once again, however, Kobs' explanation is to be preferred, since the subjunctive 'sollte können' already expresses the implied unreality of 'scheinbar' and thus makes the combination of the two, if not impossible, at least extremely unlikely (cf. Ramm, 1971:20).

Assuming that the sense of 'scheinbar' can be rendered by 'in Wirklichkeit nicht', Kobs' next step is to paraphrase the second sentence as "In Wirklichkeit liegen sie nicht glatt auf und eigentlich sollte man sie mit kleinem Anstoß wegschieben können" (ibid.:8f.). From this he then reaches the hardly surprising conclusion, "daß hier tatsächlich eine Unstimmigkeit besteht (...). Obwohl es schon als sicher gilt, daß hier von nur Scheinbarem, nicht Wirklichem die Rede ist, geraten in der zweiten Hälfte des Satzes die Bereiche des Scheinbaren und Wirklichen durcheinander. Der bloße Schein strebt nach der Wirklichkeit des 'Eigentlichen' (...)" (op.cit.:9). There are, however, two very basic errors in this argument. The first pertains to the meaning of the term 'scheinbar'. When used with precision, this adverb or adjective always denotes an opposition between the outward impression created by a phenomenon and its actual reality. Absolutely essential to the notion, therefore, is the implicit contrast between misleading appearance and real fact. Consequently, its meaning cannot be reduced to 'in Wirklichkeit nicht', since such an expression omits the fundamental aspect of misleading appearance (*Schein*), so that its only exact equivalent is 'dem Schein(e) nach'. Kobs' second cardinal mistake is to equate 'eigentlich' with 'wirklich', when the two are plainly distinct, the latter simply asserting or even emphasising that something is actually or in reality so, while the former denotes that, despite factors which may create a different impression, something is actually or really so. It is because of this important difference that clauses containing the adverb 'eigentlich' are frequently preceded or followed by an adversative (e.g. 'aber') or a concessive (e.g. 'obwohl'). Once these necessary distinctions have been drawn, it becomes obvious that there is no logical confusion whatever in the sentence at issue. But the point becomes even clearer when it is also recognised that the two halves of the sentence are actually causally related, the second half constituting

94

a logical inference from the first, so that the whole could, in fact, be accurately paraphrased as 'Da sie scheinbar (dem Scheine nach) glatt aufliegen, sollte man sie (eigentlich) mit kleinem Anstoß wegschieben können'. And since Kobs' theory of a linguistically embedded, 'paradoxical' circle depends entirely on his misconstruction of this second sentence, it totally collapses once the rational validity of that sentence has been demonstrated.

Before *Die Bäume* can be reinterpreted, however, there are two further issues that need to be clarified. The first is the matter of the opening phrase ("Denn wir") which, in Kobs' opinion, "an einen anderen Sachverhalt anzuknüpfen scheint, damit aber ins Leere greift, denn es gibt keinen solchen Anknüpfungspunkt" (op.cit.:8), a view that is shared, with some modifications, by Ramm (1971:21) and Steinmetz (1977:90) as well. Yet, to construe the work in this way is to overlook the crucial factor of context. For, in all of its forms, whether published or unpublished, *Die Bäume* never once occurs in isolation. Within the first version of *Beschreibung eines Kampfes*, for example, it is prefaced by the following remarks from the prayerful man:

> Wir bauen eigentlich unbrauchbare Kriegsmaschinen, Thürme, Mauern, Vorhänge aus Seide und wir könnten uns viel darüber wundern, wenn wir Zeit dazu hätten. Und erhalten uns in Schwebe, wir fallen nicht, wir flattern, wenn wir auch häßlicher sind als Fledermäuse. Und schon kann uns kaum jemand an einem schönen Tage hindern zu sagen: 'Ach Gott heute ist ein schöner Tag'. Denn schon sind wir auf unserer Erde eingerichtet und leben auf Grund unseres Einverständnisses. (*BkII* 120,122)

Despite some minor alterations and additions, the same framework is also provided in the second unpublished version (*BkII* 121,123), while in the final version of *Betrachtung* it is preceded by the following, equally brief exposition called *Wunsch, Indianer zu werden*.

> Wenn man doch ein Indianer wäre, gleich bereit und auf dem rennenden Pferde, schief in der Luft, immer wieder kurz erzitterte über dem zitternden Boden, bis man die Sporen ließ, denn es gab keine Sporen, bis man die Zügel wegwarf, denn es gab keine Zügel, und kaum das Land vor sich als glatt gemähte Heide sah, schon ohne Pferdehals und Pferdekopf. (*Se* 18f.)[1]

Although the differences between these two types of framework are undeniably great, they nevertheless have one concern in common, namely, the relationship between man and the earth. In the first unpublished version, this is made quite explicit by the last sentence, the burden of the whole passage being that man's sense of security and the objects he fabricates in order to express or reinforce it are actually deceptive, since they are based solely on a tacit human agreement to regard the world in a particular, comforting manner rather than face the possible anguish or terror of viewing it otherwise. *Wunsch, Indianer zu werden*, on the other hand, creates the image of a fervently desired, even ideal human condition, characterised by total self-integration and certainty. Instantly decisive and alert, the Red Indian is so completely at one with himself and the world, as he races through the countryside on his horse, that he becomes increasingly oblivious of everything except the sheer motion in which he is utterly involved. Spurs, reins, the nature of the terrain, even the horse's head and neck: all gradually fall away, recede from his consciousness, as he attains the supreme freedom and happiness of a completely untroubled, unself-aware vision in action. Both in its original and in its definitive form, therefore, the context of *Die Bäume* clearly reveals that it is intended as a statement about the underlying nature of the human condition, the "Denn wir" of the final version serving explicitly to generalise the work's ideas and to relate them, as cause, to the preceding wish, as effect (cf. Binder, 1975:119).

The other matter that needs to be settled before this interpretation can be completed is the construction to be placed on the expression 'Baumstämme im Schnee'. According to H. Richter (1962: 76) and Kobs, these objects are to be understood as felled logs, "des Blätterschmucks der Krone entkleidet, nicht mehr im Boden wurzelnd, die liegengeblieben sind, weil man sie nicht rechtzeitig abtransportiert hat" (Kobs, 1970:13). Flach (1967:131) and Ramm (1971: 19ff.), on the other hand, evidently see them as standing in the snow, while Steinmetz (1977:90) maintains that both views are possible and that, in any case, each leads to the same outcome. However, the question cannot be dismissed so lightly, for it makes a great deal of difference whether, as H. Richter and Kobs imply, man is being compared to something already dead, something already severed from the earth, or to something living and rooted in the earth. Furthermore, if the tree-trunks are taken to mean felled logs, it makes nonsense of the notion that they could even apparently be 'fest mit dem Boden verbunden'. Steinmetz (loc.cit.) tries to overcome this difficulty by allowing for "festgefrorene liegende Baumstämme", but in doing so makes equal nonsense of the idea that one might even apparently push them aside 'mit kleinem Anstoß'. Despite the verb 'aufliegen', therefore, the tree-trunks must be interpreted as belonging to living, standing trees, unless one is predetermined to make nonsense of the work.

Viewed in the light of the preceding comments, *Die Bäume* assumes enormous importance in the understanding of Kafka's oeuvre, since it establishes one of the most fundamental characteristics of all his thought and writing, namely, the recognition of a reality superior to and masked by the empirical (cf. *Hv* 121). For, through its developed analogy, *Die Bäume* actually presents three *degrés du savoir*, to use Maritain's term. The first is that of immediate perception, which can be misleading. It is on this level that men, like tree-trunks deep in snow, may seem to resemble insecure, easily removed theatrical props, with no firm tie to the earth. But this illusion is corrected by the second degree of knowledge, the empirical, according to which men, like stands of trees, are known to be physically rooted in the earth, whatever the appearances to the contrary. However, in Kafka's judgement, one must also acknowledge that empirical knowledge, itself, is ultimately an illusion, that physical reality, far from providing man with certainty and security, actually deceives him by making him blind to the metaphysical and preternatural, which may at any moment irrupt into his life (cf. *Die Verwandlung, Der Prozeß* and many similar works), by deflecting his attention from or blocking his access to the truth, which therefore remains ultimately uncertain and unfathomable, and by encouraging him to find comfort in various types of falsehood (cf. *Hv* 39ff., aphorisms on *Sünde, Lüge, Betrug, Böse*). As Kafka was much later (probably in spring, 1923) to remark to Janouch:

Wir leben in einer Zeit des Bösen. Das ist schon daran ersichtlich, daß nichts mehr seinen richtigen Namen trägt. (...) Die Begriffe werden wie entkernte, leere Nußschalen hin- und hergeschoben. So spricht man zum Beispiel von der Heimat jetzt, in diesem Augenblick, da die Wurzeln des Menschen schon längst aus dem Boden gerissen sind. (*Gk* 81f.)

Despite his empirically demonstrable, firm ties with the earth, then, man can, like tree-trunks, be totally uprooted, and Kafka firmly believed that, in his own era, man had been so for a long time. This is the third degree of knowledge, the resolution of the apparent contradiction in the last sentence of *Die Bäume*. For this brief work is truly a paradox, in the precise, traditional and only meaningful sense of the term.

Apart from demonstrating the actual nature of the paradox, however, *Die Bäume* also helps to clarify the vexed question of reality in Kafka's fiction. According to Fingerhut (1969), almost all scholars are agreed in regarding "Kafkas Prosa" as being characterised by the fact, "daß in ihr Reales und Irreales unmittelbar nebeneinandersteht" (op.cit.:60), and his claim is supported by the more recent study of H. Kraft (1972:39ff.). Kobs (1970), on the other hand, maintains that, because the reader is bound to the vision of characters who accept themselves and their co-existents are empirically real, he, too, must "die einsinnig dargestellte Welt als empirische Realität hinnehmen" (op.cit.:53), a proposition which, if valid, would turn all fables, fairytales and science fiction into documentaries. At the opposite extreme, Walser (1961:49,140) denies the reality of the novels any empirical reference at all, and Henel (1967) agrees with him, asserting that Kafka's world is neither "Darstellung einer transzendenten Welt" nor the "Abbild oder Persiflage einer empirischen Wirklichkeit" (op.cit.:254). Consequently, to her mind, even "die Menschen in dieser Welt sind nicht der empirischen Welt entnommen" (loc. cit.), although in the remainder of her article she does not hesitate to attribute human awareness to Kafka's 'heroes' or to interpret their 'Gegenwelt' as the projection of their own repressed guilt, as if awareness, psychic projections and guilt bore no relationship whatever to empirical reality.

That most of Kafka's fiction contains elements which are clearly non-empirical, which belong to the third degree of knowledge, is undeniable. But to interpret all of his literary phenomena in this way is to distort the meaning of the term 'empirical'. Even if one ignores the ambiguity in all of Walser's criteria (op.cit.:49), it is not true that fictional characters, for example, must be "psychologisch wahr" or "anthropologisch menschlich" or "biologisch natürlich" (Henel, 1967: 254) to be empirically representative. On the contrary, if a fictional phenomenon, whether personal or otherwise, is to be classified as empirically representative, the only requirement it must meet is that nothing about it may transgress the accepted limits of the empirically possible. Consequently, despite the fact that many of Kafka's characters never question the actual existence of obviously non-empirical phenomena about them, this does not jeopardise their empirically representative status, for if it did, then one would be logically obliged to conclude that, not only every member of the Flat Earth Society, but also every believer in a god ipso facto forfeited his empirical standing, a proposition which is manifestly absurd. To ignore or deny this principle is to miss the whole point of Kafka's purpose in most of his works, that purpose being, as *Die Bäume* so well illustrates, to challenge the empirically representative or second degree of knowledge. It is for this reason that the traditional and genuine paradox plays such an important part in his fiction.

*   *   *

Reviewing Kafka scholarship in 1967, Kurz made the following observation:

> Um und nach 1950 ist in der Kafka-Forschung eine Zäsur zu verzeichnen. Die weltanschaulichen Aspekte, die meist im publizistischen und vermeintlich logischen Direktgang Kafkas Werk abgezwungen wurden, traten, wenigstens in ihrer unmethodischen Isolierung, zurück. Die ästhetischen Fragen traten als Gegenreaktion und Zeichen des kritischeren Werkbewußtseins in den Vordergrund. (Kurz, 1967:66)

If the deliberations of this chapter and their ensuing conclusions have any validity at all, then clearly they demonstrate the accuracy of Kurz's assessment. At the same time, however, they also confirm the obvious fact that to be in the foreground is not necessarily to be in focus. For, contrary to the opinion of Gaier (1969) and the many other advocates of *Vieldeutigkeit*, it is not the intrinsic nature of Kafka's works which has led to such a bewildering divergence of opinions or 'chorus of lies' about their meaning, but rather the sheer inadequacy of the critical theories with which they have been approached. Now that those shortcomings have been revealed and, it is to be hoped, suitably remedied, an attempt can finally be made to provide a sound basis for the interpretation of what is, after all, the overriding concern of this study: Kafka's *Landarzt* collection.

3. TOWARDS A RHETORIC OF THE COLLECTION

At the beginning of the preface to his monumental study, Booth (1961) explains:

> In writing about the rhetoric of fiction, I am not primarily interested in didactic fiction, fiction used for propaganda or instruction. My subject is the technique of non-didactic fiction, viewed as the art of communicating with readers — the rhetorical resources available to the writer of epic, novel, or short story as he tries, consciously or unconsciously, to impose his fictional world upon the reader.

Among Kafka scholars since Beißner (1952), however, these resources, as revealed by the preceding chapter, have been taken to mean principally, if not exclusively, the author's use of narrative perspective. Furthermore, in adopting this very restricted view of fictional rhetoric, such scholars have the unequivocal support of authority. Lubbock (1921), for example, argues that the "whole intricate question of method in the craft of fiction" is "governed by the question of point of view" (op.cit.:251), and Kayser (1948) agrees with him, when he maintains of the *Erzählhaltung*: "Ihre rechte Erfassung ist für das Verständnis eines Werkes von größter Bedeutung" (op.cit.: 204; s.a. Kayser, 1956:231).

Yet, without in any way underestimating the significance of point of view, examination of *Einsinnigkeit* and fictional perspective in general has disclosed that it is not of primary importance, that narrators, expositors and reflectors may be quite demonstrably unreliable, that their point of view may be undermined or overruled by a whole range of unobtrusive and covert devices at the author's disposal. Consequently, any consideration of fictional rhetoric which attempts to adequately represent the actual nature of its subject matter must give precedence to these other, more subtle elements of the fictional enterprise, since they are the factors which collectively provide the author's indirect commentary and ultimately establish the implicit norms of his work. Regrettably, within the limits of the present study, it will not be possible to treat all of these elements in detail. Nevertheless, some have already been discussed, others will inevitably be mentioned in the later, extensive analysis of the texts, and a few will simply have to be adumbrated as possible corollaries of others. All that the following observations aim to achieve is an accurate and reasonably objective description of the principal means employed by Kafka in the *Landarzt* collection as he attempts to create and 'impose his fictional world upon the reader'. Furthermore, in pursuing this objective, they lay no claim to exclusive validity. Nor do they pretend to be totally unengaged in interpretation, since that is impossible in an account of any author's rhetoric. Nonetheless, their primary concern is to describe, to explain the main premises on which the subsequent, lengthy interpretations are based, and to allow the reader to judge them for himself, in advance and as a separate issue.

Structure

In literary commentary, it is not uncommon to find the term 'structure' construed in an architectural sense, as the set of building-blocks with which some fixed edifice is erected and left to stand, statically, on its own. Stanzel (1955), however, rightly opposes this notion, insisting that the structure of a novel should be understood as "das Zusammenwirken, die Abhängigkeit voneinander und die Einheit aller am Roman beteiligten Aufbauelemente" (op.cit.:7). More recently, Moffat/McElheny (1966) have reasserted this interpretation of the concept, with an even more active emphasis:

> The best means to keen understanding is what learning psychologist Jerome Bruner has called 'structure' and what Alfred Whitehead long ago called 'seeing the woods by means of the trees'. That is, any field of knowledge one might care to name is a field because of certain basic relations that operate throughout it, lines of force that magnetise it. This set of relations shifts; it is dynamic. (op.cit.:578)

Viewed from this more dynamic standpoint, and in the light of the remarks made earlier about the nature of reality in Kafka's works, all the pieces of the *Landarzt* collection exhibit a common structure, in that each of them creates a set of relations in which one or more representatives of historically conditioned, empirical reality are confronted with a phenomenon which constitutes such a disturbing, radical departure from customary norms and values, interpretations and assumptions, that it induces the various representatives of empirical reality, and the reader with them, to attempt to come to terms with it. In *Das nächste Dorf*, it is true, the element of *Auseinandersetzung* on the part of the empirically representative, only slightly personalised expositor would seem to be entirely lacking. However, from the fact that he obviously considers his grandfather's repeated saying worthy of public record, but fails, himself, to indicate whether or to what extent he agrees with it, one can reasonably infer that, in some way, he, too, is still trying to come to terms with it, and that he expects the reader to do the same. Consequently, at least by implication, this very brief work may also be regarded as conforming to the defined, basic structure. Similar allowances must also be made in the case of *Ein Bericht für eine Akademie* where, apart from Rotpeter's reference to a journalist's comment about his self-exposure in public (*Se* 148f.), there is no explicit attempt at *Auseinandersetzung* by his empirically representative, learned listeners, although it is clearly implied by the academy's actual invitation to Rotpeter and the topic on which they ask him to address them. Another somewhat anomalous piece is *Ein Brudermord*, where the entire action and all the main characters, with their highly typifying names, are so radically stylised that the work seems to contain no acceptable representative of empirical reality at all. In this instance, however, that role is assumed by the narrator who, though scarcely personalised, nevertheless speaks directly to the reader on two occasions, both times passing comment on the unfathomable nature of the reality he is presenting. Furthermore, although it may seem from his narrative that he defies the limits of empirical reality by displaying omniscience, it must not be overlooked that he is merely providing his own version of what is allegedly proven fact. As his opening sentence states: "Es ist erwiesen, daß der Mord auf folgende Weise erfolgte: (...)" (*Se* 144). Essentially, therefore, this work, too, confirms the uniform structural principle underlying each piece of the collection.

Within this uniformity, however, there is clear and very significant diversity, the basic structure taking shape in one of four different ways, according to the specific nature of the radically disturbing phenomenon encountered. Perhaps the most obvious of these variations is constituted by those works in which empirically representative reality is confronted with the physically actual, yet empirically inexplicable agents of a transcendent, moral authority. At its most palpable, this structure is exemplified by *Vor dem Gesetz*, where the forbidding, elusive doorkeeper not only confounds all the countryman's assumptions about the Law, but is also characterised as its direct, albeit distant servant and, unlike the countryman, defies the limits of the empirically possible by not aging. Despite all appearances to the contrary, the same set of relations also underlies *Ein Landarzt* and *Ein altes Blatt.* That these works portray phenomena which are to be accepted as physically actual, yet empirically inexplicable, few will dispute, since the evidence of the fiction is unequivocal: two mysterious horses and a groom that suddenly appear from a small, dilapidated, long disused pigsty; a boy's hideous, yet beautiful and incurable wound, crawling with worms of no know phylum; and nomads of no recorded human type accompanied by carnivorous horses. Many, however, will need to be convinced that, like the doorkeeper before the Law, these phenomena, too, are to be construed as the agents of a transcendent, moral authority. Yet, within the texts, themselves, support for such an interpretation is unmistakable. Quite apart from the fictional fact of their trans-empirical or preternatural nature, the horses and groom, for example, are directly attributed by the doctor to the intervention of the gods (*Se* 125), and the later neighing of the horses is taken to be "höhern Orts angeordnet" (*Se* 127). Similarly, the boy's wound is related by the doctor to a loss of faith among his patients and their abuse of him "zu heiligen Zwecken" (*Se* 127), the boy, himself, says that he was born with it and that it is his "ganze Ausstattung" (*Se* 128), while the doctor later explains it in terms of a fatal, existential weakness common to many men (*Se* 128). Finally, in the case of the nomads and their horses, although the cobbler states that the way of life and institutions of the empire they have invaded are incomprehensible and a matter of utter indifference to them (*Se* 130), he nevertheless also maintains that the reason for their presence, the focus of their attraction, is the seat of the emperor, the earthly representative of the Law: "Der kaiserliche Palast hat die Nomaden angelockt, versteht es aber nicht, sie wieder zu vertreiben" (*Se* 131). When one further considers that, despite their apparently irresistible force, the nomads never once attack the palace, it becomes evident that their primary function is to reveal, simply by the effect of their presence, some hidden truth about the nature of the relationship between the Law, its earthly representative and his subjects. Thus here, as in *Ein Landarzt*, there are distinct, if not conclusive indications that these other physically actual, yet empirically inexplicable phenomena are also to be interpreted as the agents of a transcendent, moral authority, however unlikely it may at first appear. As more detailed analysis will show, these indications are strengthened by the total context of the collection.

Kafka's second variation on the fundamentally uniform structure of the *Landarzt* pieces is to confront empirically representative reality with a partially, but essentially humanised animal or thing. Examples of this particular structure are provided by *Der neue Advokat*, in which Alexander the Great's battle-charger, Bucephalus, is resurrected and made a fully qualified member of the modern legal fraternity; *Schakale und Araber*, where a traveller "aus dem hohen Norden" (*Se* 133), journeying with Arabs through the desert, suddenly finds himself face to face with an extremely eloquent jackal; *Die Sorge des Hausvaters*, which deals with a somewhat reticent, utterly elusive, childlike creature, composed of an odd assortment of bits and pieces and bearing the enigmatic name Odradek; and, finally, *Ein Bericht für eine Akademie*, the attempted autobiographical report to the members of a learned academy by an educated, talking ape, an established star "auf allen großen Varietébühnen der zivilisierten Welt" (*Se* 148). Each of these characters, too, is physically actual, yet empirically inexplicable. However, to have grouped them with those already mentioned would have been to ignore certain very crucial differences between the two. First, there is nothing violent or sinister, forbidding or punitive about these beings. On the contrary, they co-exist at ease with man, and each of the works in which they appear has a strong element of almost lighthearted irony about it. Second, and more important, instead of opposing or threatening, misleading or abusing man, they seem to reveal, in an admittedly extreme form, an actual affinity with him, bringing into high relief an important aspect of his modern existence. And, in two of the works concerned, this kinship is quite openly stated. At the end of *Der neue Advokat* (*Se* 124), for example, the empirically representative expositor takes the human-equine Bucephalus' reaction to his forlorn, contemporary situation as a possibly valid example for all humans to follow. Similarly, early in his report and despite his acknowledged human-simian nature, Rotpeter explicitly generalises the significance of his condition, applying it to all earthly creatures: "Ihr Affentum, meine Herren, sofern Sie etwas Derartiges hinter sich haben, kann Ihnen nicht ferner sein als mir das meine. An der Ferse aber kitzelt es jeden, der hier auf Erden geht: den kleinen Schimpansen wie den großen Achilles" (*Se* 148). It will be the task of interpretation to show that the jackals and Odradek possess a similar relevance for modern man, and that both also provide him with the opportunity of gaining insight into his own desolate condition, as Kafka saw is.

In a third group of pieces, Kafka varies his basic structure again, this time by confronting the empirically representative with a hypothetical reality: a vision, a legend or a dream. This is the case in *Auf der Galerie, Eine kaiserliche Botschaft* and *Ein Traum*. Furthermore, in each of these works, the attempt of the empirically representative character to come to terms with the phenomenon confronting him is expressed in one brief sentence at the end. Of the actual circusgoer in the gallery, for example, the reader is simply told: "da dies so ist, legt der Galeriebesucher das Gesicht auf die Brüstung und, im Schlußmarsch wie in einem schweren Traum versinkend, weint er, ohne es zu wissen" (*Se* 129). Similarly, knowing the emperor's message will never arrive, the lowliest subject still goes on sitting and dreaming: "Du aber sitzt an Deinem Fenster und erträumst sie Dir, wenn der Abend kommt" (*Se* 139). Finally, and even more briefly, Josef K.'s dream of his own suicide by self-burial concludes with the lapidary phrase: "Entzückt von diesem Anblick erwachte er" (*Se* 147).

The fourth and last variation on Kafka's basic structure in the *Landarzt* pieces is more difficult to define, since the phenomenon confronting the empirically representative neither defies the limits of the empirically possible nor consists in anything explicitly hypothetical or unreal. Rather, it is a question here of commonplace empirical reality trying to come to terms with a radicalised and distanced form of itself. Illustrative of this category is the attempt of the miners in *Ein Besuch im Bergwerk* to grasp the nature of the mine's ten, young chief engineers and their haughty attendant, all of whom appear "als etwas Unverständliches" (*Se* 138) in their esteem. Then there is the already mentioned case of the grandfather's repeated, radical view of time as an uncontrollable, terrifyingly rapid process of inorganic change in *Das nächste Dorf.* A further example is provided by *Elf Söhne*, where the radicalisation consists in the highly improbable number of sons (especially given the lack of any reference to a mother or daughters), the fact that the father only ever adverts to his allegedly beloved children by number rather than name, and the one characteristic which the father regards as common to them all, namely, their incapacity to fulfil what he considers to be their potential, a surely extreme case among so many siblings. Finally, as indicated earlier, *Ein Brudermord* also belongs to this category, the radicalised nature of the phenomena confronting narrator and reader being heightened by the fact that the expectations associated with the title are confounded by the details of the story, the work's classical allusions are totally at odds with the actual content, and the murder is given no apparent motivation whatever.

In one of four different ways, then, each of the *Landarzt* pieces displays a structure in which, to use the terminology of earlier analysis, the second or empirically representative degree of knowledge is always confronted with one or more phenomena belonging to the third or trans-empirical degree of knowledge, entities which constitute a radical departure from or denial of the former's norms and values, interpretations and assumptions.[1] Either explicitly or implicitly, therefore, each of these works challenges the validity of the empirically representative, and from his advantaged position, outside the fiction, the reader is invited, if not provoked to untertake the same task here as in the case of *Die Bäume*, that is, to resolve the evident contradictions by fully exploring the implications of the trans-empirical phenomena so deliberately placed before him. For among the present texts, as in so much, if not all of Kafka's fiction, his essential literary structure is that of the rhetorical figure so prominent in the writings of some of his favourite thinkers, from Plato (*Bf* 693; *Bo* 108; *Tb* 673; *Gk* 190) to Meister Eckhart (*Br* 20; cf. Pasley, 1966) and Kierkegaard (*Br* esp. 224ff.; *Bo* 108; *Tb* esp. 511ff.; *Gk* 117, 215), namely, the paradox, as traditionally understood.

Owing to the nature of their underlying structure, the pieces comprising the *Landarzt* collection are also likely to convey ironies of various kinds. Needless to say, many scholars have already drawn attention, at least in passing, to this conspicuous aspect of Kafka's fiction, but no-one has yet analysed the subject on the basis of a comprehensive theory, such as that elaborated by Muecke (1969; 1970) or Booth (1974). Sokel (1964), for example, discusses the question primarily in terms of Sophoclean tragedy, while Glicksberg (1969) and H. Kraft (1972) are more concerned with Kierkegaard's definition, that is, with what Muecke (1970:66ff.) calls "general irony" and Booth (1974:240ff.) "unstable irony". Unfortunately, limitations on length prevent further consideration of the matter here. Nevertheless, where appropriate, instances of irony will certainly be noted in the following interpretation of the collection. Whenever the concept is used in that context, however, it is to be construed in the sense expounded by Muecke (1970:24ff.), which may be summarised as the quality resulting from the detached presentation (source) and reconstruction (recipient) of a discrepancy between appearance and reality, expressed as a confindent unawareness (feigned by the ironist, actual in the victim) of this discrepancy, and thus producing a comic effect of some kind, from black humour to belly-laughter.

Another obvious corollary of the fundamental structure employed in the *Landarzt* texts is the potential for grotesqueness, a further matter that can be dealt with only very briefly in the present discussion. Kassel (1969) has already devoted an entire volume to this feature of Kafka's work. However, his analysis is seriously flawed

108

by its thoroughly inadequate definition, which asserts as the essential characteristic of the grotesque the "unvermittelte Zusammenfügung von Unvereinbarem" resulting in "die ästhetische Möglichmachung des ontologisch Unmöglichen" (op.cit.:26). But if this were true, it would mean that, in the field of religious art, for example, not only every devil, but also every angel would have to be classified as grotesque, a proposition which, itself, is worthy of the epithet. Meanwhile, one of the most grotesque works in the whole of Kafka's oeuvre, *Ein Brudermord*, would go totally unnoticed, as it is by Kassel. Consequently, when used in this study, the term 'grotesque' is intended, not as Kassel understands it, but in the sense elaborated by Thomson (1972:20ff.), namely, that which alienates by presenting an unresolvable clash of incompatible, concrete phenomena and arousing an unresolvable clash of emotions, the latter tending simultaneously towards some form of aversion (dislike, revulsion, horror) and amusement (laughter, mirth, ridicule).

Finally, in this examination of structure, it needs to be emphasised that, so far, the notion has been considered only in regard to each of the *Landarzt* pieces as an individual entity. Within the collection itself, however, the concept assumes an additional dimension, for there it also refers to the dynamic set of relations underlying the actual sequence of the texts, the quite specific order in which, Kafka insisted, they should be published. What the principal elements of the author's structure in that sense might be, only an interpretation of the collection as a whole will reveal.

Point of View

If, as already argued, the structure of a work of fiction is to be understood as a set of dynamic relations, it should be evident that, although point of view, in the sense defined earlier, may be opposed or overruled by structure, the two can never be entirely separated. On the contrary, in any successful work of fiction, the one is closely attuned to the other. Consequently, it should come as no surprise to find that, with very few exceptions, Kafka's choices in the matter of point of view, at least among the *Landarzt* pieces, are governed by the general principle that it should provide the most effective and economical means to the desired end of challenging the validity of the empirically representative. Thus, no matter what particular point of view he may employ in any of these works, his fundamental practice remains almost invariably the same, and constitutes a synthesis of four main technical elements.

The first of these consists in binding the reader as closely as possible to the mind of the figure who is the principal or sole representative of empirical reality in a given narrative or exposition. Most commonly, therefore, Kafka simply relays his works directly through these figures, having them communicate with the reader in the first person, singular or plural. Eight of the *Landarzt* pieces exemplify this procedure: *Der neue Advokat, Ein Landarzt, Ein altes Blatt, Schakale und Araber, Ein Besuch im Bergwerk, Das nächste Dorf, Die Sorge des Hausvaters* and *Elf Söhne*. A somewhat deviant and ultimately unsuccessful form of the same technique is to be found in *Ein Brudermord*, where the empirically representative narrator does not actually use the first person, but twice directly addresses the reader, clearly establishing his own personal presence as a cynical and sensational crime reporter. On some occasions, however, this method of personalised narration or exposition proves unsuitable for the communication of the particular material in question. Obvious cases in point are the three pieces that deal with a hypothetical reality. In these instances, Kafka adopts his much less frequent, alternative technique of having the work transmitted by a highly impersonalised, psychologically advantaged expositor or narrator, but limiting unequivocal inside views of characters to the figure representing empirical reality, so that the reader is again bound very largely to the latter's mind and perspective, although all the other devices associated with the reflector technique remain at the disposal of these narrators and expositors as well, so that the resultant works are by no means uniform in nature.[2] Apart from *Auf der Galerie, Eine kaiserliche Botschaft* and *Ein Traum, Vor dem Gesetz* is also relayed in this manner.

The one, very obvious exception to this and most of the other basic elements in Kafka's use of point of view among the *Landarzt* pieces is the last work of the collection, *Ein Bericht für eine Akade-*

mie. Here the deviation consists in the fact that the story's personalised narrator, far from representing empirical reality, takes the form of an essentially humanised ape. The ostensible reason for such a complete reversal of Kafka's normal procedure is, of course, the academy's request for Rotpeter's report. However, the real justification lies in the author's motives behind the work. For, as later, detailed analysis will attempt to show, in this, the culmination of the collection, it was Kafka's intention to bring the existential quest implicit in the preceding works to a positive, albeit paradoxical conclusion. And since that conclusion was to entail a startling revaluation of empirical reality, there was an obvious logic in having it communicated by a representative of trans-empirical reality, while at the same time inducing the reader to identify with him as closely as possible, both emotionally and intellectually. It was evidently with considerations such as these in mind that Kafka chose to give Rotpeter a hybrid human-simian nature, while personalising him to a far greater extent than any other of the collection's narrators or expositors and having him explicitly equate his manifestly quite exceptional condition with that of all creatures, including man (*Se* 148). For apparently the same reason, he also endowed him with qualities which arouse considerable sympathy and trust, not the least being his frankness in frequently and openly drawing attention to the narrative act, warning the reader about possible distortions and misunderstandings. This characteristic places him in a category unique among the *Landarzt* narrators and expositors, in that it makes him aesthetically self-aware.

The second main element in Kafka's normal choice and use of fictional perspective in the *Landarzt* collection may be seen as a re-inforcement of the first. For, instead of providing the reader with anything approaching a detailed portrayal of his empirically representative figures, be they narrators, expositors or reflectors, he consistently avoids the sense of difference or otherness such a procedure would almost inevitably create, and deliberately reduces them, for the greater part, to the level of an anonymous medium of sensory perception, emotional reaction and intellectual speculation, a technique which might also be expected to facilitate the reader's identification with them. Thus, apart from a brief reference to the stiffening, shrivelled body of the dying countryman at the end of *Vor dem Gesetz* (*Se* 132), no information whatever is given about the external appearance of the thirteen figures now being considered, and only one of them, Josef K. of *Ein Traum*, is actually known to the reader by name, the remainder being identified purely functionally, in terms either of their social status (a probable member of the legal community, a country doctor, a cobbler, a man from the country, a miner, the lowliest imperial subject, a crime reporter) or of their familial position (a grandson, a family man, a father of eleven sons), or of their present activity (a circusgoer in the gallery, a European traveller in the desert).

To draw attention to these shared features of Kafka's empirically representative figures, however, is not to suggest that they are all alike in their degree of personalisation. On the contrary, one need only compare the circusgoer in the gallery with the man from the country or the grandson with the country doctor to be aware that a sense of personality is conveyed by far more than names, appearance, social standing and current pursuits. Other factors of particular significance are actions, attitudes, types and degrees of emotion, and the extent of intellectual insight. Taking these into account, one can recognise that the most personalised of these representative figures is clearly the country doctor and by far the least is the grandson, while all the others occupy positions somewhere in between. Yet, despite these unmistakable differences, it is also obvious that the range of variation is not great, and that the majority of these figures bear less resemblance to the country doctor than to the insubstantial imperial subject of *Eine kaiserliche Botschaft*, that "winzig vor der kaiserlichen Sonne in die fernste Ferne geflüchteten Schatten" (*Se* 138). Consequently, the divergence in degrees of personalisation does not invalidate the already stated, general principle that, in the *Landarzt* collection, Kafka's marked tendency is to minimise the distinguishing personal qualities of his empirically representative figures, even when they assume the role of narrator or expositor, and that their general lack of detailed, individual traits facilitates the reader's identification with their mentality.

If it is true that the first two principal constituents of Kafka's point of view in the *Landarzt* collection are calculated to reduce the distance between the reader and the minds of the figures representing empirical reality, then it is equally true that the remaining two tend to work in the opposite direction. And the reason for this counter-effectiveness is that they both concern the relationship between the representative figures and the disconcerting, even baffling phenomena confronting them, a matter which, in turn, significantly affects the relationship between the reader and the figures to whose mentality he is so closely bound. Thus the third main element consists in the relatively stringent limitations Kafka places on his empirical representatives' ability to actively participate in, to influence and even to understand the situations and events with which they are faced.

Of the reflectors, for example, only two play an active role in the events of their stories: the man from the country and Josef K.. The former initiates the action by his arrival and request for admittance to the Law, but soon submits to the mysterious and frightening doorkeeper's will by deciding to wait. Thereafter his participation is limited almost exclusively to verbal acts: importunity, cursing, grumbling, questions and answers; and none of them has the slightest influence on the doorkeeper's attitude or the story's outcome: the protagonist's death without gaining admittance. For the greater part of *Ein Traum*, Josef K. is even more passive than the countryman, as he is transported to a festive burial scene and then simply observes. It is only towards the end of the dream, when he finally recognises the burial as his own, that he actively participates by digging his way into the grave and taking up his expected position. Thus his only influence on the events is temporarily to retard their irresistible flow and the ultimate fulfilment of his implied death-wish. Nevertheless, by his act of self-burial, Josef K. shows a more direct and clear understanding of his situation than do any of his fellow reflectors. The imperial subject is allowed merely to indulge in idle dreams, the countryman's assumptions all prove to be false and his questions futile, while the man in the gallery is not even granted the awareness that he is actually weeping.

Among the nine empirically representative narrators and expositors, the extent of active involvement is still more limited, with only three playing a direct, physical role in the works they communicate: the country doctor, the cobbler and the traveller in the desert. Of these, the cobbler participates the least, ever more rarely running out of his shop to clear away the worst of the nomads' mess and co-operating with his business colleagues in financially supporting the tormented butcher, but otherwise keeping as far out of harm's way as possible and preferring simply to observe. Although no more willing an active participant than the cobbler, the traveller in the desert is forced into considerably more physical involvement, as he is surrounded and pinned down by a pack of jackals, with whose leader he then engages in a rather lengthy conversation. At the end of the story, he is also prompted to further action, when he restrains the Arab leader from continuing to lash the jackals with his whip. However, by far the most physically involved of all three is the country doctor, who stands at the very centre of his story's action, briefly directing it at the beginning, then becoming increasingly its sufferer, as brutish agents of the preternatural take control and ultimately transport him, naked, through wastes of snow to his inevitable ruin. Thus, like the cobbler and the traveller, he influences the course of events only minimally and has no effect whatever on the nature of the phenomena or the situation confronting him.

Unlike almost all the other empirically representative narrators and expositors, however, the country doctor does give evidence of an unusual degree of intellectual insight. Indeed, apart from the expositior of *Der neue Advokat*, he is the only one to display a broad and penetrating understanding of his era, its difference from previous times, and its relation to the alien phenomena with which he is suddenly faced. Together these two figures therefore come closest to grasping the true significance of the trans-empirical element in their particular situations. Nevertheless, the tentative conclusion of the one and the final self-pitying despair of the other clearly indicate the limits of their comprehension. As for the remainder of the empirical representatives, although the extent of their insight into reality varies significantly, from the family man, the father and the traveller to the miner, the cobbler, the crime reporter and, finally, the grandson, they are generally even more at a loss to understand the disturbing phenomena confronting them, and most of them openly admit it.

By placing such relatively severe restrictions on the participation, influence and understanding of his empirical representatives, Kafka tends to maximise the distance between them and the various troubling phenomena with which, explicitly or implicitly, they attempt to come to terms. At the same time, however, he also sets up a tension in the relationship between the reader and these representatives. For although the former may be closely bound to the minds of the latter, he is not necessarily subject to their intellectual limitations and may, therefore, not be content to accept their interpretations or their degrees of bafflement.

It is as if to increase this tension, to provoke the reader into transcending the understanding and reactions of his empirical representatives, that Kafka adds a fourth basic element to the point of view employed in all of the first thirteen *Landarzt* pieces. This consists in the technique of devoting the greater part and, in some cases, virtually the whole of each work to a detailed account of its particular, disconcerting phenomenon, so that the latter assumes a strongly tangible quality and cannot be lightly dismissed, while at the same time it is made as elusive as possible. To achieve this last end, Kafka not only invents the mysterious types of beings already described, he generally also imposes severe restrictions on the extent to which they may directly present or reveal themselves. The only major exceptions to this practice are *Vor dem Gesetz, Schakale und Araber* and *Das nächste Dorf*, where such considerations as immediacy evidently outweigh the desire for maximum distance and puzzlement. In those works containing empirically inexplicable figures, Kafka further reinforces the enigmatic quality of these entities by simply having the fact of their existence taken for granted. Not one of his empirical representatives, not even the most intellectually aware, ever questions the fact that such creatures could exist. Instead, they are made to concentrate on the possible significance of the fact that they do exist, and the reader is clearly expected to do the same.

In summary, then, Kafka's use of point of view in all but the last of the *Landarzt* pieces constitutes a synthesis of four techniques. First, he binds the reader as closely as possible to the mind of the principal or sole figure representing empirical reality in the work. Second, he facilitates the reader's identification with the mind of that figure by reducing the latter very largely to an anonymous medium of sensory perception, emotional reaction and intellectual speculation. Third, he places relatively stringent restrictions on the extent of the representative figure's participation, influence and understanding, so that a tension is established between him and the reader, who is not necessarily subject to the same limitations, at least on the emotional and intellectual levels, and may therefore not be content to identify completely with the representative's reactions and interpretations. Finally, he heightens this tension between reader and representative by devoting the greater part, if not almost the entirety of each work to an account of its particular, disturbing phenomenon, thus rendering the latter strongly tangible in quality, but simultaneously making it as elusive as possible, not only by giving it an empirically impossible, hypothetical or radicalised form, but on most occasions also by limiting to an extreme degree the extent of its direct self-presentation or self-revelation and, in the case of the non-empirical entities, never once allowing the fact of their existence to be doubted.

As indicated earlier, because Kafka's choice of fictional perspective throughout most of the *Landarzt* collection is determined by the need or desire to include all of these four elements, one of its major effects, like that of the basic structure inherent in each of the texts, is to provoke a radical questioning of empirical reality, encouraging the reader to go beyond the intellectual limits of each empirically representative figure and to arrive at a more penetrating, cohesive and dispassionate understanding of the situations and events presented. At the same time, however, because the point of view generally also works to establish at least a strong and continuing emotional tie between reader and representative, it frequently has the further effect of creating a lasting ambivalence towards the latter, an effect which has all too often been ignored by those who, in the interests of unequivocal interpretations, feel obliged to like or dislike, approve or disapprove without qualification. Finally, because the information presented in these works is subject to the various types and degrees of limitation already mentioned, similar restrictions will also and inevitably be imposed on the reader's ability to unriddle, explain and interpret, so that a residual element of mystery and uncertainty is to be neither regretted nor denied, but simply accepted as an integral part of Kafka's literary purpose and its implicit world-view.

To complete this examination of point of view in the *Landarzt* collection, there are two further, very significant aspects of the topic that need to be considered, and both are relevant to all fourteen of the works at issue. The first is the matter of mental or psychological advantage, what Booth (1961:160) calls "privilege", by which he means knowledge that the narrator or expositor communicates as fact, although he cannot possibly have learned it "by strictly natural means" (loc.cit.) such as perception, formal learning, experience or reasonable inference. "Complete privilege", Booth further explains, "is what we usually call omniscience", while the "most important single privilege is that of obtaining an inside view of another character" (loc.cit.).

From what has already been said, it will be evident that, in the present collection, the only extensive use of advantaged knowledge is to be found among the impersonalised narrators and expositors, all of whom regularly provide a relatively detailed inside view of one of their characters (the circusgoer, the countryman, the imperial subject, Josef K.) and one or more ambiguously direct glimpses into the mind of another figure as well (the ringmaster, the doorkeeper, the dying emperor, the headstone engraver).[3] However, since this technique, its purpose and effects have been discussed at some length in earlier sections of this study, further elaboration is unnecessary here. Instead, attention will be concentrated on four statements which differ substantially from inside views, but which constitute the only remaining examples of advantaged knowledge in the *Landarzt* collection. Three of them occur in personalised works, and all of them are of considerable moment for the would-be interpreter.

The first and most obvious instance is encountered in the last paragraph of the collection's title-story. There the country doctor laments: "Niemals komme ich so nach Hause; meine blühende Praxis ist verloren; ein Nachfolger bestiehlt mich, aber ohne Nutzen, denn er kann mich nicht ersetzen; in meinem Hause wütet der ekle Pferdeknecht; Rosa ist sein Opfer; ich will es nicht ausdenken" (*Se* 128). Taking into account the uncanny nature of preceding events and the doctor's horses, most of the phrases in this rather staccato sentence can be attributed to reasonable inference. However, the apparently contradictory claims about an alleged successor simply cannot. Why Kafka felt it necessary to have his deeply involved narrator make these advantaged assertions will become clearer only from a thorough analysis of the whole work. For the moment, suffice it to say that they eliminate a possible misunderstanding of the ending and reinforce the underlying significance of the story's events.

Because this first example of advantaged knowledge derives from one of Kafka's most intellectually perceptive narrators and in a context where levels of reality are increasingly confused, it is more readily accepted than the second, which is uttered by the cobbler of *Ein altes Blatt.* In the fourth paragraph of this piece, the reader is told in some detail about the total inability of the expositor and his countryman, even by the use of sign language, to communicate with the nomadic invaders. In the same paragraph, the reader is also informed that the institutions of the cobbler's country are a matter of complete indifference to the nomads. Yet, in the last paragraph, the expositor is rather clumsily allowed the totally advantaged remark: "Der kaiserliche Palast hat die Nomaden angelockt" (*Se* 131). Given the contents of the preceding statements, there is no possible, natural means by which the cobbler could either know or infer the substance of this claim. Furthermore, like the doctor's advantaged allegations, it contains an apparent contradiction. For, if the institutions of the cobbler's country are a matter of complete indifference to the nomads, how can one of the most important of these institutions have attracted them? Again it will be the task of interpretation to resolve this apparent contradiction, which is obviously crucial to a comprehensive understanding of the nomads and their horses and, thus, of the work as a whole.

The next example of advantaged knowledge is the phrase: "Da das Tor zum Gesetz offensteht wie immer" (*Se* 131) in *Vor dem Gesetz.* However, since the remark and its implications have already been considered in the preceding analysis of unobtrusive, direct commentary, there is no need to re-examine it here. Instead, one can move on to the last instance of this phenomenon in the collection, a piece of advantaged knowledge which, though equally as crucial as the others, is probably the most skilfully concealed of all, but is nevertheless to be found in *Elf Söhne*. Discussing his second son's hidden, but deep-seated flaw, the father describes it as "irgendeine Unfähigkeit, die mir allein sichtbare Anlage seines Lebens rund zu vollenden" (*Se* 141). The nature of the advantage here resides not so much in a form of knowledge which could not be gained by strictly natural means as in the assertion that it is accessible to only one person. After all, if the son's potential is capable of being perceived by the father, there is no valid reason whatever for assuming that it cannot also be discerned by others, including the son himself. That the father nonetheless makes this claim to exclusiveness reveals that the alleged knowledge is actually nothing more than an arbitrary, subjective judgement. Furthermore, since he quite explicitly extends the significance of the supposed failing in his son, maintaining that it is "gleichzeitig der Fehler unserer ganzen Familie" (*Se* 141), himself included, it also becomes evident that the real source of his extremely critical attitude towards his children is, in fact, the personal conviction that his own shortcomings have simply been perpetuated in them. Through his assertion of advantaged knowledge, therefore, the father implicitly turns his whole commentary against himself, as well as the notion of paternity as a possible means of self-transcendence or vicarious self-fulfilment.

In general, then, it can be said that, although the extent of advantaged knowledge in the *Landarzt* pieces is by no means great, it is nevertheless of considerable importance whenever it does occur. For, in the form of inside views, it plays an extremely influential role in establishing Kafka's desired degree of identification, tension, ambivalence and uncertainty between reader and reflector, while in its other form it is decisive in focussing the complex intellectual and moral issues raised by the works concerned. Thus it constitutes a crucial element of Kafka's fictional point of view and cannot be ignored in any interpretation with pretensions to thoroughness.

The final aspect of point of view that needs to be examined in this context is ultimately of more relevance than any other to the task of interpretation and judgement. Yet it is also the most difficult to define and assess. Booth (1961) explains the matter thus:

> If the reason for discussing point of view is to find how it relates to literary effects, then surely the moral and intellectual qualities of the narrator are

119

more important to our judgement than whether he is referred to as 'I' or 'he', or whether he is privileged or limited. If he is discovered to be untrustworthy, then the total effect of the work he relays to us is transformed. (op.cit.:158)

He then continues:

> Our terminology for this kind of distance in narrators is almost hopelessly inadequate. For lack of better terms, I have called a narrator *reliable* when he speaks for or acts in accordance with the norms of the work (which is to say, the implied author's norms), *unreliable* when he does not. (ibid.:158f.)

Furthermore, as already pointed out, somewhat earlier in his study Booth also makes the following, overstated, but related generalisation: "In so far a novel does not directly refer to this (implied) author, there will be no distinction between him and the implied, undramatised narrator." (ibid.:151)

Adapted to the concepts of the present study, reliability refers primarily to the emotional, intellectual and moral dimensions of the relationships constituting fictional point of view, and the critic's task in attempting to assess it is twofold. First, he must try to establish what values inform the attitudes and actions of a particular narrator or expositor, as reflected in the content and manner of his communication. Then, by comparing those values with the total structure of the work in question, he must endeavour to indicate the extent to which the author implicitly affirms or negates them, for reliability is always a matter of degree, especially in such elusive works as Kafka's.

Because this task requires nothing less than a detailed analysis of each specific work in the collection, it will not be undertaken here. However, as the following chapter will reveal, several general principles concerning reliability do emerge from the *Landarzt* pieces, and they may usefully be formulated at this point. First, since all of Kafka's impersonalised narrators are generally so to a high degree, and also display considerable mental or psychological advantage, the differences between them and the author, at least in terms of literary image and values, may be taken as minimal, so that they are to be construed as reliable. Second, although Kafka's impersonalised

120

narrators or expositors communicate much of their works through the minds of reflectors, there is always an implied or stated gap of awareness between the two, so that none of the reflectors can be assumed to be entirely reliable. Third, the more dispassionate, well-informed and intellectually perceptive a personalised narrator or expositor happens to be, the more reliable he is likely to be. And, finally, self-pity in a narrator, expositor or reflector is an infallible sign of unreliability.

Symbol

Although a close examination of structure and point of view does much to provide a sound basis for an interpretation of the *Landarzt* pieces, it still leaves certain fundamental questions unanswered. At its most obvious, this is to be noted in the case of recurring motifs. How is one to construe, for example, Kafka's deliberate choice of the number eleven in the composition of *Elf Söhne* and *Ein Besuch im Bergwerk*? Why do horses and circus or variety performances figure so prominently in the collection? And why, of all the famous horses in history, should he select Bucephalus to transform into a modern lawyer? Behind these and many similar questions that might legitimately be raised, there lies the general issue of the author's artistic intention, the purpose informing his fiction and determining the resources he employs. Already it has been argued that this issue is not to be resolved by reference to allegory or, with two exceptions, parable. Consequently, in opposition to Anders (1951), Emrich (1958;1960;1968)[4], Henel (1967) and, more recently, P. Richter (1975:206-217), but in support of the position consistently adopted by E. Heller (1948;1974), a resolution will be sought in terms of symbol.

Immediately, however, one is faced with the problem of an acceptable definition. And here the difficulty is even greater than in the case of allegory, for 'symbol' has also become the common property of mathematics, the physical sciences, philosophy, psychology, anthropology (cf. Firth, 1973), and semiotics (cf. Lyons, 1977:99ff.). Sörenson (1972), Todorov (1977) and Kobbe (1980) have all reviewed the relevant literature and clearly demonstrated the historical relativity of Goethe's still widely accepted definition (cf. Emrich, Frenzel, P. Richter). But the only alternative they offer consists of Kobbe's explanation that the *Symbolisant* is "eine para-semiotische Größe innerhalb des Feldes der ontologischen Semantik des Realen" (op.cit.:325) and the *Symbolisat* is "eine ontologische Instanz in der 'Tiefe' der menschlichen Erfahrungswelt oder 'jenseits' der menschlichen Seinsordnung" (ibid.:330). While both of these statements are undoubtedly true and Kobbe's study, as a whole, is a remarkable example of scholarship, it is difficult to imagine such notions becoming part of the literary critic's vocabulary. Nor are they really sufficiently specific to be of practical use. Like E. Heller (1974:116), one is therefore led to conclude that, at the present time, a certain personal arbitrariness in the definition of this term is inescapable.

As understood in the present study, a literary symbol is any fictional phenomenon, from a single object or action to a whole work, which, while retaining its literally denoted reality, nevertheless becomes so charged with meaning as to suggest a more general or abstract reality beyond, yet related to itself. Thus, in E. Heller's words (loc.cit.), the symbol "possesses a double reality". The means by which this added reality is created resides in context: not simply that of the particular work itself, but also that of the historical period and the whole cultural tradition within which the work is composed. Furthermore, because this wider meaning is only suggested, symbols are generally characterised by a "degree of complication of relationships, and their quality, especially of emotion or sentiment in the thing represented", so that the "interpretation of symbols is usually a much more difficult matter than interpretation of signs" (Firth, 1973:65). Finally, some symbols may be private, what Martini (1954:323) calls "Existenzsymbole" and others *Chiffren* (cf. Frenzel, 1963:37f.), in the sense that their added reality may be specific to a particular author (e.g. windows and bachelors in Kafka's earlier works), while others may be public, that is, common to a particular group or culture. Concerning this last point, it is not without significance for Kafka's work that, in the western tradition, horses have long been regarded as symbolic

122

of "the blind forces of primigenial chaos", of "intense desires and instincts" (Cirlot, 1962:144f.) and the number eleven of "imperfection aiming at perfection" (Abbot, 1962:79). Taking due account of these and all the other, previously considered elements of Kafka's rhetoric, a reinterpretation of the *Landarzt* collection can now be undertaken in full.

4. EIN LANDARZT. KLEINE ERZÄHLUNGEN: AN INTERPRETATION

Introduction

To the best of contemporary knowledge (*Bo* 228ff.; Bezzel, 1975; Binder, 1975; 1979), two of the *Landarzt* pieces, *Ein Traum* and *Vor dem Gesetz*, were composed as early as the second week of December, 1914. Then, after a gap of more than two years, another seven were written during the first two months of 1917, while the remaining five were completed during March and April of the same year. Thus, as a whole, the collection spans one of the most turbulent periods in all of Kafka's life.

The most obvious cause of the author's concern at this time was naturally the First World War, in which his two brothers-in-law, Josef Pollak and Karl Hermann, were actively engaged, and which was to result in the complete dissolution of the Hapsburg monarchy, as well as the Austro-Hungarian empire. Kafka, himself, was exempted from military service on the grounds that he was performing 'an essential civilian function' (cf. Brod, 1954:164). However, he frequently expressed a strong desire to enlist (cf. *Bf* 632f.,638,640,644; *Tb* 499f.) and on 21st June, 1916, actually underwent an army medical examination that declared him fit for "Landsturmdienst mit der Waffe" (Bezzel, 1975:112), although within two days this decision had been overruled and his call-up deferred "laut Erlaß des k.k. Staathaltereipräsidums auf unbestimmte Zeit" (loc.cit.). Instead, therefore, he was obliged to devote more of his time to the family's asbestos factory, which ultimately closed down in March, 1917 (*Hv* 432), and to his own official position at the semi-nationalised Arbeiter-Unfall-Versicherungs-Anstalt, where two extra business hours were introduced from March, 1916.

Because of the war, Kafka was also obliged to move from his parental home, giving up his room early in August, 1914, to his eldest sister, Elli, and her children. At first he stayed in the apartment of his other married sister, Valli, who was temporarily resting with her parents-in-law in Böhmisch-Brod. Then, in September, he shifted to Elli's apartment in Nerudagasse. But finally, on 10th February, 1915, he asserted his independence by renting a room of his own in the same building as the apartment of his sister, Valli Pollak, in Bilekgasse. And although, as a result of his sensitivity to noise, he subsequently moved to Lange Gasse during March, 1915, and from 26th November, 1916, regularly spent each afternoon at a small house in Alchimistengasse, leased and placed at his disposal by his youngest and favourite sister, Ottla, he did not return to his parents' house until the first clear signs of the tuberculosis, from which he was to die, began to manifest themselves, at the beginning of September, 1917. Given the extremely tense nature of the relationship between Kafka and his domineering father, this interval of relative distance between the two is obviously unlikely to be without its significance.

The period during which Kafka composed the *Landarzt* pieces encompassed the second phase of his tormented courtship of Felice Bauer as well. After their first engagement had ended on 12th July, 1914, Kafka did not resume his voluminous correspondence with her until about the beginning of November, 1914, and they met again for the first time late in January of the following year (*Tb* 495f.; *Bf* 624). In early July, 1916, they then spent almost a fortnight together in Marienbad, where they agreed to marry soon after the end of the war, to live in Berlin, and for each to be financially self-supporting (*Br* 140), although Kafka's continuing nagging doubts about the matter are clearly evident from the list of arguments for and against marriage entered in his notebook at the end of the following month (*Hv* 238). Nevertheless, the second offical engagement took place in Prague at the beginning of July, 1917. By August, however, Kafka had begun spitting blood (*Bm* 160), and his illness provided a means of finally resolving the issue, so that his correspondence with her apparently ceased in September and the engagement was officially dissolved on 28th December, 1917: "Als Auflösungsgrund der Verlobung gilt nach außen hin nur die Krankheit, so habe ich es auch dem Vater gesagt" (*Bo* 47).

These facts are mentioned here, not in order to deduce the meaning of the *Landarzt* collection from them, but simply in order to establish the background against which the individual pieces were composed and arranged (cf. Binder, 1975:233f.). To what extent any of these

126

events and experiences fell within Kafka's artistic range will only become evident once the collection has been analysed in its own right. For, as Liddell (1947) has accurately remarked:

> Our evidence for a writer's 'values', for what he thinks important, can (...) only be drawn from his writings. If we know, for example, from other sources that a writer was in the *maquis*, or that he was with Pétain, we should forget it as a piece of irrelevant gossip. If it was not a part of his experience that fell within his range, it has nothing to do with his work; if it fell within his range as a writer, he will himself tell us what we need to know about it — he cannot avoid it. (op.cit.:39; cf. Walser, 1961:17)

Der neue Advokat

Although *Der neue Advokat* (Jan., 1917)[1] is more gently ironic than most of the pieces that follow, it nevertheless establishes the basic concern of the collection from the outset. Raising Alexander the Great's warhorse from its grave beside the Hydaspes (now Jhelum), Kafka creates of it an equivocal, human-equine figure, confers upon it a doctorate of laws, and places it in the midst of the modern legal community, an apparent member of which reports and comments on the strange Dr. Bucephalus's situation.

The effect of the expositor's commentary is twofold. First, in lighter view, it tilts at the imperturbable, unimaginative legal mind as it rationalises its general approval of Bucephalus's admission to the bar: "Mit erstaunlicher Einsicht sagt man sich, daß Bucephalus bei der heutigen Gesellschaftsordnung in einer schwierigen Lage ist und daß er deshalb, sowie auch wegen seiner weltgeschichtlichen Bedeutung, jedenfalls Entgegenkommen verdient" (*Se* 123). But, more important, it also serves to define the nature of modern times by comparison with the past.

In this context, the figure of Alexander assumes a symbolic significance. For although his times were not without their share of violent destruction and are not, therefore, represented as a spotless ideal, they were nevertheless shaped by an energetic, unequivocal, absolute power[2] which pointed the way towards a clearly defined, though distant and ultimately unattainable goal. Alexander, as the embodiment of the Law, had imparted to his people a vital sense of purpose and direction, which man has since lost. Consequently, although the present age seems to resemble his in some respects,[3] the similarity is purely external. Without the authority and grandeur of design a figure such as he could give, life has become constricting, confusing and uncertain, an empty ritual: "Heute[4] sind die Tore[5] ganz anderswohin und weiter und höher vertragen; niemand zeigt die Richtung; viele halten Schwerter, aber nur, um mit ihnen zu fuchteln; und der Blick, der ihnen folgen will, verwirrt sich" (*Se* 123f.). Nor is true aid to be found in the existing legal system, which, far from substituting for the law of Alexander, has evidently proved impotent as a human guide, and thus forms an essential part of modern society's profound wretchedness.

In his transformed state, Bucephalus, too, develops a symbolic stature. Without Alexander, he has lost his previous *raison d'être*. He is isolated, uprooted, lacking in certainty and definite direction. In this respect, he is representative of modern man as seen by the expositor. Thus, in the last paragraph of the piece, his reaction to the situation in which he now finds himself is proposed as a possibly valid course for all to follow: "Vielleicht ist es deshalb wirklich das beste, sich, wie es Bucephalus getan hat, in die Gesetzbücher zu versenken" (*Se* 124).

The nature of Bucephalus's occupation is extremely significant. Since the passing of figures like Alexander the Great, man has lost continuing contact with and faith in a grand, purposive, authoritative life-principle. He has become divorced from any vital law transcending, yet informing individual existence. This he must now seek to rediscover or replace, if he is to overcome the deep loneliness and uncertainty of modern existence, the negative freedom with which he has been left and in which Bucephalus pursues his studies: "unbedrückt die Seiten von den Lenden des Reiters, bei stiller Lampe, fern dem Getöse der Alexanderschlacht (...)" (*Se* 124).

The basic problem, therefore, is one of finding a positive *modus vivendi* in the face of spiritual isolation and confusion, a moral means of coming to terms with the unhappy reality of an age which has lost sight of any ultimate goal and, with its empty ritual, hinders the individual's attempts to regain sight of it. Directly or indirectly, it is this search for existential purpose and value that informs the whole of the *Landarzt* collection and constitutes its fundamental source of unity. Whether such a *modus vivendi* is to be found in a thorough study of the law or in a preoccupation with one's circumscribed *Beruf* remains an unanswered question at this stage, although it is already clearly implied that no definite or helpful direction is to be expected from the prevailing system of laws. Bucephalus's accommodation to the forlorn circumstances of his new existence is perhaps, but not necessarily, the best solution. It is the effect of the following narratives and expositions to test its general validity by defining in more detail the nature of life's uncertainty, by examining more closely the various elements of Bucephalus's present situation (*Beruf, Gesetz, Freiheit*), and by proposing alternative resolutions to the problem of existence in modern times.

Ein Landarzt

The title-piece of the collection (Jan./Feb., 1917)[1] initiates the more detailed treatment of the socio-historical view presented in *Der neue Advokat* by directly relating the troubles of this "unglückseligsten Zeitalters" (*Se* 128) to man's loss of religious faith: "So sind die Leute in meiner Gegend. (...) Den alten Glauben haben sie verloren; der Pfarrer sitzt zu Hause und zerzupft die Meßgewänder, eines nach dem andern; aber der Arzt soll alles leisten mit seiner zarten chirurgischen Hand" (*Se* 127). From ultimate reality the people have turned to immediate matter, from a search for salvation (*Heil*) to a contentment with physical cure (*Heilung*),[2] from the metaphysical to the medical. And the country doctor finds himself cast in the impossible role of substitute saviour.

But instead of rejecting this role, which he recognises as being utterly false, he devotes himself unsparingly to his *Beruf*, considering the demands of his patients before all else: "Ich bin vom Bezirk angestellt[3] und tue meine Pflicht bis zum Rand, bis dorthin, wo es fast zuviel wird. Schlecht bezahlt, bin ich doch freigebig und hilfsbereit gegenüber den Armen" (*Se* 126). Thus, in the depths of winter, although he has already worn out one horse through his devotion to

129

duty, he still insists on answering the night-call of a seriously ill patient, and is "zerstreut, gequält" (*Se* 124) when, for want of a horse, he sees no possibility of making the visit. The reason for this self-sacrificing diligence is not a lack of awareness, on the doctor's part, of the deception that is being practised. Rather, in his view, it is a lack of any real alternative: "'(...) Nun bin ich aber Arzt. Was soll ich tun?'" (*Se* 128). And, in fact, the whole story takes shape in a world of helplessness, futility and bitter despair, from the opening situation that is "aussichtslos" and "zwecklos" (*Se* 124) to the final lament: "es ist niemals gutzumachen" (*Se* 128).

However, the hopelessness of this fundamentally deceitful situation cannot be attributed merely to the age in which the doctor lives and the type of people he serves. In part it also derives from his own submissiveness. As he says of himself: "Ich bin kein Weltverbesserer (...)" (*Se* 126). Finding it difficult, if not impossible, to come to an understanding with the people, he prefers to acquiesce in their self-deception: "Rezepte schreiben ist leicht, aber im übrigen sich mit den Leuten verständigen, ist schwer" (*Se* 126). Thus he continues to devote himself untiringly to his *Beruf*, to allow himself to be used "zu heiligen Zwecken" (*Se* 127): in short, to support the people in their godlessness and false faith. Basically, then, there is a contradiction in the *modus vivendi* the doctor has chosen, a contradiction which he recognises, but feels unable or loth to resolve. It is this combination of lucid awareness and a somewhat self-pitying acquiescence that makes of him, as narrator-agent, a complex mixture of reliability and unreliability and creates a certain moral ambivalence towards him.[4]

In order to reveal the true nature of the doctor's position and its inevitable outcome, Kafka employs in this story his peculiar device of actualised, preternatural agents which rush the situation headlong to its inherent and inescapable conclusion. Here these agents take the form of a groom and two horses which suddenly appear from a dilapidated, long disused pigsty[5] that the doctor kicks, in tormented frustration, when his maid returns with no horse.

Though surprised by the sudden, inexplicable appearance of these creatures, the doctor does not hesitate to make use of them as a means of dutifully pursuing his *Beruf*. Even when the groom has

130

demonsrated his bestiality by laying hold of the maid and biting her on the cheek as she helps him harness the horses, the doctor is still not prepared to reject him: "'Du Vieh', schrie ich wütend, 'willst du die Peitsche?', besinne mich aber gleich, daß es ein Fremder ist; daß ich nicht weiß, woher er kommt, und daß er mir freiwillig aushilft, wo alle andern versagen" (*Se* 125). However, these second thoughts are to prove fatal. For although the doctor is well aware of the groom's brutal intent and insists on their driving together to his patient, he is no sooner in the gig than the groom claps his hands and he is whirled away by the horses, while the groom bursts into his house in order to find and take his pleasure with Rosa, the maid who had fled from him and hidden herself behind locked doors "im richtigen Vorgefühl der Unabwendbarkeit ihres Schicksals" (*Se* 125).

The first effect, then, of these brutal agents is to violate the doctor's trusted, indefatigable servant, "dieses schöne Mädchen, das jahrelang, von mir kaum beachtet, in meinem Haus lebte" (*Se* 126). And the significance of her violation is clearly seen by the doctor, although he places the blame for it on his patients, who torture him through the use of his nightbell. Rosa is the victim of his *Beruf*. In faithfully carrying out his medical duties, the doctor has relied unquestioningly on her aid and has not hesitated to use her in pursuing a course which he frankly regards as false, as founded on deception and dishonesty. In fact, he has come to rely on her to such an extent that she has become an indispensable part of his equivocal *modus vivendi*, so much a servant that, despite her many years in his household, he has hardly noticed her as a human being. And now, when as a human being she needs his help, he is prevented from providing her with it.

In separating the doctor from his maid and in violating her, the groom makes brutally actual a concealed fact of the doctor's life, namely, that in the interests of his *Beruf* and in spite of himself he has sacrificed his servant as human being, and for an end which he himself sees as almost worthless, certainly deceptive. In this respect, too, his *Beruf* had been based on a lie, and the truth is violently revealed by the groom's action, the thought of which continually haunts the doctor, since it attacks him at the very basis of his existence. When, therefore, he is later abused by the people he has been

131

whirled off to serve, he does not resist, for he no longer cares: "was will ich Besseres, alter Landarzt, meines Dienstmädchens beraubt!" (*Se* 127).

The second effect of the unearthly, uncontrollable agents is to confront the doctor with a patient he is powerless to heal. This whole episode, with its swift changes of direction, its confusing mixture of natural and unnatural, its grotesque details and bizarre ritual, is one of the most elusive and repulsive Kafka ever wrote.

His thoughts in a turmoil, the doctor is rushed from his gig into the smoky, almost unbreathable atmosphere of the boy's room, where the lean, feverless patient immediately whispers in his ear: "'Doktor, laß mich sterben'" (*Se* 125). Embittered by the sacrifice this apparently pointless errand has caused him, the doctor curses the gods for their co-operation and feels ill at ease in the presence of the simple-minded family, who have no idea of what has happened to him or of what their son has just said, and would probably not believe the doctor if he told them. In particular, he is troubled by the father, whose thoughts are so fixed on the welfare of his son that he is prepared to sacrifice his "Schatz" (*Se* 126), his rum, in the hope of making the doctor comfortable and better able to perform his duty. In view of the boy's whispered request and the doctor's first impression of his condition, the father's thoughts are indeed narrow. And by comparison with the other thoughts whirling around in the doctor's head, they are even more so. Little wonder, then, that the doctor refuses to drink the rum, that the thought of doing so should nauseate him. For, in accepting the drink, he would be committing himself to the father's "engen Denkkreis" (*Se* 126), thus betraying the latter's "Vertraulichkeit" (*Se* 126) and adding still further to the mutual deception underlying their relationship.[6]

However, beckoned by the mother, he goes to the bed, where he listens to the boy's breathing and heartbeat, while one of the horses, which have somehow loosened their reins and thrust their heads through the window, neighs loudly to the ceiling. Convinced by this cursory examination that the boy is perfectly healthy, the doctor prepares to return home, finding it difficult not to vent his anger on those who have called him out on yet another needless

132

errand, one which this time has cost him his maid. But, moved by the sad, disappointed looks of the family and a heavily blood-stained handkerchief held by the daughter, he suddenly feels obliged to concede that perhaps the boy is sick after all. And on re-examining him, while both horses neigh in unison, he discovers that this is in fact so, that in the area of the right hip the boy has a large wound:

> Rosa, in vielen Schattierungen, dunkel in der Tiefe, hellwerdend zu den Rändern, zartkörnig, mit ungleichmäßig sich aufsammelndem Blut, offen wie ein Bergwerk obertags. (...) Würmer, an Stärke und Länge meinem kleinen Finger gleich, rosig aus eigenem und außerdem blutbespritzt, winden sich, im Innern der Wunde festgehalten, mit weißen Köpfchen, mit vielen Beinchen ans Licht. (*Se* 127)

This wound has been variously linked with others in a similar position: Rotpeter's (Emrich, 1958:131), Jacob's (loc.cit.) and Christ's (Sokel, 1964:280).[7] But, through the use of the word *Rosa* and the curious participation of the horses, the immediate association within the work itself is with the opening events of the story, and the association proves to be of vital importance. For a comparison of this scene with the opening episode reveals a close parallel between the plight of the boy and that of the doctor. Both have a fatal weakness which, though at first hidden, is ultimately brought to light, and in both cases this weakness inheres in the very nature of the person's existence; it is his "ganze Ausstattung" (*Se* 128), his sole *raison d'être*, his vocation in life. As a source of inescapable ruin, this weakness naturally gives rise to bitter lament, but the discontent is futile and must ultimately give way to submission, resignation. In both cases, the revelation of this fatal flaw is also associated with *Rosa* and mysterious, unnatural, destructive forces (the horses and groom; the worms), which go beyond man's control, assert themselves at the expense of others, and are at once beautiful and repulsive.[8] The ritualistic scene in which the doctor is first stripped of his clothing and then placed in bed beside the boy merely underscores, in a grotesque way, the links that have already been established between the two characters. Both fall victim to a materialistic age whose false values, deceptive security and underlying impotence are brutally exposed by the irruption of destructive, trans-empirical agents into the physical sphere.

Although the doctor does not directly relate the boy's wound to his own situation, he does show an awareness of its general implications as he tries to calm the boy and reconcile him to his fatal weakness:

'Junger Freund', sage ich, 'dein Fehler ist: du hast keinen Überblick. Ich, der ich schon in allen Krankenstuben, weit und breit, gewesen bin, sage dir: deine Wunde ist so übel nicht. Im spitzen Winkel mit zwei Hieben der Hacke geschaffen. Viele bieten ihre Seite an und hören kaum die Hacke im Forst, geschweige denn, daß sie ihnen näher kommt'. (*Se* 128)

In his explanation, the doctor is not trying to deceive the boy by underrating the seriousness of the wound, which he has already silently diagnosed as incurable and fatal. He is simply trying to reduce the intensity of the young patient's reaction to it. Faced with the impossibility of providing him with physical remedies, the doctor tries to comfort him in the only other way he can in an age of unbelief, that is, by reducing the uniquely personal significance of the wound in the boy's eyes and thus helping him to accept it. This he succeeds in doing by relativising the wound's degree of nastiness and by giving it a tangible, yet symbolic frame of reference.

The analogy underlying the explanation is one that also occurs in the very early piece *Die Bäume*, namely, that between men and trees, though here the specific details and implications are naturally different. Like trees, many men expose themselves to the danger of a fatal blow to their existence and remain almost totally unaware of their approaching doom until it is too late. In the doctor's eyes, then, the boy's wound is representative of a fatal existential weakness common to many men.

From this it should be evident that the doctor is not preaching some "Auserwähltheit des Kranken" (Sokel, 1964:280) in his analogy. For the boy is one of the many, not one of the few. Similarly, there is no justification for interpreting the doctor's attitude to the wound as "erzromantisch, todesmystisch" (loc.cit.). In fact, to do so is not only to miss the bitter irony behind the use of the words *Blume* and *schön* in this scene, but also to overlook the socio-philosophical framework of the story as a whole. The people have lost all faith in the gods, and the doctor, himself, curses them and their emissaries as violent, wilfully frustrating forces. Within such a framework, it is inconceivable that he should preach some form of *Todesmystik* or that the boy should be convinced by it. On the contrary, when the doctor actually is moved to speak of death (*Se* 126), he does so in terms of an end to his futile existence, to the torture of his profession and especially to the troubles arising from the appearance of the unearthly groom and horses. He does not see it as a joyful, mystical going-beyond, for he recognises that these horses and their groom, who have brought ruin upon him, come from the beyond.

Although the doctor's "Überblick" (*Se* 128) indirectly defines his own existential position and succeeds in pacifying the incurable boy, it does not bring a similar calm to the doctor himself. Having done all he can to help the boy, he now turns to thoughts of his own *Rettung*, hurriedly gathers up clothes, bag and fur-coat, throws them in a heap into his gig and leaps on to one of the horses, expecting to be carried home as speedily as he had been swept away. But for the third time he is cheated by the unearthly horses, which have already prevented him from helping his defenceless maid and have carried him to a patient he is powerless to cure. Now, instead of showing their original speed, they move raggedly, at the pace of decrepit old men, through the wastes of snow, and the doctor senses his ultimate, protracted defeat: "Niemals komme ich so nach Hause; meine blühende Praxis ist verloren; ein Nachfolger bestiehlt mich, aber ohne Nutzen, denn er kann mich nicht ersetzen; in meinem Hause wütet der ekle Pferdeknecht; Rosa ist sein Opfer; ich will es nicht ausdenken" (*Se* 128).

As already mentioned, much of this statement is completely advantaged knowledge and, as such, accentuates the story's constant shift away from normal points of orientation, the increasing confusion of levels of reality. For here the reader is not only presented with information the doctor cannot possibly know by natural means, he is also called upon, in the first part of the sentence, to imagine the passing of a considerable amount of time in a moment, while in the second half the story's normal time-values seem to apply.

However, the chief difficulty lies in the apparently contradictory claims made by the doctor about his successor. If he has a successor, then it would seem that, profesionally, he not only can be, but already has been, replaced. Similarly, if the successor is robbing the old man, then financially the former is most certainly profiting by the latter's absence. Unless, therefore, one is to adopt the view that the doctor's claims are totally nonsensical, it is evident that *ersetzen* and *ohne Nutzen* must be understood as referring to a level other than the physical or material. Construed in this way, the statement forms an important part of the story's total view, in that it eliminates a possible misunderstanding of the ending and reinforces the true significance of the events.

In the old doctor's absence, a successor has taken over and is reaping financial gain from the flourishing practice to which the narrator, as a result of the disastrous flaw in his chosen way of life, can never return. However, his successor's gain, his triumph over the old doctor, is not to be taken as ultimate profit or gain. His success is purely material and presents no valid alternative to the ruinous path the old doctor has chosen, a path which he must now follow, helplessly, to its desolate end:

> Nackt, dem Froste dieses unglückseligsten Zeitalters ausgesetzt, mit irdischem Wagen, unirdischen Pferden, treibe ich mich alter Mann umher. Mein Pelz hängt hinten am Wagen, ich kann ihn aber nicht erreichen, und keiner aus dem beweglichen Gesindel der Patienten rührt den Finger. Betrogen! Betrogen! Einmal dem Fehlläuten der Nachtglocke gefolgt — es ist niemals gutzumachen. (*Se* 128)

With extreme succinctness, the doctor's last cry summarises the story's moral view, at the centre of which lies deception. This deception derives, in the first instance, from the nature of the times, which find their embodiment in the doctor's simple, but materialistic and godless patients. In supposing that life can be lived securely and morally without a belief in some ultimate, transcendent reality, modern man deceives himself. So, too, do the country folk who seek a substitute for salvation in medication. Thus their ringing of the doctor's nightbell, that "Zeichen und Instrument seines Berufs" (Sokel, 1964:276), is informed from the very beginning by a misguided faith, a fundamental lie, which is powerfully exposed by the nature of the boy's wound and their reaction to it. Their calls are a 'Fehlläuten' not only in the sense that they frequently bring the doctor out needlessly, but also in the sense that they arise from false values. The patients deceive themselves, albeit unwittingly, and ruthlessly use the doctor as a part of their deception. To this extent, the old man is justified in feeling that they have cheated him and in referring to them as 'Gesindel', when, despite his unswerving devotion to them, they make no effort to help him retrieve his coat.[9]

Nevertheless, as already pointed out, it would be a mistake to imagine that the doctor is simply the innocent victim of a godless society and age. On the contrary, in submitting to the will of his clients by conscientiously answering their calls, even at night and in the depths of winter, he both encourages his patients' deception and betrays his own moral awareness. Thus, from the first time he answered their *Fehlläuten*, he committed himself to a series of consequences which were to lead inevitably to his own ruin. The particular false call with which the story is immediately concerned is but the culmination of many (cf. *Se* 126) and, as such, provides a quintessential statement of their significance.

Insofar as he deliberately acquiesced in deceit, the doctor is morally culpable, and the function of the horses and groom, which also constantly cheat him, is to reveal and punish this guilt by reducing his circumstances to their underlying, desolate reality. At the same time, it cannot be denied that, to a large extent, the doctor's guilt results from a lack of any real alternative. For, if he had neglected or ignored those in need of him, he would have been equally, if not more culpable. In effect, then, he has chosen what is probably the lesser of two evils. But evil it remains and therefore ruinous, in spite of extenuating circumstances.

In several ways, *Ein Landarzt* recalls aspects of Kafka's earlier writings. The scrupulous moral view, the concern with deceit and deception, the ruthless punishment of the central character, are all to be found in such works as *Das Urteil* and *Die Verwandlung.*

The bitter despair and fatalism, too, are not uncommon. But, in other important respects, it is also quite unique among the works he had produced so far in his career. Its open concern with religion as a social force and the success with which the author establishes an ambivalent attitude towards the narrator-agent are two of its more unusual features. Another, and probably its chief source of individuality, is the particular form in which the trans-empirical is introduced into the action. Here, for the first time in Kafka's shorter fiction, it appears in violently physical, uncontrollable, animal form in order to have its moral effect.

But, quite apart from its originality, the work also assumes a particular significance within the framework of the present collection, in that it provides a bleakly negative answer to one of the questions posed at the end of *Der neue Advokat*. The complete preoccupation with *Beruf* does not, of itself, lead to a genuine *modus vivendi* in modern times. On the contrary, its inevitable outcome, as experienced by the doctor, is utter ruin.

In view of the story's originality and its significance within the collection, its historical value is considerable. But, intrinsically, its merit is doubtful, largely because it becomes uncontrolled and overstated. Kafka's exploitation of the irrational, the unnatural and the repulsive is, of course, one of the hallmarks of his mature writing. But here it seems to exceed the demands of the work's realised intention. Particularly in the episode with the young patient and his family, one has the impression that the author is wilfully indulging mood and technique, that he is almost wallowing in grotesquerie, apparent contradiction and confused levels of reality. The excessive horror and mystification of the episode serve only to distort the story's artistic intention and thus to reduce its aesthetic value.

Auf der Galerie

By contrast, *Auf der Galerie* (Jan./Feb., 1917),[1] which resembles the preceding story in its flowing, almost breathless movement, provides an excellent example of controlled effect. Taking as his

138

point of departure a circus performance, Kafka gives new expression, in the two long sentences of this piece, to the general problem of existence informing *Ein Landarzt*. That is to say, he again portrays man's inability to come to terms with the underlying reality of existence because that reality is firmly masked by an intractable and deceptive surface.

But, even at this most general level, there are several important differences between the two works. In *Ein Landarzt*, man's inability is also, to some extent, his unwillingness; the mask of deception is largely of his own making and therefore gives rise to questions of guilt. This, in turn, leads to punishment, which occurs when the brutal agents of trans-empirical reality irrupt into the physical sphere, thus causing the inner truth of human life, the desolate underlying reality, to reveal itself at the expense of misleading appearance. These developments are not to be found in *Auf der Galerie*, where sight and vision remain intact, because they are kept apart.

The work's first paragraph, which is cast in the form of a lengthy hypothesis, presents the possible reality underlying a circus performance. It is a vision of unrelenting oppression, imminent peril, meaningless ritual, infinite despair. And in the centre of this vision stands the frail, consumptive individual performer, destined to go through a never-ending act staged by a threatening, potentially violent force, to the applause of an insatiable, automaton-like mass. If this possible reality underlying the performance were to become actual, if in all its horror it were to become concrete reality, then perhaps one could come to grips with it, perhaps *a young* circusgoer in the gallery would rush headlong into the ring to put a stop to it.

But, in actuality, the vision remains unrealised. The colourful surface of unceasing solicitude and gentle devotion, of love and admiration, continues to mask the possible underlying reality with such force that the latter is nowhere apparent. And because this is so, the person who sees through the postulated mask, *the* circusgoer who is actually witnessing the performance, remains powerless before both the surface and the possible reality. Laying his head on the railing and "im Schlußmarsch wie in einem schweren Traum versinkend, weint er, ohne es zu wissen" (*Se* 129). As the performance comes to an end, the possibility that surface and projected underlying reality might coincide also passes, together with the opportunity for an active *Auseinandersetzung* between the penetrating observer and reality. Thus the spectator is left, immersed in the profoundly sad intuition of the continuing and unalterable disparity between vision and actuality, between a terrifying inner potentiality and a rosy outward appearance. This disparity is underscored by his weeping without knowing it.[2]

Despite its close thematic and emotional links with *Ein Landarzt*, *Auf der Galerie* differs from the preceding story not only in the respects already mentioned, but also in that its ultimate effect is to cast some doubt on the view of life embodied in the previous work. For the disparity between surface and underlying reality, which is taken for granted in *Ein Landarzt* and leads to such drastic consequences, here becomes uncertain. What was previously regarded as actually inherent in and perilous to modern existence is now only possibly so. This change in viewpoint, though scarcely more consoling than the original firm conviction, is reflected in the hypothetical form the vision of inner reality is now made to take. In keeping with such a shift in focus, surface reality gains in strength. But it is not thereby vindicated at the expense of the original vision. Nor is there any question of the one's cancelling the other out. Rather, the two remain equally equivocal; and the individual, in his new, distant position, up in the gallery, is left as the centre of this tense equipoise, a fact which is emphasised by the close balancing of details between the first paragraph and the second.

Auf der Galerie is an example of Kafka's mature art at its best, of his ability to convey an intense and complex view of life in a form which is outwardly very simple and in a style which is all the more poignant for its firm control. At the same time, this piece, like *Der neue Advokat*, is of particular importance in the author's artistic development (cf. Kraft, 1972:160f.; Henel, 1979), since it indicates, however tentatively, his gradual movement away from a point of desperate, sometimes indulgent self-involvement towards a position of restrained, often ironic distance, from an all-pervasive, sometimes unbalanced preoccupation with guilt and punishment towards a tense, melancholy, but viable uncertainty. Furthermore,

140

its central image, the circus or variety performance, is one that recurs and assumes a decisive role in *Ein Bericht für eine Akademie*, as well as the later *Hungerkünstler* collection.

Considered apart from its individual value, however, *Auf der Galerie* assumes the additional significance of combining with the preceding two pieces in order to reveal certain basic structural principles which, it will be shown, inform the whole *Landarzt* collection. As already suggested, *Der neue Advokat* serves to pose the general problem of the collection and to indicate some of its more important elements: *Beruf, Gesetz, Freiheit.* Together with *Ein Bericht für eine Akademie*, which proposes a final resolution of the problem, this first piece may therefore be seen as defining the framework of ideas within which the following twelve pieces are to move. This is the most basic structural principle of the collection (cf. H. Richter, 1962:126; Binder, 1975:235).

Within the framework provided by *Der neue Advokat* and *Ein Bericht für eine Akademie*, the first principle governing the arrangement of the remaining narratives and expositions is that established by the title-piece and *Auf der Galerie*, namely, the grouping of these individual works in pairs according to the particular aspect of modern life's uncertainty they portray and its implications in the search for positive existential purpose (cf. Binder, 1975:235f.; Kittler, 1979: 212ff.). Thus, despite the abovementioned development between *Ein Landarzt* and *Auf der Galerie*, a development which not only characterises the collection as a whole, but also operates, as a second principle of arrangement, within each thematic pair, these two works were nevertheless both concerned with a single problem, that is, with the difficulty, if not impossibility, of achieving a genuine *modus vivendi* in modern times because of the disparity between appearance and underlying reality, between actuality and vision, the second and third degrees of knowledge. Such is the persuasive power of empirical reality that it is capable of becoming the sole object of human awareness, the only concern of human existence. Though nothing more than a mask,[3] it is so convincingly deceptive[4] that life's inner truth ultimately remains hidden, even from the searching visionary, who is thus prevented from clearly grasping its nature and from coming to terms with it before it is too late.

The same bleak view of existence also informs the next two pieces. But here the terms are more specific and the range of artistic vision is, accordingly, more limited. This gradual reduction in scope,[5] the increasing restriction to a more narrow and particular aspect of existence, constitutes the final basic principle of arrangement within the collection. As the quest for positive existential value proceeds, the possible areas of hope become ever fewer, and man is confined with increasing intensity to his own isolation and uncertainty. If one were to juxtapose *Ein Landarzt* and *Ein Traum*, for example, this principle would be readily apparent. However, its influence can also be seen in the fourth and fifth pieces of the collection, where the problem of establishing a genuine *modus vivendi* is linked, more specifically, with the relationship between the individual and the Law, the latter in the sense of an absolute authority which, though external to and remote from man, nevertheless exerts a decisive influence on the entire course of his existence.

Ein altes Blatt

In *Ein altes Blatt* (mid/end March, 1971)[1] this authority is vested in a human representative of the ultimate Absolute, the Emperor. On him the ordinary inhabitants of the country rely completely for protection from external threats to their livelihood. But the faith on which the artisans and merchants have founded their apparently secure way of life is seriously questioned when the capital of their country is mysteriously invaded and its centre occupied by a group of "Nomaden aus dem Norden" (*Se* 130).[2]

These armed nomads with their wild, carnivorous horses represent the very antithesis of the expositor, a cobbler who speaks in the name of his fellow countrymen. They are alien not only in that they come from over the border, but also in that they constitute a violent denial of all established values in the imperial homeland. Instead of trying to found an orderly, civilised community, they roam about as lawless, primitive marauders, show no regard for cleanliness or hygiene, abhor houses, communicate with one another like screeching jackdaws, grimace as if possessed, and have no understanding of or interest in the language, way of life or institutions of the country they have invaded. Before such mysterious, uncontrollable and potentially ruinous beings, the cobbler and his fellow citizens are powerless. Unable to resist, they co-operate in their own downfall.

However, the influence of the nomads is not limited to the inevitable and radical changes they produce in the way of life formerly led by the Emperor's subjects. On the contrary, their effect on the ordinary citizen is dependent, in the first place, on the negative reaction they induce from the imperial power. For, instead of attempting to defend the citizens by driving the nomadic invaders out of the country, the imperial guards retreat behind the palace gate: "Das Tor bleibt verschlossen; die Wache, früher immer festlich ein- und ausmarschierend, hält sich hinter vergitterten Fenstern" (Se 131). Consequently, the ordinary citizens are left to defend themselves and the country as a whole: "wir sind aber einer solchen Aufgabe nicht gewachsen; haben uns doch auch nie gerühmt, dessen fähig zu sein" (Se 131).

By their presence, then, the nomads create a rift between the Law, as embodied in the imperial authority, and its adherents, the imperial subjects. But this situation is not fundamentally new. In fact, it differs only in degree from the relationship which had previously existed. For the withdrawal of the imperial power in upon itself had apparently been going on for some time and had come so near to being complete that the cobbler is doubtful whether the Emperor could have been brought to the window even by the deafening roar of a live ox being devoured by the nomads and their horses in the palace square:

> Gerade damals glaubte ich den Kaiser selbst in einem Fenster des Palastes gesehen zu haben; niemals sonst kommt er in diese äußeren Gemächer, immer nur lebt er in dem innersten Garten; diesmal aber stand er, so schien es mir wenigstens, an einem der Fenster und blickte mit gesenktem Kopf auf das Treiben vor seinem Schloß. (Se 131)

But although the cobbler and his fellow citizens have evidently been aware of the Emperor's withdrawal from the affairs of the country, they have not bothered themselves about it. Instead of considering the possible implications of such a withdrawal and the shift in responsibility it involves, they have continued to go about their business as if nothing had happened. Their implicit faith in the Emperor's protection proves to be blind and thus misleading.

Viewed in this light, the "Mißverständnis" (*Se* 131) of which the cobbler speaks takes on a rather different meaning, since it applies to the ordinary citizens as well. Certainly the imperial power has failed to carry out its assumed responsibilities, and insofar as it has neglected the country's defence, it could be said to have misunderstood its role vis-à-vis the people. But the people, too, have shown a lack of true understanding. For, until the nomadic invasion, they had ignored the implications of the Emperor's withdrawal and, in consequence, had failed to remedy the potentially dangerous situation in which they were placed. By continuing to act as if the relationship between them and the imperial power had not changed, they betrayed themselves.

It is the function of the nomads and their horses to bring this deceptive relationship into stark relief. Like the horses and groom in *Ein Landarzt*, they are the brutish agents of an inexorable, trans-empirical reality that irrupts into the physical sphere in order to reveal the latter's fundamental weakness, its inherent threat to life. They are, as it were, attracted by the situation, in much the same way as the court officials of *Der Prozeß* claim to be drawn towards guilt (*Pz* 15). Thus, although the "Einrichtungen" (*Se* 130) of the cobbler's country are said to be as incomprehensible to the nomads as the latter are indifferent to them, it is nevertheless also claimed, in that piece of advantaged knowledge mentioned earlier, that it is precisely the most important of the country's 'Einrichtungen' which is responsible for their presence: "Der kaiserliche Palast hat die Nomaden angelockt, versteht es aber nicht, sie wieder zu vertreiben" (*Se* 131). And the palace attracts them because it has become the focal point of a crucial weakness in the relationship between the empire's ultimate authority and its ordinary citizens.

If, as was previously suggested, *Auf der Galerie* casts some doubt on the view of life informing *Ein Landarzt*, it should be clear that in *Ein altes Blatt* all such doubt is dispelled, as the values of the earlier story are strongly reaffirmed. Reference has already been made to the similarity in function and character between the trans-empirical

144

agents in both pieces. Analogous, too, are the situations of deception and misunderstanding into which these agents irrupt, as well as the part played by the conscientious pursuit of *Beruf* in producing such situations. A further resemblance is to be found in the outcome of the preternatural agents' intervention, namely, the protracted, yet inevitable ruin of the narrator or expositor, towards whom, in each case, one retains a somewhat ambivalent attitude.

Probably less obvious than these similarities, yet of equal importance, is the link between the priest of *Ein Landarzt* and the Emperor of *Ein altes Blatt*. In their different ways, these two figures represent the impotence in modern life, as construed by Kafka, of what were formerly intermediaries between man and the Absolute.[3] Though evidently occupying a position similar in potential influence to that of Alexander, this Emperor has lost contact with his subjects. Far from inspiring in them a sense of true existential purpose based on a living awareness of the Absolute, he has allowed them to become totally preoccupied with their own narrow concerns, while he, himself, has withdrawn into a fortified, irresponsible isolation. That this situation also implies a rift between the Absolute and its earthly representative may be inferred from the very nature of the nomads and their horses. But since it is an implication that gains in definition from the insights provided by two later pieces, *Vor dem Gesetz* and *Eine kaiserliche Botschaft*, its elaboration will be delayed until after those two works have been analysed.

Despite its significant affinities with *Ein Landarzt*, however, *Ein altes Blatt* still gives some evidence of that development which has already been noted in the case of *Auf der Galerie*. For, unlike *Ein Landarzt*, it is more of an exposition than a narrative, and its speaker, though a part of the situation he presents and discusses, is more of a generalised witness than an isolated, deeply involved individual. As a result, by comparison with the doctor's narrative, there is a greater degree of emotional distance and artistic control in what the cobbler has to say.

Nevertheless, the work is not entirely satisfying, because it tends to leave one cold. The very distance granted the expositor and the natural limitations of his personality reduce the emotional intensity, so that the piece lacks sufficient immediacy to produce any strong commitment, however momentary, to the mysterious world it embodies. Rather, one is left with a certain intellectual curiosity about a situation that scarcely disguises its contrivance, an impression reinforced by the work's clumsy use of advantaged knowledge and its arbitrary, almost meaningless title.[4]

Vor dem Gesetz

Much the same impression is created by *Vor dem Gesetz* (early Dec., 1914),[1] which, in the almost rigid functionality of its components, betrays its original, didactic purpose (cf. *Pz* 255). The narrative begins in a matter-of-fact, untroubled manner: "Vor dem Gesetz steht ein Türhüter. Zu diesem Türhüter kommt ein Mann vom Lande und bittet um Eintritt in das Gesetz" (*Se* 131). Everything in this opening situation has a self-evident ring about it. The man's arrival seems to belong to the normal order of things. He comes apparently of his own free will and shows no surprise at finding a doorkeeper before the entrance to the Law, which in this context denotes the ultimate, transcendent Absolute.[2] Nor does he appear to doubt that the doorkeeper's function is to grant admittance upon request. At this stage, then, the man from the country evidently considers his relationship to the doorkeeper and the Law to be so clearly defined as to be beyond all question.

However, from the very moment the doorkeeper answers the man's first request, this sense of unequivocal normality disappears and is replaced by the confusion of conflicting interpretation. As the opening suggests, the man from the country does, indeed, approach the Law with an untroubled mind, for to him the relationship between the individual and the Law is quite straightforward. There is, he believes, but one entrance to the Law, and all men strive towards it (*Se* 132). Once they have reached it, he expects that they should be admitted, regardless of person or time (*Se* 131). But the doorkeeper, an initiate of the Law, presents a very different view. Admittance, he immediately makes clear, is not automatic upon arrival or request. Nor is it necessarily to be gained by waiting. Furthermore, there are, he implies, as many entrances to the Law

146

as there are people (*Se* 132), and admittance is controlled not by one doorkeeper, but by a hierarchy of increasingly more powerful and forbidding guardians, of whom he is but the lowest in rank (*Se* 131).

Confronted with this forceful challenge to his assumptions, the man becomes progressively more uncertain. At first his curiosity is excited by the doorkeeper's refusal to admit him. But once he has been told about the hierarchy of guardians and has carefully noted the doorkeeper's appearance of severity and mystery, his confidence is so shaken that he is prepared to sit and wait. This act of submission marks the turning-point in the story and is followed by a rapid decline.

Although the man's will to gain admittance remains as strong as ever, the reason for admittance, namely, the Law, becomes over-shadowed in his eyes by the instrument of admittance, that is, the doorkeeper. The goal becomes increasingly remote as he becomes more and more preoccupied with the immediate means to that goal. Importunity, attempted bribery, curses and grumbling: all are of no avail. With the onset of sensility, he even begs the fleas in the door-keeper's fur-collar to help him. Finally, as death approaches, his eyes grow dim, "und er weiß nicht, ob es um ihn wirklich dunkler wird, oder ob ihn nur seine Augen täuschen. Wohl aber erkennt er jetzt im Dunkel einen Glanz, der unverlöschlich aus der Türe des Gesetzes bricht" (*Se* 132). But this somewhat uncertain glimpse of the reality he has been seeking is incapable of remedying the situation. In fact, the question to which it gives rise leads only to further disillusion-ment and ultimate frustration, as the doorkeeper bellows in the man's ear: "'Hier konnte niemand sonst Einlaß erhalten, denn dieser Ein-gang war nur für dich bestimmt. Ich gehe jetzt und schließe ihn'" (*Se* 132).

At this point, one might be tempted to leave the story, agreeing with a whole body of scholars, from Neumann (1968) and Kobs (1970) to Steinmetz (1977) and Elm (1979),[3] that it presents an insoluble epistemological problem, or concluding with Rhein (1964) that it portrays the decline and fall of an existentially guilty man:

Death comes to the lonely man as it comes to the lonely K. Both become aware of the most obvious question only after they have squandered their

However, such interpretations are a considerable oversimplification in that they suppose the doorkeeper to be a reliable informant, when in fact the weight of evidence suggests the opposite.

In this regard, the impersonalised narrator assumes an extremely important role, for, as already pointed out, it is he who relates, from his position of advantaged knowledge,[5] that the door to the Law is always open (*Se* 131). Consequently, there is every reason to believe, as the priest maintains in *Der Prozeß* (*Pz* 262f.), that the doorkeeper is mistaken when he says that he is going to close it. His claim about the existence of several, if not many doors to the Law would appear to be similarly ill-founded, since the narrator consistently creates the impression of singularity: "Vor dem Gesetz steht ein Türhüter" (*Se* 131); "Da das Tor zum Gesetz offensteht wie immer" (*Se* 131); "aus der Türe des Gesetzes" (*Se* 132). While it is true that these statements do not unequivocally contradict the doorkeeper's assertion, they certainly do not support it.

As for the two remaining explanations the doorkeeper offers, their inherent weakness reveals itself. When taking each of the man's intended bribes, he says: "'Ich nehme es nur an, damit du nicht glaubst, etwas versäumt zu haben'" (*Se* 132). Since it is obvious that the intended bribes are useless, this reason for accepting them is ridiculous. It can scarcely ease the man's mind to know that he is parting with all his valuables to no purpose.

There is a similar self-contradictory element in the doorkeeper's claims about the hierarchical nature of entry into the Law. As a doorkeeper, he is within the Law, in that he is its appointed servant. This aspect of his nature is stressed by the fact that, unlike the man from the country, he does not age. One can hardly give much credence, therefore, to his statement that he finds the sight of the third doorkeeper unbearably terrifying. For this would imply that he had never gained final admittance to the Law, and if he had not, it seems unlikely that he could be its appointed servant. Furthermore, if he finds the Law ultimately inaccessible, there can be no certainty at all about his service, for he does not yet fully know the Law. Indeed, he cannot even be sure it actually exists. Thus, all that remains clear about the doorkeeper is that, by his presence before the door, a door which, the highly impersonalised, reliable narrator relates, remains always open, he prevents the countryman from gaining admittance (cf. *Pz* 257-264).[6]

The ultimate effect of *Vor dem Gesetz*, like that of so many other pieces in this collection, is to create a situation in which the extent of individual culpability remains uncertain. In fact, if wilfulness be taken as a necessary precondition of guilt, then one may doubt that the characters are guilty at all, since it is by no means clear whether their apparent self-deception is deliberate or not. As a result, the reader's attitude to both the man and the doorkeeper remains ambivalent, and this ambivalence is a crucial part of the story's realised intention. For the characters, as such, are not of prime importance in the work. They merely serve to reveal a confused and equivocal relationship, that between the individual and the Law.

Like the cobbler in *Ein altes Blatt*, the man from the country has certain preconceived notions about his relationship to the Law. Whether, ideally speaking, these assumptions are right or wrong is not a matter with which either work concerns itself. The crucial point, as presented in both pieces, is that these ideas simply do not accord with actuality. In particular, the countryman's beliefs fail to take account of the doorkeeper, that ageless and inscrutable, institutional aspect of the Law which, though taken for granted, distorts as it serves and thus becomes an obstacle in man's path to the Law. It is this deceptive mask before the Law that the individual never penetrates, partly because of his own unchanging preconceived ideas, and partly because the mask itself has such persuasive power. In consequence, the Law remains remote, to be glimpsed uncertainly only when death is near and man has fretted away his life on its doorstep, engaged in a hopeless struggle with its deluded, immovable and immortal servant. To attempt to find a genuine *modus vivendi* in total, idealistic commitment to the Law is to yield oneself up, like the man from the country, to impenetrable confusion and destructive uncertainty or, like the cobbler, to expose oneself to the danger of protracted, but inescapable ruin.

Viewed in the total context of the *Landarzt* collection, *Ein altes Blatt* and *Vor dem Gesetz* serve a like purpose, both implying that, in modern times, commitment to an ultimate Absolute, the Law, has become impossible as a means of overcoming life's uncertainty, for the very reason that the nature of the Law, itself, has become uncertain. Since the passing of figures like Alexander the Great, direct contact with the Law has been lost, so that its official guardians and representatives are no longer what they seem to be. Instead of providing access to the Law, they have become inscrutable, institutional masks, closed, but hollow systems. Although they retain the appearance and office of the Law's guardians, they in fact deceive man and form an impenetable barrier to his moral enlightenment. As an inevitable consequence, the Law has become utterly remote, unknowable and unattainable. In the words already quoted from *Der neue Advokat*: "Heute sind die Tore ganz anderswohin und weiter und höher vertragen; niemand zeigt die Richtung (...)" (*Se* 123ff.). Under such circumstances, man's assent to the Law, however natural it may be, can only compound his existing uncertainty and lead to crushing disillusionment, while Bucephalus's thorough study of old legal writings would seem to become a futile occupation.

However, despite the negative conclusions of *Ein altes Blatt* and *Vor dem Gesetz*, the possibility of finding a genuine *modus vivendi* in commitment is not entirely precluded. Although the acceptance of and reliance on an external absolute has proved ruinously deceptive as a basis for modern existence, the possibility still remains of commitment to a subjective ideal as a valid, purposeful life-principle, and it is this possibility which is explored in the next two works. By a process of reduction, the concern of the previous two pieces is, as it were, internalised and relativised.

Schakale und Araber

With an irony at first playful, then brutal, *Schakale und Araber* (early Jan., 1917) treats of an ideal that is fervently, even devoutly racialist. This ideal is the creation of the jackals, whose leader is another of Kafka's partially, but essentially humanised animals. From time immemorial, the leader explains to the narrator, jackals have hated Arabs, because in their cold arrogance the latter kill animals

150

for food and disdainfully ignore carrion, on which jackals feed. For this reason, jackals regard Arabs as the very epitome of filth and devilish horror: "'Schmutz ist ihr Weiß; Schmutz ist ihr Schwarz; ein Grauen ist ihr Bart; speien muß man beim Anblick ihrer Augenwinkel; und heben sie den Arm, tut sich in der Achselhöhle die Hölle auf'" (*Se* 134).

In despising the Arabs, the jackals see themselves not only as completely justified, but also as loftily virtuous. For their hatred is not bred of anything so ignoble as personal jealousy or fear. Rather, it derives from a powerful and instinctive aversion to impurity. Thus the very sight of a living Arab is sufficient, they claim, to drive them out into the purer air of the desert, where they have perforce made their home. Purity is the cause to which the jackals as a race are dedicated, and since they have been exiled among the Arabs, they must destroy them, if ever their ideal is to be realised:

'Frieden müssen wir haben von den Arabern; atembare Luft; gereinigt von ihnen den Ausblick rund am Horizont; kein Klagegeschrei eines Hammels, den der Araber absticht; ruhig soll alles Getier krepieren; ungestört soll es von uns leergetrunken und bis auf die Knochen gereinigt werden. Reinheit, nichts als Reinheit wollen wir (...)'. (*Se* 134)

However, the jackals' aspirations are full of contradictions (cf. Sokel, 1967), not the least among which is their inherent inability to attain the goal they have created for themselves. Owing to their nausea at the mere sight of living Arabs, they are incapable of ever killing one of them. And, in any case, such murder would only cover them in the very uncleanness they seek to eradicate: "'Wir werden sie doch nicht töten. Soviel Wasser hätte der Nil nicht, um uns rein zu waschen'" (*Se* 134). Thus, in relation to their ideal, they remain impotent, as their arid home also suggests.

Nevertheless, the jackals do not despair. On the contrary, they live in unending hope, always longing for the arrival of a messiah, whom they see as one so endowed with "Verstand" (*Se* 133) as to be capable of immediately espousing their cause and killing the Arabs for them. Anyone who is not an Arab is potentially the appointed one. Consequently, the narrator, a traveller "aus dem hohen Norden" (*Se* 133), is quickly singled out for their acclaim.

Unfortunately, however, the traveller proves to be a rather reluctant saviour. Though greeted as the fulfilment of the jackals' age-old longing, he retorts that he is in the desert only by chance and has no intention of staying for long. Not to be deterred, the jackals continue to claim him as their appointed deliverer. After all, he is from the north, where there exists that "'Verstand, der hier unter den Arabern nicht zu finden ist'" (*Se* 133). But, regrettably, he fails them in this respect as well. Far from trying to understand their situation, he prefers, like the explorer of *In der Strafkolonie*, to remain at a dispassionate distance: "'ich maße mir kein Urteil an in Dingen, die mir so fern liegen; (...).'" (*Se* 133). If, as the jackals maintain, they are engaged in a "'Streit (...), der die Welt entzweit'" (*Se* 134), then the narrator evidently belongs to another world, for he knew nothing of the quarrel till they mentioned it, and, despite their appeals, he continues to stand outside it.

By his reactions, the narrator draws attention to the inherent absurdity of the jackals' attitude. His very distance from them creates a gentle irony that becomes increasingly apparent as the conversation progresses. For the more the leading jackal says, the more ludicrous his fervid, elevated tone becomes. Thus, when the narrator complains that he is unable to stand up because two young jackals have bitten firmly into his shirt and jacket, he is told in all seriousness: "'Sie halten deine Schleppe, (...) eine Ehrbezeigung'" (*Se* 134). This irony reaches a climax in the jackal's last plaintive cry to the European: "'wie erträgst nur du es in dieser Welt, du edles Herz und süßes Eingeweide? (...) o Herr, (...) o teurer Herr, mit Hilfe deiner alles vermögenden Hände, mit Hilfe deiner alles vermögenden Hände schneide ihnen mit dieser Schere die Hälse durch!'" (*Se* 134). The incongruity between the laudatory, almost psalmic language and the person to whom it is addressed is equalled only by that between the messianic mission the traveller is called upon to accept and the rusty pair of scissors with which he is expected to accomplish it.

From this point, however, the irony becomes quite brutal. Having interrupted the jackals' performance, the leader of the Arabs proceeds to expose the deeper contradiction in their ideal by having a dead camel brought on to the scene. Despite their vehement protestations of loathing towards the Arabs, the jackals do not now flee into the desert, for they find the carrion irresistible. In a moment their hatred is forgotten and their chaste ideal cast aside, as their bodily appetites draw them, on their bellies, towards the reeking corpse:

> Schon hing einer am Hals und fand mit dem ersten Biß die Schlagader. Wie eine kleine rasende Pumpe, die ebenso unbedingt wie aussichtslos einen übermächtigen Brand löschen will, zerrte und zuckte jede Muskel seines Körpers an ihrem Platz. Und schon lagen in gleicher Arbeit alle auf dem Leichnam hoch zu Berg. (*Se* 135)

Such is their state of "Rausch und Ohnmacht" (*Se* 135) that they are not to be driven off, even by the Arab's whip.

The jackals' ideal proves to be a sham, mere "unsinnige Hoffnung" (*Se* 135), because it is based on a distortion, even a denial of reality. Despite their exalted claims, their dedication to 'Reinheit' is apparently nothing more than an attempt to create virtue out of their own natural instincts. Unable to resist the very flesh the Arab scorns, they try to raise themselves above his contempt by construing their physical appetites as the instrument of a lofty ideal which also demands the destruction of all Arabs. In this way they hope to rid themselves of scorn and, at the same time, to sublimate their innate instincts. They who are by nature devoted to rotting bodies, who have by nature a foul breath (*Se* 133), thus conceive and pursue an ideal which, if it were to be fully realised, would require their own annihilation as well.

It is the effect of the ending to reveal, with telling severity, the basic self-deception and contradiction in the jackals' cause. They remain "wahre Narren" (*Se* 135), born to be the Arabs' carrion-eating dogs, but aspiring to be the chosen people of a peaceful world purified of Arabs. However, though they are destined to be forever frustrated, they are not completely condemned. On the contrary, by a final irony, it is their absurd hope that endears them to the very Arabs they despise. And the reader, like the narrator when he finally stays the leader's whip-hand, is moved to share the Arabs' sentiments.

Although *Schakale und Araber* has attracted considerably more critical attention than is indicated by A. Flores (1976:166f.),[1] most commentators have shown a strong tendency to allegorise the work by simply identifying the jackals with some group or principle extrinsic to the work. In view of Kafka's background, politico-historical factors, overtones of the Old Testament and the story's concern with ritual, the most obvious possible equivalent is, of course, the Jewish race (cf. Brod, 1918; Rubinstein, 1952:59f.; 1967; Beck, 1971:179ff.; Gray, 1973:134f.; Tismar, 1975).[2] But others have argued just as convincingly for an equation of the story's opponents with various similar dualities in Nietzsche's *Zur Genealogie der Moral* (Sokel, 1967; Bridgwater, 1974:115ff.).[3] The important point, however, is that this very multiplicity of equally valid or invalid equivalents makes the whole process futile. For the jackals are at once all of these groups and none of them, in that they are symbolic of any group dedicated to a like cause. It is the penetrating clarity and suggestive control with which Kafka portrays the jackals' situation that makes this one of his most successful works.

Ein Besuch im Bergwerk

In technique, *Ein Besuch im Bergwerk* (Jan/Feb., 1917)[1] presents a strong contrast to the preceding piece, its tone being rather flat and factual, while its content is restricted to the empirical order of things. There is a similar divergence in the subjective ideals the two works embody. Unlike the jackals with their exalted, global aspirations, the miners, through their observer-spokesman, espouse a more limited ideal, namely, the apparent manner of being of the mine's chief engineers, ten[2] young men who, at the direction of the management, are making the initial survey for new galleries.

To the ordinary miners, these representatives of the highest professional ranks are a source of wonder and admiration: "Wie jung diese Leute sind und dabei schon so verschiedenartig! Sie haben sich alle frei entwickelt, und ungebunden zeigt sich ihr klar bestimmtes Wesen schon in jungen Jahren" (*Se* 136). Because of their free self-development, the engineers, with the humility that comes from extensive knowledge (*Se* 137), have achieved a clarity and certainty of being which allows them to be completely involved in what they are doing, even when they seem to be neglecting the immediate task in hand, as is the case with the sixth and seventh:

> Wie sicher müssen diese zwei Herren ihrer Stellung sein, ja welche Verdienste müssen sie sich trotz ihrer Jugend um unser Bergwerk schon erworben haben, daß sie hier, bei einer so wichtigen Begehung, unter den Augen ihres Chefs, nur mit eigenen oder wenigstens mit solchen Angelegenheiten, die nicht mit der augenblicklichen Aufgabe zusammenhängen, so unbeirrbar sich beschäftigen dürfen. Oder sollte es möglich sein, daß sie, trotz alles Lachens und aller Unaufmerksamkeit, das, was nötig ist, sehr wohl bemerken?. (*Se* 136)

In and through their *Beruf*, the engineers display a state of being which is to the miners integral and positive. The freedom in which they have developed is the freedom to be entirely themselves and to give themselves fully to whatever they are doing. It is not the negative freedom of uncertainty in which Bucephalus pursues his *Beruf*. Nor is it the arid freedom that the jackals seek. For the engineers have achieved self-fulfilment not by distancing themselves from their natural environment, but by involving themselves in it. And their humble involvement is imbued with such certainty, such confidence, that it remains undaunted, despite inevitable, accompanying worries and troubles, which have already left their mark on the features of the fifth engineer.

Although the miners regard the engineers with admiration and respect, they also find them inscrutable, mystifying. The implied distance between the engineers' manner of being and that familiar to the ordinary miners is so great that the latter are unable to understand or judge the former. Thus, after a lengthy attempt to account for the behaviour of the sixth and seventh engineers, the narrator-expositor finally concludes: "Man wagt über solche Herren kaum ein bestimmtes Urteil abzugeben" (*Se* 136). Like the nature of their companions, that of these two engineers remains ultimately "unverständlich" (*Se* 137) to the miners.

In order to reinforce the significance of the engineers in the miners' eyes, Kafka here employs a technique which is almost unique in his art, a method of presentation which has led Politzer (1962:94) to describe this work and *Elf Söhne* as "basically plotless enumerations" and, as already mentioned, Pasley (1965) to regard both works as deliberate mystifications. In choosing to refer to the engineers by number, rather than name, and in allowing numerical succession to become one of the main structural principles of the text, Kafka does, it is true, create an air of mystery. And although this enigmatic quality is in keeping with the miners' view of the engineers, it also gives rise to several problems.

Chief among these is the actual number of engineers. At first sight, the choice of ten would seem to be entirely arbitrary. However, it can also be construed as an integral part of the work's inner necessity. For, in almost all cultural traditions, but especially in the Judaic, the number ten has long been symbolic of completeness, integrity, harmony, perfection (cf. Abbot, 1962:236ff.; Cirlot, 1962:223), and it is precisely these qualities which characterise the engineers' manner of being as viewed by the miners. Accordingly, the choice of the number ten can be interpreted as a symbolic means of underpinning the ideal nature the engineers assume in the story.

If the number of engineers can be thus related to the inner necessity of the piece, so too can the set of qualities with which each engineer is endowed. Far from being a random selection, these qualities seem to have been deliberately chosen so as to arrange the engineers in complementary pairs about a central point or pivot, the fifth engineer, a determined *Einzelgänger* who is "vielleicht der oberste im Rang" (*Se* 136) and exercises a controlling influence on the movement of the whole group. Thus the first engineer's somewhat carefree, lively, wide-ranging view is complemented by the second engineer's precise, careful observation. The tense dignity of the withdrawn third engineer finds its complement in the almost insensitive loquacity of the fourth. To all appearances, the sixth and seventh, who are treated as a unit, are least attentive to their work, while the eighth is the epitome of concentration. The ninth, too, is intent on his task, often dangerously so, but the tenth, with his nonchalant control and technical understanding, prevents possible accidents. Viewed in this light, the qualities

156

attributed to each engineer and the order in which they are arranged may also be said to reinforce the ideas of wholeness, integrity, harmony. Having chosen the number ten for its traditional symbolism, Kafka then exploits the normal numerical succession in order to strengthen the number's symbolic associations.

The full significance of the unoccupied "Kanzleidiener der Bergdirektion" (*Se* 137), who accompanies the engineers, is evidently to be discovered in the same traditional, symbolic pattern. For he is the eleventh member of the group and, as pointed out earlier, eleven "is a number which in one aspect represents imperfection aiming at perfection" (Abbot, 1962:79; cf. Cirlot, 1962:223f.). Like the engineers with whom he associates, the attendant is so involved in himself as to be oblivious of the miners' actions and reactions, so that he, too, remains "als etwas Unverständliches" (*Se* 138) in their esteem. But, unlike the engineers, he is full of haughty pride about his position and his relationship to the miners, so that the latter nevertheless laugh at him behind his back. Lacking the engineers' extensive knowledge and its accompanying humility, he becomes an unconvincing, imperfect imitation of them. Thus, by contrast, he helps to define still more closely the true nature of the miners' ideal, the cause of their admiration, mystification and wistful longing:

> Heute wird wenig mehr gearbeitet; die Unterbrechung war zu ausgiebig; ein solcher Besuch nimmt alle Gedanken an Arbeit mit sich fort. Allzu verlockend ist es, den Herren in das Dunkel des Probestollens nachzublicken, in dem sie alle verschwunden sind. Auch geht unsere Arbeitsschicht bald zu Ende; wir werden die Rückkehr der Herren nicht mehr mit ansehen. (*Se* 138)

Because it is contingent upon a high level of knowledge and professional skill, the ideal embodied in the engineers remains forever beyond the reach of the ordinary miners, who, like the jackals, must yearn in vain. However, although the engineers' manner of being is necessarily limited as an ideal, it is not thereby invalidated in itself. That is to say, although the ordinary miners will never achieve the engineers' apparent certainty and freedom, their integrity and clarity of being, these qualities are nevertheless affirmed as possibilities in the engineers themselves. The principal difference, then, between this piece and the previous one resides in the fact that, intellectually speaking, the jackals' ideal is totally rejected as unattained and un-attainable, whereas the miners' ideal is affirmed as a state evidently already realised in others, but is negated as an ideal for the miners and thus for the generality of men. It remains for the last piece of the collection to redefine the engineers' mode of being in such a way as to make it universally valid and attainable.

Despite its more affirmative conclusion and its greater significance in the development of Kafka's attitude to existence, *Ein Besuch im Bergwerk* is of much less aesthetic value than *Schakale und Araber*. To a large extent, this is due to its enumerative technique which, though one may be able to explain and justify it without recourse to esoteric, allegorical equations, nevertheless reduces the work to little more than an abstract, intellectual puzzle. In part, it also derives from the character of the narrator-expositor, who is so intellectually disadvantaged that his observations lack any depth and thus tend to become boring.

Through *Schakale und Araber* and *Ein Besuch im Bergwerk*, then, the general concern of the collection is related to the particular question of subjective ideals. In other words, these two works may be said to deal with the possibility of finding valid existential purpose in the commitment to a purely personal absolute or, at least, to one which is limited to a very specific group of beings. And if this interpretation is correct, then it is evident that, with varying intensity, both works deny the possibility. In view of the conceivable range of subjective ideals, this is an extremely drastic conclusion and obviously requires a more detailed explanation, if it is to be seen in its proper perspective.

As subjective ideals, the states with which the jackals and miners become preoccupied are mental-emotional projections of and by the self, out of its existing, implicitly undesirable situation into one that is eminently desirable, but as yet unrealised by the self. To this extent, they are like all such ideals. But there is one crucial respect in which they differ. The states which the jackals and miners regard as ideal are not only non-existent in them at present, they also lie completely beyond their potentialities. Owing to their very nature, the jackals can never achieve the state of purity they so ardently desire. Nor, for the same reason, can the miners ever become the

158

chief engineers they so much admire. In fact, their preoccupation with these ideals implies a flight from the self and a rejection of it, a somewhat desperate desire for release or escape. And, in both cases, this desire must forever be frustrated, because the ideal is inherently unattainable.

If one compares the apparently broad intention underlying the *Landarzt* collection with the narrow concerns of *Schakale und Araber* and *Ein Besuch im Bergwerk*, it may seem that, in limiting his consideration of subjective ideals to those which are inherently unattainable, Kafka is being unduly restrictive. Indeed, it may even seem that he undermines the whole framework of the collection by rendering unacceptable any general conclusion drawn from such limited evidence. But these possible impressions are far from the truth. In fact, it is the very limitation of the jackals' and miners' ideals that makes them most pertinent to the general argument of the collection.

As previously stated, the basis of the *Landarzt* pieces is the view that, intellectually and spiritually, modern life lacks any certainty of direction or purpose, that it is confused and deceptive. Placed in such an intolerable situation, man may seek to overcome it, like the miners and jackals, by contemplating and even actually pursuing an ideal which embodies the opposite of his present situation. But all his endeavours in this direction are futile, because the uncertainty, as the first five pieces have shown, is an unalterable, inescapable part of the modern human condition. The engineers, it is true, appear to contradict this generalisation. However, it should not be overlooked that the reader knows them only as the ordinary miner construes them. What they are actually like in themselves, the author never indicates, so that they remain only postulated exceptions to the rule of modern life's inherent and profound uncertainty. Given this condition, to commit oneself to the ideal of intellectual-spiritual certainty is to be like the jackals and cherish an "unsinnige Hoffnung" (*Se* 135). The commitment, however natural it may be, involves a fundamental self-contradiction, since it is an implicit denial of the very reality from which it arises. As such, it can only lead to lasting frustration and discontent.

From this forlorn conclusion a certain narrowing of scope and outlook naturally follows. For in a world which permits of no intellectual-spiritual certainty, man's stature, his relative power and value, must be drastically reduced. So, too, must his possibilities of development. Indeed, if man's present estate is as Kafka implies, then one can hardly conceive of human development at all any more, because to do so is to presuppose an organic view of change and, in an unalterably uncertain world, that is impossible. Furthermore, if this is true of the intellectual, emotional and spiritual dimensions of human existence, it must also have its physical correlative, since in man all these aspects are combined and interdependent. That is to say, if man's intellect, emotions and spirit are prey to an irrevocable, existential uncertainty, then his relationship to the purely physical world must be similarly affected. This notion has already been suggested in some of the earlier pieces, especially those directly concerned with the disparity between surface and underlying reality. But its most explicit formulation is to be found in the next two works, where the author deliberately presents situations in which it is asserted that, even on the purely physical level, the conscious attempt to reach a goal, be it the most immediate or the most distant, is also subject to a profound, inescapable uncertainty, so that here, too, man can find no real hope of deliverance from his desolate situation.

Das nächste Dorf

It is one of the distinguishing features of the *Landarzt* collection that, through its narrators and expositors or, where they are different, its principal characters, the view of life it conveys is closely linked with middle or old age. Even in those pieces where this association is not made explicit, it is still suggested by social position or by some contrast with youth, as in *Auf der Galerie* and *Ein Besuch im Bergwerk*. In the second last work of the collection, it is true, this sense of age and, with it, the previously established socio-historical perspective are almost entirely lacking, especially for readers unfamiliar with Josef K. of *Der Prozeß*, as was the case during Kafka's lifetime. Consequently, at least in this respect, *Ein Traum* must be regarded as not altogether typical of the collection. However, its very atypicality accentuates the fact that the vision underlying the remaining pieces is

160

intimately related to an advanced position in life and thus in time, a position which, in the case of the speaker, permits a certain distance from immediate situations and events, enabling him to view existence in the light, however dim, of not inconsiderable experience, and to recognise some of its basic qualities. It is from this position that life has already been characterised as lacking in real purpose or value, as being fatally deceptive and profoundly uncertain. Moreover, since in these pieces the situation of the individual narrator, expositor or chief character assumes a symbolic significance for modern man, his position in time has historical as well as personal or technical implications, suggesting a culture that has lost its youth and is now experiencing a wretched decline.

A sense of age is, therefore, inseparable from the largely fatalistic view of man informing most of the *Landarzt* pieces, and the indissoluble link between these two aspects of the collection provides further evidence of Kafka's clear insight into the nature of existence. For all awareness of man as self is necessarily and closely related to a particular awareness of time.

> What we call the self, person or individual is experienced and known only against the background of the succession of temporal moments and changes constituting his biography (...). The question, what is man, therefore, invariably refers to the question of what is time. The quest for a clarification of the self leads to a *recherche du temps perdu*. And the more seriously human beings become engaged in this quest, the more they become preoccupied and concerned with the consciousness of time and its meaning for human life. (Meyerhoff, 1955:1f.; s.a. Church, 1963:171ff.; Harvey, 1965: 101ff.)

Within the present collection, this link between time and the self is nowhere more apparent than in the shortest piece, *Das nächste Dorf* (Jan./Feb. 1917),[1] where the desolate uncertainty of modern man finds its correlative in the view of time often expressed by the expositor's grandfather. From his position of advanced age and corresponding uncertainty, the grandfather sees time as an uncontrollable, terrifyingly rapid process of disjunctive or inorganic change. Thus, to him, life appears "erstaunlich kurz" (*Se* 138). It contracts in his memory, because it has evidently been a succession of fleeting moments unconnected by any awareness of underlying order or growth.[2]

The effect of the grandfather's sense of time, however, is not only to make his own life appear as extremely brief. It also causes him to consider as almost incomprehensible the attempt to reach a goal, no matter how near and tangible it may be. For even under normal, favourable circumstances, the attempt is inevitably subject to the passage of time, which, once viewed in all its swiftness, assumes a force sufficient to make the mind shrink from the undertaking. Between will and goal, resolution and realisation, there is a necessary distance, which an intense awareness of transience perpetuates through fear.[3]

In principle, the grandfather's awareness of time and its significance for life is entirely consistent with the vision of human uncertainty conveyed by earlier and later pieces of the collection. Consequently, in principle, it must be imputed to the author as well. This does not mean, however, that Kafka also shares or affirms the intensity of the old man's awareness. On the contrary, through the introductory sentence, "Mein Großvater pflegte zu sagen: (...)" (*Se* 138), his expositor clearly relates this intensity to an age much in excess of his own, and leaves completely in doubt whether and to what extent he is to be identified with the grandfather's extreme, even morbid sentiments. Indeed, if it were not for the context of the collection, it would be impossible to establish a clear association at all between the grandfather's view and that of the expositor or the author. Thus the work must be taken as indicating a direction of thought and emotion, rather than a fixed or unequivocally defined position. But the guiding principle remains plain enough, namely, the awareness that, in a world where time is experienced increasingly as transient, the possibility of purposive action, even on the purely physical level, is correspondingly reduced, as man becomes the helpless victim of his own paralysing fear and uncertainty.

Eine kaiserliche Botschaft

A similarly extreme view of the modern human condition is embodied in the story *Eine kaiserliche Botschaft* (early March, 1917),[1] which originally formed part of Kafka's much longer, posthumously pub-

162

lished work, *Beim Bau der chinesischen Mauer* (s. *BkI* 77f.).[2] Through two of its principal figures, the Emperor and his helpless subject, this brief narrative immediately calls to mind *Ein altes Blatt* which, as already noted, also has close links with the same original. But apart from obvious similarities in subject matter, the two pieces actually have little in common. One need only compare the psychologically advantaged, almost totally impersonalised narrator of the one with the intellectually and emotionally very limited, yet clearly personalised expositor of the other to be strongly aware of their differences, especially in their impact on the reader.

It is on the moral level, however, that these differences are most striking and significant. Unlike *Ein altes Blatt*, *Eine kaiserliche Botschaft* shows no concern with responsibility or guilt, and thus lacks any punitive element corresponding to the nomads. For here the remoteness of the Emperor is not the result of withdrawal on his part. Nor has it been brought about by a preoccupation with *Beruf* on the part of his subjects. Rather, it is inherent in the very nature of the imperial position. As the centre of his own solar system, the Emperor is that vital, illuminating point about which all life within his empire revolves and arranges itself in descending order. Thus he is necessarily and increasingly distant from his subjects.

The effect of this inevitable distance is to make direct communication ultimately impossible. Although on his deathbed the Emperor entrusts a robust, faithful servant with a message for his lowliest subject, the sheer weight and extent of intervening physical reality, the "Dazwischen" (Mühlberger, 1960:20), is such that, despite the servant's unflagging efforts and the co-operation of others, the message can never be delivered. The unending mass of imperial institution frustrates the dying Emperor's wish and causes the loyal messenger to strive in vain:

> (...) wie nutzlos müht er sich ab; immer noch zwängt er sich durch die Gemächer des innersten Palastes; niemals wird er sie überwinden; und gelänge ihm dies, nichts wäre gewonnen; die Treppen hinab müßte er sich kämpfen; und gelänge ihm dies, nichts wäre gewonnen; die Höfe wären zu durchmessen; und nach den Höfen der zweite umschließende Palast; und wieder Treppen und Höfe; und wieder ein Palast; und so weiter durch Jahrtausende; und stürzte er endlich aus dem äußersten Tor — aber niemals, niemals kann

es geschehen — liegt erst die Residenzstadt vor ihm, die Mitte der Welt, hochgeschüttet voll ihres Bodensatzes. Niemand dringt hier durch und gar mit der Botschaft eines Toten. (*Se* 138f.)

Here, as in *Das nächste Dorf*, there is a necessary gap between will and goal, resolution and realisation, a gap which, owing to the very nature of modern existence, cannot be bridged.

Thus the imperial authority and its indefatigable emissary prove ultimately powerless before the physical and institutional reality of which they are a part. And if they are powerless, how much more so is the solitary individual, reduced in stature from the beginning to "dem jämmerlichen Untertanen, dem winzig vor der kaiserlichen Sonne in die fernste Ferne geflüchteten Schatten" (*Se* 138). Utterly insignificant and isolated, knowing of the imperial message only through legend and, therefore, uncertain of its very existence, he is incapable of action, almost of willing. Unlike the countryman, who confidently approaches the entrance to the Law, is only gradually brought into physical subjection and never accepts final defeat, this anonymous 'Du' is resigned from the outset to waiting in vain for a messenger of the absolute authority to approach him. His lot, like that of the actual circusgoer in *Auf der Galerie*, is a lasting, melancholy helplessness, as he sits in idle dreams and gazes out into the evening, imagining the message that might have been.[3] Though more wistful than desperate, in essence he nevertheless corresponds closely to the grandfather's vision of man in *Das nächste Dorf*. And again, as in that piece, the speaker's relationship to him remains somewhat ill-defined, though evidently tending towards complete identification.

Of all the *Landarzt* pieces, *Eine kaiserliche Botschaft* is, aesthetically speaking, one of the best, combining stylistic simplicity, directness and control with a strong undercurrent of emotional involvement which clearly distinguishes it from the cold virtuosity of some earlier pieces. At the same time, it is probably also the most typical, in that more than any other of these works it is suggestive of the whole, providing a focal point not only for much of the collection's imagery, but also for its principal themes. Among the latter, perhaps none is of more importance than the relationship between man and the Absolute, since it may be said to provide a framework for all the rest.

And because it is of such importance, an attempt to summarise the author's views on the matter has been deliberately delayed until now, when all the *Landarzt* pieces directly related to them have been analysed.

Excursus: The Law

According to many, if not most critics, the fundamental principle of Kafka's world-view is to be discovered in *Eine kaiserliche Botschaft* or, more precisely, in the figure of the Emperor, whose emblem is the sun and who is finally said to have died, as the Emperor Franz Joseph had done on 21st November, 1916. This, they maintain, is obviously an imaginative representation of the Nietzschean dictum: "Gott ist tot".[1] Consequently, the author must be an atheist, albeit "verschämt" (Anders, 1951:71ff.).[2] However, to arrive at such a conclusion is not only to distort Kafka's views and to oversimplify Nietzsche's,[3] it is also to make several erroneous assumptions about this story and one of its principal characters.

In the first place, it is false to assume that, because his emblem is the sun, the Emperor is therefore to be identified with God. Indeed, to make such an assumption is to confuse a traditional, public symbol with allegory. That the imperial emblem naturally and immediately suggests the Divine is hardly to be doubted. But this does not make the Emperor God, any more than a flag with skull and crossbones transforms a pirate into Death. The emblem merely establishes a direct, conventional link between the two; it does not make them identical. Thus, in the present case, the sun indicates that Emperor and God are alike in being a gravitational centre which is at the same time a source of life-giving light, warmth, and so on. It does not suggest that they are alike in other respects or that, even in the mentioned respects, there is no difference between the types of light, heat and gravitational force each possesses.

It is also false to assume that the individual Emperor is to be equated with the imperial office and dignity. In other words, it does not follow from the death of a particular Emperor that the 'Kaisertum' disappears with him. On the contrary, the story clearly implies that the imperial system is so firmly established as to be immovable. And, in *Beim Bau der chinesischen Mauer*, the speaker makes the point quite explicit before relating the parable of the imperial message. The Emperor "als solcher", he explains, is "groß durch alle Stockwerke der Welt", but "der lebendige Kaiser" is only "ein Mensch wie wir" (*BkI* 76). Thus, although "der einzelne Kaiser" may decline and fall, the "Kaisertum" remains "unsterblich" (*BkI* 77). Obviously, there can be no question here, either, of equating the Emperor's death in Kafka's story with the news announced by Nietzsche in *Die fröhliche Wissenschaft* (1882). Consequently, for want of further evidence, one must conclude, in terms of the abovementioned argument, that Kafka is not an atheist, 'verschämt' or otherwise.

But to infer from this that he is therefore a theist, a deist or even an agnostic would obviously be rash. His attitudes and values are much too unorthodox for that. Indeed, their lack of orthodoxy is such that, if it is to be conveyed with any accuracy, definitions specifically relating to God are probably best omitted altogether from the discussion, since they will usually imply much more than is either appropriate or intended (cf. W. Kraft, 1968:65-78).

Insofar as Kafka conceives at all of a metaphysical absolute, he does so in terms of the Law. Even the rare references to divinity in his works[4] are coloured by this idea. In other words, for him the ultimate reality of life is an absolute, transcendent authority which is the final seat of judgement and the real source of all genuine existential value.[5]

When figures like Alexander the Great were alive, however, the Law was not only transcendent, but clearly immanent as well, working through its temporal representative, who transmitted its spirit to his subjects.[6] As the absolute head of an earthly empire, Alexander imparted to those below and about him a genuine and unequivocal sense of value, purpose and direction. In accomplishing this, he acted as a true representative of the Law, arousing and sustaining in his subjects a vital awareness of the Ultimate and their relationship to it.

But, with the passage of time, this situation has been drastically altered. The 'Kaisertum' or its equivalent, be it church or legal system,[7] has of course remained, because it is immortal. However, immortality is no guarantee of immutability,[8] as the Christian doctrine

166

of the soul also recognises. And the first effect of this apparently inevitable change has been to create a rift between the people and the Law's earthly representatives. Instead of playing a role similar to Alexander's, these mediators have withdrawn into themselves (*Ein altes Blatt*), or have fallen victim to their own institutional existence (*Eine kaiserliche Botschaft*), or have simply been deserted by man, as he has become increasingly preoccupied with his own materialistic concerns (*Ein Landarzt*). Whatever the cause and the extent of guilt (if guilt there be), the distressing fact nevertheless remains that these supposed intermediaries between man and the Law have become utterly remote, inscrutable, misleading and functionally impotent (*Vor dem Gesetz*). Far from imparting a vital awareness of value, purpose and direction to their subjects, they create uncertainty, confusion, frustration or despair.

Thus they have ceased to be true representatives of the Law. Like the doorkeeper, they retain the office and appearance, but lack the substance.[9] Between surface and underlying reality there has arisen a deceptive, potentially ruinous disparity. Consequently, the very nature of the Law, itself, has become uncertain.

Faced with this situation, man may experience some form of anguish or eventually arrive at a wistful resignation, as in *Eine kaiserliche Botschaft*.[10] On the other hand, however, he may also be lulled into a false sense of freedom and security,[11] choosing to ignore the Law or even to deny its actual existence. But he does so at his own peril. For although the Law may no longer work through its immortal representatives, it is still capable of directly asserting itself. With inexorable force, it may at any moment irrupt into the physical sphere, transforming the existing empirical (*Die Verwandlung*; *In der Strafkolonie*)[12] or assuming the form of trans-empirical, violent, vengeful creatures that call to mind the Erinnyes (*Ein Landarzt*; *Ein altes Blatt*). In this way, it continues to establish its values, especially by revealing and punishing both human deception and the evasion of personal responsibility, two of the capital sins in Kafka's world-view (cf. *Hv* 39ff.).

Why Kafka should have construed the Law in this way, one can only speculate, as many already have,[13] since even his extra-literary utterances on the subject provide no unequivocal clues (cf. *Tb* 21f.,

549,554f.; *Hv* 84; *BkI* 283; *Gk* 227,231,242f.). That his overbearing, social-climbing, philistine father implanted in him a strong sense of guilt and authoritative arbitrariness is scarcely to be doubted, whatever the acknowledged legalistic tricks employed in Kafka's *Brief an den Vater.* Nevertheless, this Oedipal dimension of the issue has clearly been much exaggerated, especially when one considers, for example, that the very first of Kafka's fictional judges, Herr Bendemann of *Das Urteil*, condemns to death the very type of son Kafka's father would unquestionably have preferred, rather than the determined bachelor and sickly, unsuccessful businessman, Georg's friend in Russia, whom he calls a "Sohn nach meinem Herzen" (*Se* 29). This same fact must also create deep reservations about theories which associate Kafka's Law with the Torah's injunctions against bachelorhood (cf. Walther, 1977:143), although the Old Testament's emphasis on the Law and its partial image of Yahweh as a rigorous judge and ruthless avenger, even a warrior (Ex. 15:3ff.), are extremely unlikely not to have affected Kafka's outlook, and certainly did occupy his attention for a time about six months before most of the *Landarzt* pieces were written (Bezzel, 1975:112ff.). E. Heller (1948; 1974) has consistently argued that Kafka's world-view, including his notion of the Law, also contains a distinctly Gnostic or Manichean element, and there is much in the author's writings, especially the aphorisms, to support such a proposition (e.g. matter is inherently evil, demonic intruders, etc.). However, according to available evidence, it is highly improbable that Kafka became acquainted with Gnosticism, let alone Marcionism (cf. Anders, 1952:87f.; Kuna, 1974:45ff.), before 1921 (Wagenbach, 1958:263). A more plausible explanation of his work's apparently Gnostic features would therefore seem to lie in the related teachings of neo-Platonism (cf. Copleston, 1946:207-228, esp. 222ff.), a tradition with which Kafka was undeniably familiar, if only through the work of Meister Eckhart (*Br* 20; Pasley, 1966), and St. Augustine (*Hv* 446), although Walther's study (1977) of the subject, because of his schizophrenic and oneiric bias (op.cit.:10ff., 72ff.), fails to explore the matter at all.[14]

A link between these psychoanalytical or religio-philosophical speculations and possible socio-historical influences is provided by Nietzsche, whose ideas had aroused Kafka's interest as early as 1900-

1901, that is, during his last year at school (P. Heller, 1971; Bridgwater, 1974). In the third of his *Unzeitgemäße Betrachtungen*, a treatise significantly devoted to "Schopenhauer als Erzieher", of whose works Kafka was evidently also an avid reader (cf. Wagenbach, 1958:260), Nietzsche (1874) gives the following analysis of his own era:

Wenn es aber einseitig sein sollte, nur die Schwäche der Linien und die Stumpfheit der Farben am Bilde des modernen Lebens hervorzuheben, so ist jedenfalls die zweite Seite um nichts erfreulicher, sondern nur um so beunruhigender. Es sind gewiss Kräfte da, ungeheure Kräfte, aber wilde, ursprüngliche und ganz und gar unbarmherzige. Man sieht mit banger Erwartung auf sie hin wie in den Braukessel einer Hexenküche: es kann jeden Augenblick zucken und blitzen, schreckliche Erscheinungen anzukündigen. Seit einem Jahrhundert sind wir auf lauter fundamentale Erschütterungen vorbereitet; und wenn neuerdings versucht wird, diesem tiefsten modernen Hange, einzustürzen oder zu explodieren, die constitutive Kraft des sogenannten nationalen Staates entgegenzustellen, so ist doch für lange Zeiten hinaus auch er nur eine Vermehrung der allgemeinen Unsicherheit und Bedrohlichkeit. Dass die Einzelnen sich so gebärden, als ob sie von allen diesen Besorgnissen nichts wüssten, macht uns nicht irre: ihre Unruhe zeigt es, wie gut sie davon wissen; sie denken mit einer Hast und Ausschliesslichkeit an sich, wie noch nie Menschen an sich gedacht haben, sie bauen und pflanzen für ihren Tag, und die Jagd nach Glück wird nie grösser sein als wenn es zwischen heute und morgen erhascht werden muss: weil übermorgen vielleicht überhaupt alle Jagdzeit zu Ende ist. Wir leben die Periode der Atome, des atomistischen Chaos. (op.cit.:367)

Nothing, it seems, could be more evocative of Kafka's relationship to his own time than this passage, a period when the Austro-Hungarian empire was crumbling and about to be totally dissolved, when Kafka, a fully qualified lawyer and reluctant employee of a semi-nationalised workers' insurance company, educated in German, but surrounded by increasingly nationalistic Czechs, reared in Judaism, but encircled by ever more bitter and violent Christians, rightly sensed the underlying lawlessness, emptiness and aimlessness of his epoch (cf. Mühlberger, 1960; Stern, 1976; Hilsch, 1979; Stölzl, 1979). As he was later to explain to Janouch:

Das Volk der Bibel ist die Zusammenfassung von Individuen durch ein Gesetz. Die Massen von heute widersetzen sich aber jeder Zusammenfassung.

> Sie streben auseinander auf Grund der inneren Gesetzlosigkeit. Das ist die Triebkraft ihrer rastlosen Bewegung. Die Massen hasten, laufen, gehen im Sturmschritt durch die Zeit. Wohin? Von wo kommen sie? Niemand weiß es. Je mehr sie marschieren, um so weniger erreichen sie ein Ziel. Nutzlos verbrauchen sie ihre Kräfte. Sie denken, daß sie gehen. Dabei stürzen sie — auf der Stelle marschierend — nur ins Leere. Das ist alles. Der Mensch hat hier seine Heimat verloren. (*Gk* 232)

It is in revelation of and opposition to this awareness of his era's underlying reality that Kafka creates his own image of the Law, with its utterly deceptive, impotent earthly representatives and its violently punitive, trans-empirical emissaries.

Already it has been suggested, however, that Kafka's vision, even of such an important reality as the relationship between the individual and the Law, is by no means a static or fixed set of insights. Rather, it shows a distinct development. As the author becomes more deeply aware of the nature and extent of life's uncertainty, the ruthlessly severe outlook informing works like *Die Verwandlung* and *Ein Landarzt* gives way to a broader, more balanced view, so that after *Ein altes Blatt* the motif of destructive moral atonement does not recur in the works Kafka published in his own lifetime. Instead of limiting himself to a somewhat morbid preoccupation with guilt and horrific punishment, he now adopts a more gently ironic, ambivalent, but not indifferent attitude, focussing his attention on situations of enduring tension and anguish, independent of guilt. Even in *Ein Brudermord*, where the central act is again violent and destructive, there is no simple reversion to the moral values of preceding works.

An essential part of this shift in focus is a decisive change in Kafka's characteristic literary technique of juxtaposing, in tangible form, two different levels of reality or modes of being. In *Die Verwandlung*, *In der Strafkolonie*, *Ein Landarzt* and *Ein altes Blatt*, man is confronted with a materially actual, yet physically inexplicable phenomenon, which imposes itself forcibly and irrevocably upon one or more of the work's central figures. And, in each case, the effect of this imposition is to establish some moral value through the physical ruin of the figures concerned. Thus, as indicated earlier, these strange phenomena may be regarded as passing judgement on a situation that is morally confused and misleading. For this reason and because of their trans-empirical nature, they may also be interpreted as issuing from the Law.

However, with creatures like Bucephalus and the jackals, this is no longer the case. For although, as partially humanised animals, they too are materially actual, yet physically inexplicable, they nevertheless lack the irresistible, destructive, moral force of such phenomena as the horses and groom. Far from reflecting or representing the values of a merciless, transcendent Absolute, they display a close affinity with the specifically human condition of modern times, at least as Kafka saw it. Instead of ruthlessly exposing and punishing man's guilt, they embody, in a concentrated, generally extreme form, some fundamental, yet problematical aspect of his existence, and thus provide him with the possibility of gaining insight into his own nature.[15] In form and function, therefore, they have much in common with the characters of literary fable,[16] and are, like them, mere fabrications of the author's mind for a literary purpose, whereas figures like the nomads and their horses, which point to a primal, relentless reality beyond themselves and the author, belong more to the world of *Erlkönig* and similar ballads.

Die Sorge des Hausvaters

It is with this distinction in mind that one should approach the next *Landarzt* piece, *Die Sorge des Hausvaters* (end April, 1917),[1] for its central character is one of Kafka's fabular[2] creatures and differs from others in the collection only in being a partially, though essentially humanised thing, rather than an animal. Odradek, the character in question, is closely related to a theme which is clearly enunciated in *Der neue Advokat* and which forms the basic premiss of the following pieces, namely, the view that modern life lacks any real purpose, value or meaning. Convinced of such a lack and of the absolute necessity to remedy it, Kafka has undertaken, in and through the *Landarzt* collection, an implied quest for these fundamental life-principles. But, from one work to the next, the possibility of ever finding them has been progressively reduced, so that one might already be tempted to conclude that modern life is unalterably lacking in them. It is this possible conclusion, divorced from any desire for its opposite, that the creature Odradek apparently embodies. That is to say, it represents a state which, in the eyes of the expositor, the 'Hausvater', seems to be purely, even positively valueless, purposeless and meaningless.

To all outward appearances, nothing about the being Odradek makes sense. Though it can comprehend and make intelligent use of human discourse, it seems to lack the most vital human organs and is not even remotely human in its physical form. Rather, it is a conglomerate of disparate parts which, though they may resemble familiar concrete objects, are now so far removed from their original function that the 'Hausvater' is at a loss to know what their present purpose might be and thus whether Odradek has or ever had any purpose either. "Es ist Ding und zugleich Nicht-Ding, Mensch und zugleich Nicht-Mensch" (Emrich, 1958:95). In manner and habits, it is equally elusive, moving about too nimbly to be caught, never settling in one place, often staying away for months on end, and alternating in mood between a wry reticence and a wooden silence. Even its name is apparently without sense or meaning. Some claim that it is of Slavonic origin, others that it is derived from German and only influenced by the Slavonic. "Die Unsicherheit beider Deutungen aber läßt wohl mit Recht darauf schließen, daß keine zutrifft, zumal man auch mit keiner von ihnen einen Sinn des Wortes finden kann" (Se 139).

If this apparent lack of sense, meaning and purpose were an unequivocal description of Odradek's nature, then he might easily be dismissed as unworthy of human attention, especially since he is quite harmless. But the description is not unequivocal. On the contrary, like all the expositor's attempts to interpret Odradek's nature, it is totally uncertain. For the most remarkable thing about this strange creature is that, while he certainly gives the impression of lacking sense, meaning and purpose, at the same time he also appears to lack nothing. What the human mind naturally construes as a negative state is, in his case, evidently no privation at all: "das Ganze erscheint zwar sinnlos, aber in seiner Art abgeschlossen" (Se 139). In other words, it would seem that in him a basic assumption of human life either is transvalued or simply ceases to be relevant. For if he is pointless, then he is so purely and positively, and that is obviously a contradiction in terms.

In every aspect of his being, then, Odradek completely eludes the grasp of the family man. Yet, for all his harmlessness, he cannot be dismissed as a mere nonsense, since the fundamental notion of sense appears peculiarly irrelevant to this whole nature. Consequently, he has the effect of challenging the very basis of the father's existence, casting serious doubt even on the validity of his normal mental processes. In particular, he brings into question the family man's implicit, indeed instinctive assumption that all creatures must have some 'Sinn' and that this 'Sinn' may be found in the procreation and nurturing of a family. Thus, when the speaker compares his own purposeful life with Odradek's, he is filled with care:

> Vergeblich frage ich mich, was mit ihm geschehen wird. Kann er denn sterben? Alles, was stirbt, hat vorher eine Art Ziel, eine Art Tätigkeit gehabt und daran hat es sich zerrieben; das trifft bei Odradek nicht zu. Sollte er also einstmals etwa noch vor den Füßen meiner Kinder und Kindeskinder mit nachschleifendem Zwirnsfaden die Treppe hinunterkollern? Er schadet ja offenbar niemandem; aber die Vorstellung, daß er mich auch noch überleben sollte, ist mir eine fast schmerzliche. (*Se* 140)

Confronted with the possibility of pure purposelessness, the family man senses the very real uncertainty of all he stands for. Odradek becomes, as it were, his 'Sorgenkind', since by his existence he makes the value of fatherhood, family life and any purpose whatever seem fundamentally equivocal.

Ironically, therefore, this strangely elusive creature does have a 'Sinn' after all, and paradoxically it consists in his very appearance of 'Sinnlosigkeit'. The same is also true of his name, as Emrich (1958) has discovered:

> Im Tschechischen (und allgemein Westslawischen) gibt es das Verbum 'odraditi' (= jemandem etwas abraten). Dieses Wort stammt etymologisch aus dem Deutschen (rad = Rat). Die slawische 'Beeinflussung' erstreckt sich danach auf das Präfix od (= ab, weg von) und auf das Suffix -ek, das eine Verkleinerung ausdrückt. Aber auch die erstere Ansicht ist ja berechtigt, wonach das Wort ein rein slawisches Gebilde ist und sich auch aus dem Slawischen in seiner 'Bildung' ganz erklären läßt. Odradek würde nämlich

danach ein kleines Wesen bedeuten, das jemandem etwas abrät, bzw. überhaupt immer abrät. (op.cit.:92f.)[3]

Since Kafka, as the creator of the word Odradek, was evidently also
aware of its hidden meaning, one may be led to wonder why he
should have deliberately withheld this information from both the
family man and the general reader. And the reason is, of course, that
the mystification is absolutely necessary to the work's embodied
intention. For, if the expositor had not been denied this information,
Odradek would not have completely eluded his grasp. Nor would he
have seemed to be entirely or positively 'sinnlos'. Thus he would
have failed to have the effect that his name implies, that is, he would
have failed to dissuade the expositor from taking for granted the
validity of the values on which the whole idea of 'Hausvater' is based.

However, although Odradek's mysterious nature implicitly casts
doubt on the very basis of the family man's existence and thus ultimately assumes an extremely important 'Sinn' for expositor, author
and reader, it must be remembered that this 'Sinn' is no more than a
description of the effect produced by the weird creature's appearance.
It does nothing to define his actual nature, which still remains a mass
of apparent contradictions and, therefore, as equivocal as the values
his appearance brings into question. Consequently, it would be a
mistake to assume, as Emrich (1958:95) and Politzer (1962:97) do,
that Odradek is intended to represent a valid or viable alternative to
the family man's purposeful existence. On the contrary, the author
affirms the values neither of the one nor of the other. Rather, through
the invention of an utterly elusive being, he suggests a possibility that
renders uncertain even the most fundamental of human assumptions,
namely, that 'Sinn' is a positive quality and that life without it is
unthinkable. Whether this assumption is, in fact, wrong is neither
stated nor implied. The important point is that it may be wrong and
that in a world separated from the Absolute there is no way of knowing whether it is or is not.

Because of its brevity, its largely unemotional tone and the
necessary limitations of its expositor, *Die Sorge des Hausvaters* may
fail to elicit any positive response at all from the reader. In fact,
despite the mysterious quality of its central figure, it may seem

altogether slight, dull and hardly worthy of attention (cf. Sokel, 1964). But this surface impression is deceptive. Certainly the work is narrow in compass and mainly intellectual in appeal. It is also imbued with the spirit of Kafka's chilling humour, the effect of which is perhaps best described by the family man's reference to Odradek's laughter: "es ist (...) nur ein Lachen, wie man es ohne Lungen hervorbringen kann. Es klingt etwa so, wie das Rascheln in gefallenen Blättern" (*Se* 140). Yet, within these limits, the piece shows a brilliance of conception and execution that is seldom equalled in Kafka's shorter fiction. Probably nowhere else among these works is a similarly elusive insight conveyed with such imaginative economy, originality and utter precision.

In view of its intrinsic merits and its direct relevance to the general theme of the foregoing pieces, *Die Sorge des Hausvaters* naturally assumes a position of considerable importance in the *Landarzt* collection. However, as yet the extent of that importance has not been fully outlined. For there still remains the question of the work's particular position in the total scheme of the collection, and that can only be answered by means of a more specific comparison with the two immediately preceding pieces.

Though very different in structure, style and subject matter, *Das nächste Dorf* and *Eine kaiserliche Botschaft* are closely related in the view of life they embody. Both suggest that man is no longer master of the physical reality to which he belongs. Rather, he has become its helpless victim. Consequently, even on the purely physical level, any conscious attempt to reach a goal, be it the most immediate or the most distant, is subject to a deep-seated, ineluctable uncertainty. Thus the possibility of achieving a purpose, even on this same level, becomes so remote that the attempt seems futile and, with some certainty, a negative result can be foretold.

A very similar awareness also informs *Die Sorge des Hausvaters*. However, here the concern is no longer with conscious will or resolution. Instead, by the usual process of reduction, the author again narrows his focus, this time to consider the possibility of establishing and achieving some valid purpose through physical instinct. Under normal circumstances, to become a 'Hausvater' is to perform an innate, physical function and thus to fulfil a natural, intuitive purpose of the human person. At the same time, insofar as the parent lives on in all his descendants, it is also to transcend the limits of individual mortality. For both these reasons, parenthood might well be regarded as providing human life with the secure, unequivocal, even ultimate value which man sees as necessary to his existence. However, as already pointed out, it is the effect of Odradek to challenge this intuitive assumption by suggesting the possibility that the very notion of purpose is uncertain, that it may not even be a positive value, let alone an ultimate one.

Elf Söhne

In dealing with the relationship between a father and his children, *Elf Söhne* (end March, 1917)[1] raises the same issue as the preceding piece. It also arrives at a similarly negative conclusion. But here the challenge to the assumed value of fatherhood derives not from a fabular creature like Odradek, but from the father's sons, as they appear in his regard.

Although, in the characterisation and assessment of his sons, the father affirms his love for all of them, he also makes very plain the dissatisfaction and disillusionment which, in varying degrees, they all cause him. Indeed, at times he is so conscious of their alleged failings and so intent on fault-finding that one may wonder just how much charity there really is in his love. Be that as it may, it is quite clear that he does not see them as the fulfilment of a positive life-purpose, however innate and instinctive. Nor does he find in them the consoling promise of a continuing family line. For the seventh son is the only one whom he would really like to see become a father, and he shows not the slightest interest in the opposite sex, while the only son to display any concern at all for his father's future is the eleventh, and he is so frail, so otherworldly that the father trusts him least of all, realising that his characteristics are calculated to destroy the family.

To the head of this family, then, paternity is far from representing an unequivocal, enduring existential value. Rather, it appears to him largely as the propagation of imperfection. Thus, despite his

176

professed love for his sons and his awareness of their good points, he recognises in all of them, as their one common characteristic, a general family weakness, which he defines in reference to his second son's defective left eye:

> Es ist natürlich nicht dieser körperliche Fehler, der mir weh tut, sondern eine ihm irgendwie entsprechende kleine Unregelmäßigkeit seines Geistes, irgendein in seinem Blut irrendes Gift, irgendeine Unfähigkeit, die mir allein sichtbare Anlage seines Lebens rund zu vollenden. Gerade dies macht ihn allerdings andererseits wieder zu meinem wahren Sohn, denn dieser sein Fehler ist gleichzeitig der Fehler unserer ganzen Familie und an diesem Sohn nur überdeutlich. (*Se* 141)

However, although the father is conscious of this failing in the whole of his family, there is no indication that the sons share his awareness. Indeed, if they are all like the second, they cannot possibly share it, since the father alone is aware of the potentiality that is never fully realised. From this one may conclude, as argued in the earlier discussion of advantaged knowledge, that the supposed general weakness in the sons is merely a projection of the father's own self-awareness. Thus, when one considers the extremely critical and disappointed attitude he nevertheless adopts towards them, it becomes clear that the real source of his discontent is not so much the particular faults of each son as the knowledge that in them he has failed to overcome himself. The positive fulfilment he had evidently hoped to find in procreation has been denied him. In his sons he has merely propagated his own imperfection.[2]

As if to highlight this somewhat concealed, yet crucial aspect of the father's position, Kafka employs here a technique essentially identical with that in *Ein Besuch im Bergwerk.* That is to say, in this exposition, as in the preceding one, he reinforces the significance of the situation by the use of a traditional numerical symbol. In choosing the otherwise arbitrary, not to mention improbable number of eleven sons, and in causing the father to refer to them exclusively by number, rather than name, Kafka draws attention to the fact that the father represents 'imperfection aiming at perfection'. This suggestion may seem to entail a complete contradiction of the symbolic principle. After all, it is the sons who are eleven, not the father. However, the appearance of contradiction is deceptive. For it must be remembered that, unlike the engineers' attendant, the father strives to achieve his goal not in and through himself, but in and through his sons. Consequently, they are eleven, not he, because they are the symbolic embodiment of his purpose, as well as its actual frustration.

Within this framework of traditional symbolism, the specific numbering of the sons is governed by the principle that each succeeding son shall contrast with the previous one.[3] Even where the two are alike in some respects, the total effect will still be one of contrast. The first two sons, for example, are both 'klug', but whereas the first displays his cleverness within narrow limits and never comes to terms with the world, the second combines it with broad experience and worldly wisdom. Similarly, the second and third are both handsome, but differ in the type of handsomeness each possesses. By these means, using the sons' outward appearance, temperament and relationship to their socio-historical environment as specific terms of reference, the author creates an organic whole.

Yet, while one may rightly speak of inner unity and necessity in *Elf Söhne*, there is also considerable justification for the view that, in a manner curiously opposed to the rigid functionality of the work's enumerative technique, its detail often exceeds the demands of its unifying intention. In other words, although the father's remarks may all be construed as directly or indirectly relevant to the underlying purpose of the work, at times they are so elaborate that the construction itself becomes improbable. As a result, one is left with the impression that, in the case of the second son, for example, much of the detail is unnecessary and thus distorts the work's apparent intention. Certainly the detail creates a more plastic quality and some emotional intensity in a work which, in other respects, tends to be abstract and flat. But it also confuses, makes the whole piece seem obviously contrived, and lends weight to that otherwise demonstrably unjustified allegoresis of the father and sons as Kafka and eleven of his stories.[4] For these reasons, despite its intrinsic interest and its special significance within the collection as a whole, *Elf Söhne* proves to be of little aesthetic merit.

In terms of the search for a positive *modus vivendi* in an age of spiritual, intellectual and emotional uncertainty, *Die Sorge des Haus-*

178

vaters and *Elf Söhne* thus clearly provide no more grounds for hope than the preceding pieces of the collection. Despite its fundamental relevance to life and the promise it holds of unequivocal purpose and enduring value, fatherhood is shown to be no less a source of disillusionment and anguish than absolute earthly authority or subjective ideals. Consequently, in a last desperate reduction of scope, the author now focusses on thoughts of release through death. If modern life is so intractably uncertain that even procreation becomes equivocal in purpose and value, then perhaps man's only remaining hope lies in the destruction of that life. Since the detailed examination of the human condition has failed to reveal any other means of affirming existence, it may be that man's only real alternative is to affirm it by physically negating it, that is, to attempt to create sense by destroying the embodiment of senselessness. It is this utterly extreme and paradoxical undertaking which provides the link between the next two pieces, the last thematic pair of the *Landarzt* collection.

Ein Brudermord

Assuming the guise of a crime reporter, Kafka first gives expression to this drastic possibility in *Ein Brudermord* (Jan./Feb., 1917).[1] The story is brief, yet one of the most intricate and perplexing of the whole collection. In no small measure, this is due to its peculiar style, which is a perverse mixture of factual sobriety, sensationalism and Classical allusion.

The work opens in the manner of an official report, but soon begins to display characteristics more typical of delinquent journalism. Complex sentence structure gives way to staccato phrases, past tense to present historic, unembellished information to lurid detail, dispassionate narrative distance to overtly emotional involvement, as the story acquires a thrilling, almost melodramatic quality.[2] Stylised characters, prolonged suspense, large gestures, semi-hysterical soliloquy, extreme pathos: all form part of a highly coloured development, which, with the murderer's arrest, comes to a halt in one last, incomplete sentence: "Schmar, mit Mühe die

179

letzte Übelkeit verbeißend, den Mund an die Schulter des Schutz-mannes gedrückt, der leichtfüßig ihn davonführt" (*Se* 145).

With a similarly grotesque perversity, the significance of the work's title is also radically altered as the events unfold. For although the murderer is sufficiently familiar with his victim to know the where-abouts of his office and home, the hour at which he finishes work, certain details of his domestic life and the Christian name of his wife, it is nevertheless obvious from their surnames that the two men are not full blood-brothers. On the contrary, the indication is that they are nothing more than close friends and drinking companions. In this light, the title is suddenly transformed, and the significance of the action with it. For here fratricide refers not to a family crime in the usual sense, but more generally to a fatal attack by man on his fellow man. Primarily, therefore, the murderer and his victim are opposed representatives of the human family, rather than individual persons at enmity. It is presumably in order to reinforce the sense of their representative function that the author gives them such stylised, typifying names.

Wese, the victim, suggests the essence or substance (*Wesen*) of the good, ordinary citizen and human being. A diligent, evidently successful office-worker, he is also happily married, friendly, convivial, and capable of taking a simple delight in the beauty of nature. Apparently untroubled by questions of ultimate reality and their concomitant anguish in modern times, he leads the limited, but relatively serene life of the unaware or naive, at peace with the world, loved and loving. Together with his utterly devoted wife, he represents the ideal of fraternal humanity.

At the opposite extreme stands the murderer, Schmar, whose name aptly calls to mind both the action and the effect of stabbing (cf. *Schmarre*, dial. *Schmarr*).[3] In his impassioned treachery and wanton destructiveness, he is the epitome of man's inhumanity to man. By killing his close friend, he travesties the very notion of a universal human brotherhood, a concept which gained wide currency during the Enlightenment and developed into the *Humanitätsideal* of German Classicism.

This travesty is nowhere more appearant than in the emotion he experiences immediately after the murder: "Seligkeit des Mordes!

180

Erleichterung, Beflügelung durch das Fließen des fremden Blutes!" (*Se* 145). The soaring emotion which Schiller regarded as informing the brotherhood of man, joy, which was for him "die starke Feder/ In der ewigen Natur", binding men together with its "sanfter Flügel" (*An die Freude*), is here perverted into the estatic thrill accompanying the destruction of a fellow human being. And when the thrill has passed, the resultant disillusionment is again expressed in terms which are a base mockery of their literary origins. Faced with the continuing reality of his friend's bloodstained corpse, Schmar wishes that he could immediately make it disappear altogether, but realises that this is impossible: "Nicht alles wird erfüllt, nicht alle Blütenträume reiften, dein schwerer Rest liegt hier, schon unzugänglich jedem Tritt" (*Se* 145). Prometheus, the embodiment of a humanly creative force in Goethe's poem of the same name, he whose dreams had been of powerfully affirming human life, independent and defiant of the gods, is now quoted by his grotesque moral opposite,[4] Schmar, whose wish had been the complete annihilation of his brother-man.

Between the poles represented by Schmar and Wese stands the callous, righteous spectator, Pallas, the private citizen who knows the murderer (cf. *Se* 145) and is evidently aware of what he is about to do but makes no attempt to intervene. Though not viciously destructive, he nonetheless also acts in a manner utterly opposed to the fraternal ideal, and thus provides a grotesque reflection of the Classical spirit with which his name is traditionally associated:

> Offensichtlich soll diese Gestalt in ihrer sensationslüsternen Neugier, menschlichen Gleichgültigkeit und hämischen Genugtuung post festum den seines Wesens beraubten, philiströs und unmenschlich zugleich gewordenen Rest von Pallas Athene darstellen, der mächtigen und klugen Göttin der Weisheit und Kultur, der Beschützerin der Staaten in Krieg und Frieden, die als Hüterin der Ordnung und Humanität, als 'Stadtschirmerin' ihren festen Platz in Athen und vielen anderen Städten der Antike hatte. (H. Richter, 1962: 153)

Of all the characters in the story, Pallas occupies a position which is visually nearest the narrator's. Yet, morally, the two are most distant. For Pallas is the only character of whom the narrator unequivocally and consistently disapproves. Indeed, so strong is his antipathy towards this embodiment of heartless, morbid curiosity that it gives rise to his first direct and emotional comment on the action, as Pallas watches Schmar's gruesome preparations for murder: "Warum duldete das alles der Private Pallas, der in der Nähe aus seinem Fenster im zweiten Stockwerk alles beobachtete? Ergründe die Menschennatur!" (*Se* 144). Though applied to nature rather than man, it is this same incomprehension before the sheer callousness of existence which also finds expression in the narrator's only other personal, interpretative comment. Before Wese turns the street corner where Schmar is waiting, he pauses to enjoy the gold and blue of the night-sky:

> Unwissend blickt er es an, unwissend streicht er das Haar unter dem gelüpften Hut; nichts rückt dort oben zusammen, um ihm die allernächste Zukunft anzuzeigen; alles bleibt an seinem unsinnigen, unerforschlichen Platz. An und für sich sehr vernünftig, daß Wese weitergeht, aber er geht ins Messer des Schmar. (*Se* 145)

From this second intrusion, it is clear that the narrator, as the author's ostensible spokesman, does not regard Wese with the disapproval he obviously shows towards Pallas. Rather, it would seem that he feels considerable sympathy for him, an attitude which the action and the ending are calculated to arouse in the reader as well. Yet it would be a mistake to assume from this that, in the present instance, the relationship between narrator and character is one of complete moral-emotional identification. For the same comment also shows that the narrator views the world with an awareness and bitterness apparently lacking in Wese. Thus, at the very moment of the murder, he is able to distance himself entirely from the innocent victim and describe his death-rattle in terms which are peculiarly repulsive and powerfully destructive of sympathy: "Wasserratten, aufgeschlitzt, geben einen ähnlichen Laut von sich wie Wese" (*Se* 145).

The complementary effect of this analogy is, of course, to create a sense of identity between the narrator's and the murderer's moral-emotional outlook. That is to say, here the narrator appears to be actually sharing Schmar's gruesome delight in the destruction of a good, fellow human being. In view of Schmar's character, this may seem to be an inexcusable indulgence of aberrant sentiment on the

182

narrator's part. Yet, perverse though it be, the sentiment in fact forms a crucial part of the work's attempted system of values.

In murdering Wese, Schmar makes the brotherhood of man seem to be an empty, absurd idea and thus confirms, in an extreme way, the narrator's own interpretation of modern life as callous and inhuman. At the same time, however, the murder may also be construed as an attack on the apparent absurdity of the fraternal ideal, an attempt to overcome its assumed emptiness by destroying at least one of its embodiments. Whether this is, in fact, Schmar's motive for the crime is neither stated nor unequivocally suggested, for the nature and degree of his awareness remain somewhat of a mystery, much to the work's detriment. Nevertheless, from the fact that he deliberately chooses to kill a close friend and from the positive value he attaches to the thrill of murder, there is at least some justification for inferring that through the crime he is seeking release from a fraternal bond which, for an unspecified reason, he feels to be stifling. And because his otherwise wantonly destructive act permits of such an interpretation, regardless of his real motives, it may be seen in this respect as holding a certain natural attraction for the narrator, since it represents a possibly meaningful response to the oppressive senselessness he quite plainly perceives in man and nature. It is from this point of view that the narrator is able to identify himself, to some extent, with Schmar and thus to deliberately cultivate a style which mirrors the latter's values, especially the desire for thrilling experience as a relief and release.

There is, however, a third dimension to the fratricide. Although it reveals the apparent absurdity of the fraternal ideal in modern times and may be simultaneously construed as an attempt to overcome that absurdity, it also necessarily reinforces the same absurdity, because it adds to life's inhumanity. In choosing to murder his friend, therefore, Schmar confirms the very senselessness he is evidently seeking to escape, and Wese's corpse, with its mute question, becomes the symbol of his murderer's renewed and lasting frustration. As a result, arrest and nausea quickly follow the feeling of liberation and soaring ecstasy, while the possible paradox of the story is reduced to a mere vicious circle.

Ultimately, then, Schmar's actions and implied values prove to be simply destructive, a travesty of human brotherhood and a delusive source of emotional relief. Far from overcoming life's oppressive inhumanity, they reinforce it, even to the point of granting Pallas the opportunity to indulge his hypocritical self-righteousness. Seen in this light, the ending evidently supports the narrator's view that man is incomprehensible in his callousness and inhumanity.

However, one has only to recall the largely sensational style of the work and the extent of the narrator's sympathy with Schmar to be aware of the profound ambiguity underlying this final appearance of clarity. And when, in addition, one considers that, despite Wese's murder, the values for which he stands have not been destroyed, that they in fact live on in his wife's grief and the public's concern, the ambiguity is only intensified. For the endurance of these values, not to mention their existence in the first place, brings into question the whole moral basis of the work, namely, the narrator's general assumption that life is absurdly inhuman. Evidently the narrator is mistaken. Consequently, all his values and judgements become suspect. Furthermore, since he apparently speaks for the author as well, the whole work tends to dissolve in a haze of confusion, and one is left with the suspicion that the haze conceals nothing but a turbid reality born of a perverse misanthropy. Needless to say, such qualities are not the hallmarks of good art.

Ein Traum

In contrast to *Ein Brudermord, Ein Traum* (early Dec., 1914)[1] is a model of artistic clarity and simplicity. Through the very brief, introductory sentence, which also establishes a somewhat overworked link with *Der Prozeß* (s. esp. Sokel, 1964:282-286; 1977), the author immediately, though indirectly, defines the narrator's point of view as impersonalised and extremely advantaged. From this the remainder of the work develops naturally, the narrator retaining his distant position, but limiting his psychological advantage almost exclusively to direct knowledge of the central character's mental processes. Together with the title, the few words of introduction also clearly indicate the level of reality on which the following narrative is to be understood. Here, as in all of his shorter fiction, when Kafka wishes something to be understood as a dream, he makes it quite explicit (cf. Emrich, 1958:270). Because the irrational and fantastic are readily accepted in dreams, this distinction between levels of reality obviously makes the author's and reader's task much easier. In the present story, it also has an important bearing on the significance of the ending.

No sooner has Josef K. begun to dream than he finds himself involuntarily transported, in fine weather and with consummate ease, to a cemetery. Carried along "wie auf einem reißenden Wasser in unerschütterlich schwebender Haltung" (Se 146), K. willingly cooperates with the force of attraction, adopting the role of a keen, almost fascinated spectator. In particular, he feels irresistibly drawn towards a fresh grave, where there are signs of jubilant ceremony. On arriving at the spot, he leaps from the path that races on beneath his feet, and falls on his knees before the mound of earth, whereupon two men at the other end immediately set the headstone immovably in place, while a third, a stone-engraver, appears and begins the inscription, eagerly watched by Josef K.

Initially, then, the dreaming K. limits the significance of his involuntary attraction, tacitly assuming that its goal is merely the close observation of a grand burial ceremony, the ritualistic trappings of death. Despite his keen interest, he remains at a certain secure distance, presuming that it is a matter of someone else's burial, of death as a state already achieved in another. But this limitation and its underlying assumption are very soon challenged when the artist, having begun the inscription with great skill and beauty, becomes embarrassed by K.'s presence and cannot bring himself to engrave the name of the deceased. Suddenly the ease of the opening is replaced by a feeling of frustration and helpless confusion, as the whole ceremony goes awry and K. begins to weep "untröstlich über die Lage des Künstlers" (Se 147). Once K. has calmed himself, the artist, finding no other way out, very reluctantly resumes his work, but breaks off before completing the first pale letter: "Es war ein J, fast war es schon beendet, da stampfte der

Künstler wütend mit einem Fuß in den Grabhügel hinein, daß die Erde ringsum in die Höhe flog" (*Se* 147).

Through this angry gesture, the engraver finally brings home to K. the truth of the situation, the real reason for the ceremony and the underlying cause of the original attraction, namely, the dreamer's desire for his own death.[2] Instantly K. responds to the sudden awareness. From engrossed, distressed spectator, he changes to eager, leading participant. Death becomes for him a total, self-willed engagement in the act of dying, and the joyful ease of the opening returns, intensified. For, in burying himself, K. acknowledges and achieves the real goal of his initial attraction to the cemetery, thus finally giving sense to the ritual prepared in his honour, a ritual which immediately races to its own logical conclusion: "Während er (...) unten, den Kopf im Genick noch aufgerichtet, schon von der undurchdringlichen Tiefe aufgenommen wurde, jagte oben sein Name mit mächtigen Zieraten über den Stein" (*Se* 147).

For the dreaming Josef K., then, death ultimately becomes a self-willed and self-executed act, the fulfilment of an intense, though initially latent desire, providing blissful release from embarrassment, apparently insoluble misunderstanding and emotional distress, while lending significance to an otherwise empty ritual. Because it assumes all these aspects, it is also a source of delight to the waking K.. However, while the delight is actual, its source is not. For, as a dream, K.'s vision of his own suicide remains unrealised and, in its specific detail, unrealisable within the normal, empirical order of things. Consequently, for all its delightful effect, it presents no real alternative to the life which, by implication, it rejects: the life K. has led before the dream and from which his death-wish arises. Rather, like the dreams referred to in *Auf der Galerie* and *Eine kaiserliche Botschaft*, it remains an idle fancy.

Although, as already indicated, *Ein Traum* differs considerably in technique, content and aesthetic value from *Ein Brudermord*, the two works are nevertheless alike in suggesting the general conclusion that the physical destruction of human life, whether as murder or as suicide, provides no genuine relief or release from the nature of modern existence and no real means of affirming or coming to terms with it. In the case of murder, the validity of this generalisa-

186

tion is self-evident, since by their very nature the act and its desired end are irreconcilable. However, where suicide is concerned, such a general inference may seem unjustified on the mere basis of *Ein Traum*. It is, after all, no difficult task to imagine circumstances under which suicide is not only a realisable act, but also one which, because it puts an end to the individual's human existence, appears to be entirely consonant with any desire he may have for lasting relief and release from life's senselessness. Yet, on further reflection, it becomes evident that, even under these circumstances, the above generalisation remains valid, as the following remarks should demonstrate.

Regardless of the conditions in which suicide occurs, it implies an utter despair about existence and a consequent intense desire to be rid of it. In other words, implicit in every act of suicide is the view that death provides sense where life provides none. But this view, as Schopenhauer realised, is obviously contradictory. For death as the source of sense can only signify the existence of something meaningful beyond the physical, and if such metaphysical meaning existed, then life itself would not be without sense, even for terminally ill patients. Consequently, where life is seen as utterly senseless, death, whether it be by suicide or not, can only form part of that senselessness. Certainly it constitutes an end to an individual's physical existence. But that is no guarantee of relief or release from senselessness. On the contrary, it is a final surrender to that senselessness.[3]

If the *Landarzt* collection had concluded with *Ein Brudermord* and *Ein Traum*, there can be little doubt that the reader would have been left with a powerful sense of the author's failure to find the existential purpose and value he has been seeking. *Beruf*, vision, external absolutes, subjective ideals, physical goals, fatherhood, death: all have proven impotent as a means of affirming or coming to terms with the reality of modern existence. Yet, in the midst of all this failure and continuing uncertainty, the author has also established certain grounds from which a form of positive resolution may still develop.

In the first place, by implicitly rejecting self-destruction as a meaningful alternative to living, he necessarily recommits himself to his own existence in the modern world, despite his profound awareness of the anguish such a commitment involves. Thus, from his contemplation of the most extreme of possible human negations, a certain affirmation nevertheless arises and leads to a revaluation of all that has been established so far. Throughout the entire quest represented by the preceding *Landarzt* pieces, the author has constantly proceeded on the assumption that those aspects of existence which he naturally construes as negative are to be overcome only by gaining the positive, that is, by discovering some valid life-principle through which all that is now experienced as negative will be transformed into its opposite: uncertainty into certainty, senselessness into sense, and so on. But no such principle has been discovered. Consequently, in keeping with the possibility suggested by the figure of Odradek, the author, cast back on life, is now able to view the negative not as a privation, to be overcome, but as a necessity, to be accepted (cf. *Pz* 264). And, to this extent, he is able to affirm existence, in all its uncertainty, for that uncertainty is, paradoxically, the only certain thing he has (cf. Brod, 1954:183; Gray, 1976:174).

Needless to say, such an affirmation is not to be compared in strength or vigour with that of Nietzsche or even of Kierkegaard, to name but two of Kafka's possible influences in this matter. The extreme tension underlying the resolution, the continuing powerful awareness of the negative and of the limitations it places on existence naturally precludes the fervour of vitalism or religious faith. But within this admittedly tense and confined world, purposeful development is still possible. Though caged, as it were (cf. Foulkes, 1976: 81ff.), man feels free to act and achieve, because, in coming to terms with his imprisonment, he has created from it his own sense and value. In other words, the manner of being which characterised the chief engineers of *Ein Besuch im Bergwerk* has now been divorced from a high level of skill and knowledge and has thus become a universal possibility, the embodiment of which is to be found in the longest and probably the best piece of the present collection, the work with which it concludes.

Ein Bericht für eine Akademie

The borderline narrator of this work (early April, 1917),[1] an unusual performing ape, has been invited by an academy to present a report on his "äffisches Vorleben" (*Se* 147), that is, on the life he had led before being captured on the African Gold Coast by an expedition from the Hagenbeck Zoo (*Se* 148). In itself, the request for this report is not only a reflection of the esteem in which the chief character is held by society; it is also a formal and, presumably, learned recognition of the extent to which he has become humanised. For, in making its request, the academy has obviously taken for granted that it is dealing with one who has achieved both an adequate level of awareness to be capable of surveying his life and sufficient mastery of linguistic skills to be capable of giving expression to that awareness. Yet, at the same time, the invitation also indicates that the narrator is quite a rare creature, possessing knowledge which the academicians lack, but wish to acquire. And it is here that the inner contradiction of the request becomes evident.

In asking for a report on the narrator's existence before his capture, the academicians assume not only a high degree of humanisation in this performing ape, but also a continuity of awareness between his former manner of being and his present one. In other words, they assume that, although the narrator has now developed the thought processes and speech habits specific to human beings, he is still capable of mentally returning to the world of his former, purely simian existence and of then giving it expression in human terms. However, as the narrator quickly points out, such an assumption is completely unjustified, indeed contradictory, so that, with the best will in the world, he simply cannot comply with the academy's request. For the very abilities he has acquired, those which the invitation presupposes and which enable him to provide any report at all, are specifically human abilities. As such, they naturally played no part in his former existence and are applicable only to that period of his life in which he has ceased to be the pure ape about which the academy is anxious to hear. Consequently, the fact that he is able to present any report whatever to human beings automatically precludes the possibility of a report on his 'äffisches

Vorleben'. In his present condition, his former, purely simian nature and way of life must remain inwardly as inaccessible to him as to the academicians (cf. *Se* 148).

Insofar, then, as the narrator has become human, he is prevented from providing the type of information desired by the academy. Instead, he must limit himself to reporting on that period of his life in which he has ceased to be a mere ape. And, even within this reduced scope, his account is subject to certain inevitable and important reservations. In the first place, because the human skills he now possesses have developed only gradually over almost five years, he is largely dependent on others for information about the early stages of the change in his condition (*Se* 148, 149). Furthermore, in learning to think and speak like a human being, he has naturally adopted certain human attitudes that prejudice the accuracy of his report, much of which must needs consist of back-projections, that is, attempts to describe the earlier stages of his development in terms of and in relation to the state of awareness he has now achieved: "Ich kann natürlich das damals affenmäßig Gefühlte heute nur mit Menschenworten nachzeichnen und verzeichne es infolgedessen, aber wenn ich auch die alte Affenwahrheit nicht mehr erreichen kann, wenigstens in der Richtung meiner Schilderung liegt sie, daran ist kein Zweifel" (*Se* 149f.). Because it often leads to an incongruity in tone between the action or state described and the language of the description, this distorted nature of the report is the chief source of its humour. On one occasion, for example, the narrator tries to convey the turning-point in his adjustment to captivity by characterising it as the decision to cease being an ape, and then, caught up in the human view of his development as a progression from primitive to refined mental processes, he immediately adds the absurd comment: "Ein klarer, schöner Gedankengang, den ich irgendwie mit dem Bauch ausgeheckt haben muß, denn Affen denken mit dem Bauch" (*Se* 150).

Because he draws attention to the inevitable shortcomings of his report, the narrator of *Ein Bericht für eine Akademie* is, as previously explained, aesthetically self-aware and thus occupies a position unique among the narrators and expositors of the fiction Kafka published in his own lifetime. On the emotional level, the effect of this narrative candour is to arouse in the reader a strong feeling of sympathetic

190

trust in one who is so frank with him. Intellectually, however, the same self-awareness also establishes a certain distance between the narrator and his report, a distance the reader is expected to share, if he is to avoid misunderstanding the narrative.

As already indicated, the need for this distance arises from the fact that the narrator is attempting to account, in human terms, for a phenomenon which is totally foreign to human experience, namely, the existence of a creature which is both ape and man. Such is the nature of the report he has undertaken to present that human thought and language are bound to prove somewhat inadequate to the task. However, since they are the only means at his disposal, he has no choice but to employ them, and the reader is therefore warned to make due allowance for inevitable distortions.

This critical, intellectual distance is especially necessary when it is a question of trying to grasp the narrator's actual nature. For, owing to the fact that the reader is aware of him principally as mind and voice, the natural tendency is to disregard the obvious evidence of his continuing simian physique and, instead, to think of him as a complete human being. Moreover, on several occasions, this tendency is actually, if unintentionally, encouraged by the narrator, who, in attempting to describe his development, naturally adopts the viewpoint of full humanity and refers to it as the abandonment of his simian nature (*Se* 148), as ceasing to be an ape (*Se* 150), as a struggle against his simian nature (*Se* 153), which rushed head over heels from him (*Se* 154). In fact, however, these descriptions cannot be taken as anything more than approximations, since they are based on human preconceptions. What his simian nature is or was in itself, he cannot possibly know, because by definition that nature is inaccessible to human thought. Consequently, in describing his development as he does, he merely identifies himself with the viewpoint of full humanity, thus distorting the actual reality of the change that has occurred in him. For, while it is true that he is now essentially human, in that he has become a rational animal, it is also true that, in achieving this state, he has not fully abandoned his simian nature. Rather, he has become an ambiguous, but viable mixture of man and ape,[2] as he clearly implies when discussing the wounds he received while being captured.

The first of these wounds was on the cheek and has left a scar which has caused him to be named Rotpeter, "so als unterschiede ich mich von dem unlängst krepierten, hie und da bekannten, dressierten Affentier Peter nur durch den roten Fleck auf der Wange" (*Se* 148). The ape-man objects to this name because it suggests a basic misunderstanding of his nature. Certainly he has been forced, like the mere trained ape, to modify his behaviour and to live in circumstances utterly foreign to his former simian way of life. But, unlike the mere trained ape, he has, of himself, assented to this change, and has thus made no attempt to retain his previous simian inwardness while adopting the outward signs of humanity.

However, although he differs in this respect from the mere trained ape, the second wound provides evidence that he is nevertheless not fully human, even on the mental level. Because this wound lies below the hip, it has given rise to Rotpeter's predilection for removing his trousers before visitors in order to display the scar to them, and such behaviour has led to the remark, in a newspaper article, that his simian nature is "noch nicht ganz unterdrückt" (*Se* 148). Rotpeter is infuriated by this accusation, not so much because it is untrue, but because it misses the point. It is not that he, himself, does not find his behaviour humanly unacceptable, but simply that he objects to being judged by the standard of full humanity.[3] For, although he is obviously no longer purely simian and has refused to become just a trained 'Affentier', he is also not fully human. Nor has he ever striven to be, even on the mental level. Instead, he has merely sought to cultivate that degree of humanity which will permit him to establish a positive *modus vivendi* in the human community. Thus he has become an elusive, hybrid creature. And within the limitations of this unique nature, he finds his action perfectly justifiable. Indeed, with a strong touch of irony, he explains his allegedly purely simian behaviour in terms of the highest human values: "kommt es auf Wahrheit an, wirft jeder Großgesinnte die allerfeinsten Manieren ab" (*Se* 149).

Through these references to his wounds, then, Rotpeter indirectly defines the actual nature he has now assumed and, in doing so, helps to counteract other acknowledged, possible sources of misunderstanding in his report. At the same time, by implication, he also indicates the logic informing his present nature. Although during the past five years he has deliberately developed certain essentially human characteristics, to him these characteristics, and humanisation as such, have never been an end in themselves. He has learned to think and speak, not in order to be human in these respects, but in order, as he later points out, to gain an "Ausweg" (*Se* 150), that is, a positive means of coming to terms with the impossibly unnatural position in which his capture has placed him, a form of existence which will keep alive his will to live under the intolerable conditions that have suddenly been imposed upon him. So important is this concept to the narrator that he again draws attention to the narrative act by warning the reader against possible misinterpretation. In particular, he is anxious that his desire for 'Ausweg' should not be confused with the common human desire for freedom:

> Ich habe Angst, daß man nicht genau versteht, was ich unter Ausweg verstehe. Ich gebrauche das Wort in seinem gewöhnlichsten und vollsten Sinn. Ich sage absichtlich nicht Freiheit. Ich meine nicht dieses große Gefühl der Freiheit nach allen Seiten. Als Affe kannte ich es vielleicht und ich habe Menschen kennengelernt, die sich danach sehnen. Was mich aber anlangt, verlangte ich Freiheit weder damals noch heute. Nebenbei: mit Freiheit betrügt man sich unter Menschen allzuoft. Und so wie die Freiheit zu den erhabensten Gefühlen zählt, so auch die entsprechende Täuschung zu den erhabensten. (*Se* 150)

At first sight, it may appear from this statement that, in distancing himself from a common human ideal and from his own past as conceived by men, Rotpeter is rejecting all idea of freedom. But a closer examination of the text reveals that this is by no means the case. Rather, as the narrator explains, he is concerned with a particular type of freedom, that enormous and sublime 'Gefühl der Freiheit nach allen Seiten'.[4] This kind of freedom he rejects because, as he immediately suggests, the desire for it entails a denial or distortion of one's present nature and therefore constitutes a form of self-deception, an escape from reality, like the performance of human trapeze-artists, as he sees it (*Se* 150).[5] Consequently, despite the terms of his distinction, when Rotpeter chooses an 'Ausweg' in preference to the futility of flight (*Se* 151) or "jener erwähnten

Freiheit" (*Se* 152), he may nonetheless be said to have chosen freedom. But it is the positive, purposeful freedom of being and doing what the limitations of his nature and circumstances permit. Thus, unlike Bucephalus's negative freedom, it implies a certain affirmation of actuality, an active involvement of the self in existence, despite the latter's shortcomings and restrictions.

More specifically, Rotpeter's search for an 'Ausweg' implies the need to find a way of living among men, into whose community he has been irrevocably thrust. And that, in turn, implies the need to make himself socially acceptable among humans. Imbued with the calm of the crewmen (*Se* 150), the ape therefore sets about acquiring those abilities, actions and attitudes which will bring him out of the cage (*Se* 154) into human society and will allow him to live, like the crewmen, "unbehelligt" (*Se* 151). Renouncing all stubborn adherence to his origins and to memories of his youth (*Se* 147), he begins to imitate the humans about him, learning to shake hands as a sign of "Offenheit" (*Se* 148), to spit and smoke (*Se* 152), to drink schnaps (*Se* 152f.) and to speak (*Se* 153). But, in all of this, imitation is merely a means to the end of 'Ausweg'. In themselves, the crewmen do not attract him very much. On the contrary, he finds them a rather dismal sight (*Se* 152,153). Thus he imitates, not in order to become one of them, but in order to be socially so like them as to be accepted by the human community, to get out of the cage and to create for himself the possibility of an existence, calm and unmolested like theirs, within the enforced limitations of human society. The true nature of this imitation is accentuated by the schnaps drinking. For, although Rotpeter learns to drink like the crewmen, that is, to copy the socially acceptable form among them of drinking, he finds no pleasure in the content of the act. It becomes a ritual to be performed merely as a means of gaining an 'Ausweg'.

The same purpose also informs his behaviour once he has left the ship. When handed over to an animal trainer in Hamburg, he recognises the limited possibilities open to him and unhesitatingly decides: "setze alle Kraft an, um ins Varieté zu kommen; das ist der Ausweg; Zoologischer Garten ist nur ein neuer Gitterkäfig; kommst du in ihn, bist du verloren" (*Se* 154). Sparing no effort,

194

he applies himself to learning, until he has finally achieved the average educational level of a European. But here, again, the learning has only been a means to an end:

> Durch eine Anstrengung, die sich bisher auf der Erde nicht wiederholt hat, habe ich die Durchschnittsbildung eines Europäers erreicht. Das wäre an sich vielleicht gar nichts, ist aber insofern doch etwas, als es mir aus dem Käfig half und mir diesen besonderen Ausweg, diesen Menschenausweg verschaffte. (*Se* 154)

By and large, then, Rotpeter's report is a 'success story', as Sokel (1964:341) calls it,[6] an account of the manner in which "ein gewesener Affe in die Menschenwelt eingedrungen ist und sich dort festgesetzt hat" (*Se* 148). The visible sign of this success is his unshakable position on all the great variety stages of the civilised world (*Se* 148), for this position had been the goal informing the greater part of his development from pure ape. As a variety artist, he is not, like the mere trained ape or chimpanzee, an animal trying to give the impression of being human, for essentially he is human. Nor, like the trapeze-artists, is he a human being pretending to be an ape, for the very basis of his new nature, namely, 'Ausweg', is a rejection of the deception which, in his opinion, they create, namely, 'Freiheit'. Rather, he is a viable mixture of ape and man, and as such he is a rarity, an oddity. Thus his position in the variety theatre is the true and complete expression of his new nature. As a result of his own art, he has become, as it were, a work of art and exhibits himself as such (cf. Philippi, 1966:140). Far from bringing his new existence into question, his art is of its very essence, and his success on the variety stage is its confirmation.[7]

Yet, for all this, Rotpeter's success is not unclouded, as he suggests when summing up his achievement: "Es gibt eine ausgezeichnete deutsche Redensart: sich in die Büsche schlagen[8]; das habe ich getan, ich habe mich in die Büsche geschlagen. Ich hatte keinen anderen Weg, immer vorausgesetzt, daß nicht die Freiheit zu wählen war" (*Se* 154). Although he has eluded the cage, has slipped away from the imprisonment, loneliness and confusion of the trained animal, has 'made himself scarce' as ape, in doing so he has perforce altered his old nature in order to 'enter the brushwood'[9] of the human community and its necessary limitations: "wohler und eingeschlossener fühlte ich mich in der Menschenwelt" (*Se* 147f.). While it remains true, therefore, that he has achieved what he wanted to achieve (*Se* 154), so that personally and socially he now feels completely secure (*Se* 148), there is nevertheless a constant tension underlying and restraining his sense of achievement: "Überblicke ich meine Entwicklung und ihr bisheriges Ziel, so klage ich weder, noch bin ich zufrieden" (*Se* 154).

Fundamentally, this tension inheres in Rotpeter's very nature as ape-man. But it is not merely, or even principally, a matter of the tension between human mind and simian body. Certainly Rotpeter cannot bear to see his chimpanzee companion by day, although he takes his pleasure with her at night. However, the aversion he shows in this context is not to his or her physical nature, but rather to the "Irrsinn des verwirrten dressierten Tieres" (*Se* 154), which he sees in her gaze. While being forced to perform motions inconsistent with her simian nature, she has nevertheless tried to retain her simian inwardness, has clung obstinately to her past. The alternative he rejected she has accepted. As a result, she has become bewildered, mentally deranged. Unable to be her old self and unwilling to become a new one, she exemplifies the type of living death he has avoided. Thus she is a reminder of what he might have become and of the tense inner balance he has achieved. He finds her look unbearable, not, as Philippi (1966:128,137) maintains, because he sees in it his own nature and is afraid of it, but because she represents the possibility he has overcome, and her unalterably disoriented condition troubles him.

In Rotpeter's present situation, then, the tension does not reside in any potential conflict between body and spirit, between continuing simian physique and newly acquired human mentality. Rather, it consists in his awareness of the necessary discrepancy between the achieved reality of his extremely limited present and the irretrievable potentiality of his past, his 'Affentum', as humanly conceived. In other words, the latent, inescapable weakness of his simian-human existence is to be found, as he implies towards the beginning of his report (*Se* 147.), in the tension between his knowledge of the single 'Ausweg' he has necessarily chosen and his assumption, consequent

196

upon that choice, of the freedom or numerous "Auswege" (*Se* 150) he has thereby inevitably and irrevocably forfeited.

Earlier in this study of the *Landarzt* collection, it was suggested that Kafka's partially humanised animals embody, in a concentrated generally extreme form, some fundamental, yet problematical aspect of the human condition in modern times, and that, because they possess this particular affinity with modern man as viewed by Kafka, they provide him with the possibility of insight into his own nature. Nowhere is this more apparent than in the case of Rotpeter, who, despite his unique oddity, explicitly generalises the significance of his condition: "Ihr Affentum, meine Herren, sofern Sie etwas Derartiges hinter sich haben, kann Ihnen nicht ferner sein als mir das meine. An der Ferse[10] aber kitzelt es jeden, der hier auf Erden geht: den kleinen Schimpansen wie den großen Achilles" (*Se* 148).

Adopting the human attitude towards his former simian life as virtually complete freedom, and projecting that attitude on to others about whom he can apparently know nothing with any certainty, Rotpeter interprets all human and animal existence as subject to precisely the same tension as inheres in his own nature.[11] From the lowest to the highest, all human and animal creatures are vulnerable, and in every case their basic weakness is for the one thing, namely, the titillating awareness of their 'Affentum', that is, their past construed as a state of freedom or almost unlimited possibilities. Whether all animals and human beings have at some time actually lived in such a state, Rotpeter is uncertain (*Se* 148,150). But regardless of whether they have, in fact, experienced it or not, they instinctively postulate it, insofar as they are able, and some men, he knows, long for it (*Se* 148).

However, owing to the very nature of existence, such a state, be it actual or imagined, can never be retained or regained without denying the will to live (*Se* 150,151). For, in willing to live, one necessarily assents to the general reality of life, and that implies the constant need to choose and to compromise with the circumstances of one's own existence. Consequently, to assent to life is to affirm the necessity of discarding or forfeiting certain possibilities of one's own nature and thus of abandoning freedom, in the sense already indicated. Yet, despite this affirmation, the memory, intuition or even mere assumption of freedom remains, whether one desires it or not (*Se* 150); and in remaining, it will never cease to tempt and to taunt, however much it may diminish in intensity, because it is an awareness of what has needs been lost in order that life might continue to be gained.

Applied to the concerns of the entire *Landarzt* collection, the implications of *Ein Bericht für eine Akademie* are probably best indicated by Kafka, himself, in the following notebook entry, written only some eight months after Rotpeter's report was composed:

> Er ist ein freier und gesicherter Bürger der Erde, denn er ist an eine Kette gelegt, die lang genug ist, um ihm alle irdischen Räume frei zu geben, und doch nur so lang, daß nichts ihn über die Grenzen der Erde reißen kann. Gleichzeitig aber ist er auch ein freier und gesicherter Bürger des Himmels, denn er ist auch an eine ähnlich berechnete Himmelskette gelegt. Will er nun auf die Erde, drosselt ihn das Halsband des Himmels, will er in den Himmel, jenes der Erde. Und trotzdem hat er alle Möglichkeiten und fühlt es; ja, er weigert sich sogar, das Ganze auf einen Fehler der ersten Fesselung zurückzuführen. (*Hv* 46, 94; 14. xii.1917)

Conclusion

That Kafka should have chosen to convey the accumulated wisdom of the *Landarzt* pieces through an ape, a figure traditionally associated with human folly, clearly indicates the degree of jocular self-irony he had achieved by the time he wrote much of the present collection. This aspect of the work as a totality is further accentuated once it is also recognised that, contrary to the claims of Weinberg (1963:54), Altenhöner (1964:60), Fingerhut (1969:101) and Spann (1976:122), the name of Alexander the Great's battle-charger, the central character of the collection's first piece, did not derive from any 'bull-headed' qualities on its part. Rather, according to the authority of Plutarch and Pliny, with whose writings Kafka's classical education is almost certain to have made him familiar, the horse was so called because it was "branded with an ox-head, the mark of Philoneicus's ranch: hence his name, Bucephalus" (Green, 1974:43). Apart from E.T.A. Hoffmann, it is difficult to imagine any author other than Kafka indulging in such evident and profound self-parody, deliberately allowing what he regards as the most fundamental problem of modern existence to be posed by an 'ox-head' and resolved by an 'ape'.

A much more serious form of irony, however, underlies the collection's dedication (cf. Thieberger, 1953:53). As Kafka explained to Brod at the end of March, 1918:

> Seitdem ich mich entschlossen habe, das Buch meinem Vater zu widmen, liegt mir viel daran, daß es bald erscheint. Nicht als ob ich dadurch den Vater versöhnen könnte, die Wurzeln dieser Feindschaft sind hier unausreißbar, aber ich hätte doch etwas getan, wäre, wenn schon nicht nach Palästina übersiedelt, doch mit dem Finger auf der Landkarte hingefahren. (*Br* 237)

When one recalls the complex questions with which the work is concerned and the manifestly narrow interests of Kafka's father (cf. Binder, 1979a:112ff.), as well as Kafka's undelivered confession to his father: "Mein Schreiben handelte von Dir, ich klagte dort ja nur, was ich an Deiner Brust nicht klagen konnte" (*Hv* 203), the irony of this dedication becomes all the more poignant and may well be associated with the choice of the collection's title.

Generally the matter of this choice has been related to Kafka's frequently quoted diary entry of 25th September, 1918 (*Tb* 534), and justified on the grounds of the author's personal preference for the work in question. However, the basis of this widely accepted argument or tacit assumption is extremely insecure, since it is by no means certain whether, in the diary entry, Kafka is referring to the individual title-piece or to the collection as a whole, both of which were in existence at that time. A less equivocal, alternative explanation, suggested by the preceding analyses, may be derived from the fact that *Ein Landarzt* initiates the testing of the hypothesis proposed in *Der neue Advokat*, a process which is not concluded until the resolution of the underlying problem, in *Ein Bericht für eine Akademie*. Viewed in this way, the title may be regarded as serving to reveal some of the collection's most important structural principles. However, given the irony of the dedication, another possible and likely interpretation may be inferred from the strong contrast between Kafka's father and Siegfried Löwy who, as Wagenbach (1964) remarks, was "Kafkas Lieblingsonkel, ein eigentümlicher Sonderling, Freiluftfanatiker, gebildet, belesen (er besaß als einziger der gesamten Familie eine große Bibliothek), witzig, hilfsbereit, gütig und nur äußerlich ein wenig *kalt* erscheinend, blieb Junggeselle und wurde Landarzt in Triesch (...)" (op.cit.:15).

By and large, then, the significance of Kafka's relative distance from his father during the composition of the majority of the *Landarzt* pieces can be fairly clearly defined. Regrettably, however, the same does not appear to be true of his renewed relationship with Felice Bauer, another important element of the background to the collection. For, according to recent accounts of this affair, extra-literary evidence allegedly demonstrates beyond all doubt that the primary reason for Kafka's tortured, mainly epistolary courtship of this woman and his ultimate failure to marry her or anyone else was actually his fear of sexual intimacy: "Gegenüber seiner Angst vor der Intimität sind alle andern Gründe, die er gegen die von ihm heiß ersehnte Ehe vorbringt, nur 'vorgeschoben' (...)" (Binder, 1979a:422; s.a. 129ff., 158ff.). If this is true, then it should simply be regarded, in Liddell's terms, as 'irrelevant gossip', since there is no evidence whatever that it came within the range of Kafka, the author of the *Landarzt* collection, despite the fact that two of the pieces in this work explicitly deal with the issue of paternity and two others contain female figures who are involved in sexual acts: the maid in *Ein Landarzt* and Rotpeter's chimpanzee bedmate in *Ein Bericht für eine Akademie*. What does emerge as being of relevance to both author and would-be husband is the concern with *Beruf* and the search for a valid *modus vivendi*, including the possibility of discovering the latter in fathering children, a possibility which is very significantly rejected in the fiction, but certainly not for sexual reasons.

As indicated earlier, another major factor of potential importance to the *Landarzt* collection was the First World War, during which the whole work was composed. In the opinion of Gray (1973), this event and its aftermath were of almost no significance to Kafka because, in his diaries, there are no references:

> to the fighting (except for a frank confession that he passionately wishes every kind of evil to those engaged in it), to the conditions on the home

front, which must at times have been extremely difficult, or to the revolutions which flared up in Berlin, Munich, Budapest after the Armistice, or to the inflation which followed. The misery is all within his mind, and is almost always concerned with the spiralling of his own self-criticism, or with violent self-reproach over trifles. (op.cit.:34)

Nothing could be farther from the truth than this statement and its implications. Quite apart from the references in the diaries overlooked by Gray (e.g. *Tb* 418,419,420,420f.,437,456), Kafka's letter to his publisher about *In der Strafkolonie* (*Br* 150), the composition of *Der Kübelreiter* (1916/17), and, above all, the author's conversations with Janouch (*Gk* 139,173,175,178,228f.) provide overwhelming evidence to the contrary, even if it is true that, in his published statements, he was more concerned with analysing the broader implications of the war than with recording the details of battles, uprisings, and so on. Two comments, in particular, are of extreme relevance to the present collection. The first occurs in a conversation with Janouch about a meeting of a Marxist students' league. There Kafka says:

Der Krieg, die Revolution in Rußland und das Elend der ganzen Welt erscheinen mir wie eine Flut des Bösen. Es ist eine Überschwemmung. Der Krieg hat die Schleusen des Chaos geöffnet. Die äußeren Hilfskonstruktionen der menschlichen Existenz brechen zusammen. Das geschichtliche Geschehen wird nicht mehr vom einzelnen, sondern nur noch von den Massen getragen. Wir werden gestoßen, gedrängt, hinweggefegt. Wir erleiden die Geschichte. (*Gk* 173)

In the second, Kafka reacts to some reproductions of war paintings by maintaining:

Der Krieg wurde eigentlich noch nie richtig dargestellt (...). Gewöhnlich werden nur Teilerscheinungen oder Ergebnisse − wie diese Schädelpyramide − gezeigt. Das Schreckliche des Krieges ist aber die Auflösung aller bestehenden Sicherheiten und Konventionen. Das animalisch Physische überwuchert und erstickt alles Geistige. Es ist wie eine Krebskrankheit. Der Mensch lebt nicht mehr Jahre, Monate, Tage, Stunden, sondern nur noch Augenblicke. Und selbst die lebt er nicht mehr. Er wird sich ihrer nur noch bewußt. Er existiert bloß. (*Gk* 175)

Viewed in this light and from the standpoint of Kafka's notions about the Law, the *Landarzt* collection, far from ignoring the First World War, becomes one of its most penetrating and important fictional representations.

NOTES

1. Scholarship and the Collection

1 (p.14) Although Neumann does not discuss *Vor dem Gesetz* or *Ein Traum*, since they were not composed during the period with which he is concerned, his study is nevertheless included here because its synopsis refers to the collection as a whole.

2 (p.15) Had it not been for his omission of *Auf der Galerie*, König (1954) might also have been included in this group, although his study has the added disadvantage of examining the collection's remaining pieces out of sequence, using them, instead, to illustrate various alleged structural-thematic principles of Kafka's fiction, especially "Inkongurenz zur Welt" (op.cit.: 120ff., 144ff., 154ff.). Emrich (1958), Sokel (1964) and Binder (1966), too, entirely ignore the issues of sequence and collective unity, although the first comments on ten of the collection's texts, the second on seven – four of them (*Ein Landarzt, Vor dem Gesetz, Ein Traum, Ein Bericht für eine Akademie*) in considerable detail – and the last on twelve, including seven at some length.

2. Issues in Kafka Interpretation

1 (p.22) s. Honig, 1959:15 et passim; Fletcher, 1964:322; Frye, 1965:14; Clifford, 1974:11 et passim; Quilligan, 1979:22.

2 (p.25) Although Kafka, himself, has testified to frequent meetings with Janouch (*Br* 352; *Bm* 109, 124, 147, 170f., 211), and Dora Dymant has joined Brod in vouching for the "Echtheit dieser Gespräche" because, in their judgement, the latter faithfully convey "den unverwechselbaren Stil Kafkas und seine Denkweise" (Brod, 1954:229), recent scholarship has cast grave suspicion on the contents of the collection. In particular, Binder (1979c) and Goldstücker (1980) have drawn attention to major factual errors in Janouch's alleged records and have generally raised serious doubts about the authenticity of the conversations as a whole, but especially those sections added to the second edition (1968). Despite these justified criticisms and reservations, however, the fact remains that a significant number of the comments Janouch has attributed to Kafka unmistakably bear a very close resemblance to other statements by the author in his notebooks and letters to Felice, neither of which could possibly have been plagiarised by Janouch in his initial volume (1951), since they were not published until

1953 and 1967, respectively. Obvious cases in point are Kafka's thoughts on the nature of creative writing (*Hv* 46, 93f., 104; cf. *Gk* 74f., 84, 191, 224, 231) and his derogatory remarks about allegory (*Bf* 596; cf. *Gk* 205). Furthermore, as the analyses of this study will attempt to show, there are, among the other utterances ascribed to Kafka in the conversations, more than a few which clearly reflect the same attitudes and ideas that one finds expressed in much of his fiction, above all his profoundly negative assessment of his own time (cf. *Gk* 81f., 175, 232). Given these important areas of correspondence, it would seem only reasonable to conclude that the question of Janouch's reliability is far more complex than is now generally conceded and that, for all their shortcomings, the conversations still cannot be dismissed as mere fabrications, albeit well-intentioned. Consequently, factual errors apart, wherever Janouch's testimony is consistent with the evidence of Kafka's undisputed extra-literary writings or with the implicit world-view of his fiction, it has been accepted as trustworthy, and there has been no hesitation in drawing upon it to reinforce the arguments of this study. Nevertheless, with one small exception (*Gk* 220), all such references or quotations have been deliberately limited to passages which were included in the original edition of the conversations.

3 (p.27) cf. *Bf* 700; *Br* 401; *Gk* 223f.; Wagenbach, 1958; 1964; Politzer, 1965a: esp. 53ff., 151ff.; Beicken, 1974:175ff.; Beicken, 1979a:799ff.; Binder, 1979a; Binder, 1979b:56ff.

4 (p.31) e.g. Binder, 1966, 1975; 1976; Bridgwater, 1974.

5 (p.31) This approach is adopted in some parts or the whole of all the following: K. Flores, 1955; Pasley, 1964; 1965; 1971; Sokel, 1966; Fingerhut, 1969; Thorlby, 1972; Demmer, 1973; Gray, 1973; Corngold, 1976; 1976a; 1977; Mitchell, 1974; Krusche, 1974; Binder, 1976; Sussman, 1977; Walther, 1977; Blunden, 1980.

6 (p.41) s.a. Pascal, 1982:136ff.; Elm, 1982.

7 (p.43) As the discussion of *Einsinnigkeit* and *Paradoxie* will show, *Die Bäume* (*Se* 19) satisfies all the requirements but one: it is not essentially narrative.

8 (p.44) s. Allemann, 1963a; Arntzen, 1963; Hasselblatt, 1964; Fülleborn, 1969; Philippi, 1969; Strohschneider-Kohrs, 1971; Kerkhoff, 1972; Binder, 1975; 1979b.

9 (p.51) s. Hillmann, 1964:128, 137; Sokel, 1964:21, 130f.; 1966:9, 13; 1967:169ff.; Binder, 1966:188ff., 301f., 330f.; 1979b:61ff.; Henel, 1967: 265; Fülleborn, 1969:289.

10 (p.65) To these studies must now be added Pascal's posthumous, comprehensive analysis (1982), which also argues strongly against the view that Kafka's novels and some of his stories lack a narratorial presence (e.g. op. cit.:26). However, although its objections to orthodox *Einsinnigkeit*, like its observations about the development in Kafka's narrative technique, are basically sound, and its commentaries on some individual texts provide

many valuable insights, the analysis still has some serious weaknesses. Apart from ignoring many important contributions to the debate about *Einsinnigkeit*, including Kobs (1970), Beicken (1971) and H. Kraft (1972), it also fails to elaborate an adequate theory of narration, so that it draws no distinction between narrative and non-narrative texts, its notion of the narrator is limited and sometimes confused (e.g. p.2ff. 'personal' and 'impersonal', yet 'non-personal' and a 'function'), while it disregards the crucial factor of indirect commentary almost entirely. Furthermore, despite the fact that it correctly explains the nature of the parable (p.138f.), it still insists on applying the term to works which manifestly do not conform to the essential criteria it has already defined.

11 (p.67) e.g. Friedemann, 1910:26; Petsch, 1934:111ff.; Stanzel, 1955:4f.; Kayser, 1956:236; Seidler, 1959:479; Booth, 1961:149ff.

12 (p.70) Although the use of the first-person will always imply personalisation to some extent, it is also possible for a narrator who never uses 'I' or 'we' to personalise himself indirectly through his style and subject matter. This is the case, for example, in *Ein Brudermord*, and Pascal (1982:105ff.) argues that the same is true of *Ein Hungerkünstler*.

13 (p.75) Booth's equivalent (op.cit.:160) is 'privileged', which he restricts to the cognitive dimension and wrongly opposes to 'limited', since privilege, itself, can be limited. Furthermore, as Booth acknowledges (op.cit.:160ff.), 'inside views' and 'omniscience' are really aspects of intellectual privilege or advantage, although they will generally also have emotional and moral dimensions as well.

14 (p.75) These two terms, not being limited to the emotional and/or moral, also encompass what Booth (op.cit.:153f.) calls 'narrator-agents' and 'observers', who are simply physically involved or distanced, to varing degrees.

15 (p.75) Booth's equivalent is 'self-conscious' (op.cit.:155). But since that term also has the negative connotation of 'embarrassed, shy', 'self-aware' seems preferable.

16 (p.75) Booth's separate category called "variations in support or correction" (op.cit.:159f.) is merely an aspect of the ways in which narrative reliability or unreliability may be established.

17 (p.81) On 'erlebte Rede', see Kayser, 1948:146f.; Seidler, 1959:498f.; Stanzel, 1959:7; Leopold, 1960:27; Binder, 1966:201-231. On 'narrated monologue', see Cohn, 1966; Chatman, 1978:203. Adapting the French 'style indirect libre', Pascal (1977;1982) uses the term 'free indirect speech'.

18 (p.81) Pascal (1982:23f.) interprets both of these last two examples as 'free indirect speech'. However "kurz mit aller Bestimmtheit" modifies the verbal expression "entschloß er sich" (*Se* 29) which, in Binder's terminology, is a 'Gedankenreferat' (Binder, 1966:235ff.) and derives from the narrator. The second example, it is true, could be construed as narrated monologue, but to do so would be to make nonsense of the immediately preceding, firm resolutions by Georg, as well as his subsequent attitudes and actions.

19 (p.82) Bezzel (1975:153) dates this letter as 4th July, 1920. Despite Kafka's promise, however, he seems not to have sent the letter, for on or about 7th August of the same year (cf. Bezzel, 1975:159) he wrote to Milena: "ja du kennst den Vaterbrief nicht" (*Bm* 174).

20 (p.85) Cohn (1966:112) also refers to a profound ambiguity in the use of narrated monologue, and Pascal (1982:22,25) makes much the same point.

21 (p.86) s.a. Kassel, 1969:144; Pascal, 1982:14f.

22 (p.87) e.g. Martini, 1954:319f.; Leopold, 1959; Walser, 1961:125f.; Hasselblatt, 1964:59,71ff.; Cohn, 1968; Ramm, 1971:47ff.; Krusche, 1974:119; Beicken, 1978:223.

23 (p.93) *Die Bäume* is dated by Pasley/Wagenbach (1965:81) as 1904/05. The work occurs, however, in Fassung A of *BkII* in the context of the fat man's account of his confrontation with the prayerful man. This forms a smaller framework, as it were, around the prayerful man's story (II 3c, *Geschichte des Beters*). That is to say, *Die Bäume* occurs in precisely the same context as the story, repeated in Kafka's letter to Max Brod of 28.8.1904 (*Br* 28ff.), about the answer from the woman in the garden. This story is first told by the prayerful man in Fassung A, *BkII* 90, that is, in subsection II 3b, *Begonnenes Gespräch mit dem Beter*, where it is also taken up again at the end of the subsection (*BkII* 94/96). It does not then recur until immediately after *Die Bäume* in subsection II 3d, *Fortgesetztes Gespräch zwischen dem Dikken und dem Beter* (*BkII* 122), where it marks a significant change in the fat man's attitude. The most important point, however, is that the form of this anecdote about the woman's reply, as told in Fassung A, comes closest to that repeated in the letter to Brod, and this would seem to indicate that the letter and this section of Fassung A are of the same period, namely, autumn, 1904. Thus *Die Bäume*, the published version of which is much closer to Fassung A than Fassung B, in all probability derives from the same period: autumn, 1904.

3. Towards a Rhetoric of the Collection

1 (p.107) This fact provides another possible reason for Kafka's final exclusion of *Der Kübelreiter* from the collection, since it has an entirely different structure, one frequently employed by Kafka in his earlier works, namely, the resolution of an impossibly difficult situation through a flight of fancy cf. *Kinder auf der Landstraße* (*Se* 7ff.), *Der Ausflug ins Gebirge* (*Se* 12), etc.

2 (p.110) Although, despite marked differences in narratorial distance, *Vor dem Gesetz* and *Ein Traum* distinctly conform to the earlier formulated criteria of the reflector technique, *Auf der Galerie* and *Eine kaiserliche Botschaft* do so only by implication, in that the actual details of the realities they present are not explicitly attributed to the awareness of the central character in either work. Nevertheless, from the final reaction of both the

characters in question, it must clearly be inferred that ideas at least very similar to those expressed by the expositor or narrator actually have been passing through the minds of these characters at the time of exposition or narration, and this provides sufficient justification for placing both of these works in the same category as the other two.

3   (p.117) Since the entire content of *Ein Brudermord* consists of allegedly proven facts, its obvious inside views of all the main characters cannot be regarded as advantaged knowledge and are, therefore, excluded from this discussion.

4   (p.121) In his most recent article on Kafka, Emrich (1978) gives evidence of having changed his mind about this matter, since he remarks: "Schnee, Eiseskälte, Wüste sind bekanntlich auch in anderen Dichtungen Kafkas, wie im *Schloß* oder im *Landarzt*, Sinnbilder für den *Frost unseres unglückseligsten Zeitalters*" (op.cit.:119f.). s.a. Steiner's analysis (1978) of *Amerika* in terms of symbol and contained in the same volume (Caputo-Mayr, 1978: 46-58).

4. *Ein Landarzt. Kleine Erzählungen*: An Interpretation

Der neue Advokat

1   (p.127) Although there are literally hundreds of commentaries on the *Landarzt* pieces as separate, individual works and as many as possible of such analyses have been consulted in the composition of this study, no comprehensive attempt will be made to review them in the following interpretations or these notes, because (a) the repeatedly stated, overriding concern of this study is with the collection as a whole, and all the commentaries pertinent to that concern have been examined in Chapter 1; (b) the differences between other interpretations and those presented here are ultimately due to fundamental questions of method, a topic which has been treated at considerable length in Chapters 2 and 3; and (c) detailed surveys of other analyses are readily available in Beicken (1974), A. Flores (1976) and the relevant sections of Binder (1979/II). Consequently, about *Der neue Advokat*, for example, let it suffice to say that, apart from the scholars discussed in Chapter 1, very few others have concerned themselves in any detail with this particular text, but that Binder (1966:esp 50 ff.), Fingerhut (1969:100f.), Krusche (1974:97f.) and Spann (1976:120ff.) should be added to the list in A. Flores (1976:176). The most extensive commentary is that by Binder, and the most useful are those by H. Richter (1962:128-136), Fingerhut (1969:100f.) and Krusche (1974:97f.).

2   (p.127) In theory, the old Greek cities of the motherland were not subjects of the Macedonian king, but sovereign states, which assembled at Corinth as members of a great alliance, in which the Macedonian king was included as

a member and held the office of captain-general. But, in fact, the power of this king was so vastly superior that the Greek cities were as much subject to his dictation as was the rest of the empire. Alexander was thus an absolute ruler well before he adopted the more despotic style of oriental kings. Later he was also accorded divine honours, even by the Greeks, who at this period regarded such honours as more an elaborate form of flattery than as an acknowledgement of supernatural being or powers (s. Kitto, 1951:154ff.; Green, 1974). This distinction between the transcendent Absolute and its human representative is of considerable importance in Kafka's total worldview, as the rest of the *Landarzt* pieces will show.

3 (p.128) The specific resemblances mentioned in the text are (a) the ability to murder; (b) the adroit technique of stabbing one's friend across the banquet-table; and (c) the feeling among many Macedonians that their country is too constricting, so that they curse Philipp II, Alexander's father. Of these, the second is probably a punning reference to Alexander's murder of his old friend, Clitus, at Macaranda (now Samarkand) in 328 B.C., when both were drunk. The third is discussed below.

4 (p.128) In 1910 (*Tb* 31f.), Kafka read *Taten des großen Alexander*, a work by the Russian poet and novelist Michail Kusmin (1875-1936). While examining the possible influence of this book on *Der neue Advokat*, Binder (1966:50ff.) gives the following interpretation of the word 'heute' in the text: "Dieses 'heute' kann nach dem Textzusammenhang nur die Regentschaft Philipps, des Vaters, meinen, der also nach dieser Version den Sohn überlebt (...), während bei Kusmin bezeichnenderweise Alexander vor seinem Feldzug seinen wirklichen Vater, Nektaneb, tötet, (...). Schon gleich nach Alexanders Tod konnte niemand mehr nach Indien führen, d.h. wenn wir an die (i.e. Kafkas) Lebenszeugnisse und Aphorismen denken, ein menschliches Leben erreichen. Es lebt also das Schlachtroß, das einst im Kampf voranstürmte, ein Ersatzleben, wird Jurist, wie Kafka. Gleichzeitig, meint das 'heute' natürlich auch die Gegenwart des Lesers — man wird es bei unreflektierter Lektüre nur so verstehen, vor allem weil im Präsens erzählt wird (...)" (op.cit.:51; s.a. Binder, 1975:204ff.).

There is, however, no justification at all for such a view. In response to it, the following points might be made:

(a) If the 'heute' can *only* refer to the regency of Philip, then it cannot *simultaneously* refer to the present of the reader.

(b) Although Philip II, Alexander's real father, was regent of Macedonia for several months after his brother's death, he soon assumed the title and office of king and held them till his death. When his regency ended (359B.C.), Alexander (born 356 B.C.) was not even alive, let alone dead.

(c) Philip, who was murdered when Alexander was twenty years old, raised his country from a wild, primitive, barely united land to the leadership of the Greek world before his death (Kitto, 1951:154ff.). Thus he initiated that expansionist movement that culminated in the vast conquests of his son. When, therefore, it is said in *Der neue Advokat*: "vielen ist Mazedonien zu eng, so daß sie Philipp, den Vater verfluchen" (*Se* 123), this does not require that Philip should have outlived Alexander. On the contrary, those who curse Philip today do so because *he* is the real origin of their now frustrated desire for space, their present feeling of constriction (cf. Green, 1974:44).

(d) Bucephalus died on the banks of the Hydaspes in 326B.C., that is, three years before Alexander's death in Babylon. And even if, in Kusmin's fanciful version, the battlecharger is made to outlive Alexander (though Binder does not say so), it can hardly have been as a lawyer. The very references to his admission to the bar, a 'Gerichtsdiener' and a 'Stammgast der Wettrennen' are surely sufficient to make it obvious that the 'heute' in question does not refer to the period immediately after Alexander's death, however 'unreflektiert' such a reading may be.

5 (p.128) In apparent support of the abovementioned interpretation, Binder (loc.cit.) also makes the point that, in Kusmin's work and in historical fact, Alexander reached India, whereas in Kafka's version he is said not to have done so. But, again, this is a distortion of the text. Kafka's expositor simply maintains that Alexander did not reach "Indiens Tore" (*Se* 123). What exactly he means by this expression is not unequivocally clear. However, it may be that he is referring to India's larger seaports, in which case his statement is perfectly accurate. For Alexander saw remarkably little of India, penetrating no farther east than the Hyphasis (now Sutlej) River, at which point his troops adamantly refused to march on, so that, after three days of their stubborn opposition, Alexander very reluctantly agreed to return home. This he did by marching overland, after moving down to Patala, at the mouth of the Indus (cf. Green, 1974).

Ein Landarzt

1 (p.129) With the exception of *Vor dem Gesetz*, this work has attracted more critical attention than any other piece in the collection, many of such commentaries being unequivocally Freudian in nature or allowing an allegorical psychoanalytical dimension, e.g. Neider (1948); Lawson (1957); Busacca (1958); Leiter (1958); Salinger (1961); Marson/Leopold (1964); Sokel (1964); Kurz (1967); Tiefenbrun (1973). A detailed review of the secondary literature, together with another interpretation (in terms of Kobs' alleged 'paradoxical circle'), are provided by Beicken (1974:293ff.), while a list of further studies is to be found in A. Flores (1976:156ff.), to which Spann (1976:120ff.) and the other, more recent analyses mentioned in Chapter 1 should be added. This interpretation will take issue principally with one of the most detailed, psychoanalytical commentaries, that by Sokel (1964:251-281).

2   (p.129) Throughout the story there is a constant, often grotesque play on the double associations of *heilen* and *retten* and their substantival or adjectival forms.

3   (p.129) This statement calls to mind many another character in Kafka's work who uses his occupation or profession as an excuse for evading personal responsibility or as a protective, but hollow end in itself, e.g. Josef K. and almost all the court officials in *Der Prozeß*, the shoemaker in *Ein altes Blatt*.

4   (p.130) In this respect, the present interpretation differs radically from Sokel's (1964), which construes the doctor as arrogant, cold and self-centred, and his 'tragic' situation as arising from the refusal of his fellow citizens to lend him a horse (op.cit.:276ff.). Among other things, this overlooks the doctor's need to borrow a horse in the first place.

5   (p.130) It is not improbable that this motif and that of the boy's wound were suggested by Kleist's *Michael Kohlhaas*, in which the 'Rappen' are kept in a pigsty at the Tronkenburg and one of Kohlhaas's servants suffers from the *Rose*, erysipelas. That Kafka was very familiar with and fond of Kleist's *Novelle* is attested by his diaries (*Tb* 341,705f.), his letters (*Bf* 291f.; *Br* 96,104,358) and his conversations with Janouch (*Gk* 220). s.a. Wagenbach, 1958:202.

6   (p.132) Sokel (op.cit.:276) sees this refusal as yet another example of the doctor's scorn for his fellow citizens. In part, this one-sided view may be attributed to the fact that Sokel twice substitutes "Dunstkreis" for the text's "Denkkreis" in his analysis (ibid.:273 *l*.3, 276 *l*.4).

7   (p.133) Sokel (loc.cit.) also regards the whole scene, with the horses at the window, as reminiscent of Christ's birth, and the sister's bloody handkerchief as suggesting St. Veronica's 'Schweißtuch'!

8   (p.133) cf. description of horses (*Se* 124,125) with the pigsty from which they appear and the actions of the groom. The admixture of the beautiful and the repulsive in the nature of the worms is revealed by the very description of them (*Se* 127), and is further underlined by references to them in terms of "Blume" (*Se* 127) and "schön" (*Se* 128).

9   (p.137) Sokel (op.cit.:276f.) sees the use of the word 'Gesindel' simply as the doctor's attempt to blame the people for his 'tragic' situation, as if there were not guilt or default on both sides and tragedy did not require a certain personal 'magnitude' or *grandeur d'âme* singularly lacking in Kafka's characters.

Auf der Galerie

1   (p.138) Beicken (1974:302-306) has reviewed much of the literature on this work, and further titles are mentioned in A. Flores (1976:185) as well as Chapter 1 of this study. To these should be added Binder (1966:193ff.),

Krusche (1974:28) and Spann (1976:120ff.). The most useful commentaries are those by Emrich (1958:35ff.), Philippi (1966:52-57) and H. Kraft (1972:49f.).

2 (p.140) The same motif occurs in a letter from Kafka to Grete Bloch on 14th November, 1914, where it is also associated with a contrast between youth and implied maturity or middle age: "Sie spüren kein Nachlassen der Kräfte, so dürfen Sie das nicht ausdrücken, es gibt eben eine Müdigkeit der Jugend, die das Alter zum Ersatz alles sonstigen nicht mehr kennt. Es ist kein Nachlassen der Kräfte, wenn man oben in der Gallerie (sic) der Oper weint, glauben Sie das nicht" (*Bf* 502).

3 (p.141) cf. Aphorism 54 of 8th December, 1917: "Es gibt nichts anderes als eine geistige Welt; was wir sinnliche Welt nennen ist das Böse in der geistigen, und was wir böse nennen, ist nur eine Notwendigkeit eines Augenblicks unserer ewigen Entwicklung" (*Hv* 44,91).

4 (p.141) cf. Aphorism 55 of 8th December, 1917: "Alles ist Betrug: das Mindestmaß der Täuschungen suchen, im üblichen bleiben, das Höchstmaß suchen. Im ersten Fall betrügt man das Gute, indem man sich dessen Erwerbung zu leicht machen will, das Böse, indem man ihm allzugünstige Kampfbedingungen setzt. Im zweiten Fall betrügt man das Gute, indem man also nicht einmal im Irdischen nach ihm strebt. Im dritten Fall betrügt man das Gute, indem man sich möglichst weit von ihm entfernt, das Böse, indem man hofft, durch seine Höchststeigerung es machtlos zu machen. Vorzuziehen wäre also hiernach der zweite Fall, denn das Gute betrügt man immer, das Böse in diesem Fall, wenigstens dem Anschein nach, nicht" (*Hv* 45,91f.).

5 (p.142) The term 'reduction' is used here in its normal sense and not that attributed to it by Ramm (1971), namely, 'retraction; reversion; revocation', something very akin to Walser's 'Aufhebung' (1961). What this study has in mind is closer to what Hasselblatt (1964:71ff.) calls 'destruktive Entwicklung' or what Kafka expressed in the following aphorism of 1st February, 1918: "Zwei Aufgaben des Lebensanfangs: Deinen Kreis immer mehr einschränken und immer wieder nachprüfen, ob du dich nicht irgendwo außerhalb deines Kreises versteckt hältst" (*Hv* 51,107).

Ein altes Blatt

1 (p.142) Of the nine commentaries listed in A. Flores (1976:176) and those discussed in Chapter 1 of this study, the most detailed are those by M. & E. Metzger (1966) and W. Kraft (1968:41-47). However, the most penetrating remains that by Emrich (1958:196ff.), which Flores fails to mention at all. Similarly lacking from his list is the analysis by Fingerhut (1969:148f.), who interprets the work as "eine verschlüsselte Darstellung der Wechselbeziehung von Kunst und Leben" (op.cit.:149).

2　(p.142) Motifs such as the nomads (*BkI* 68 *e*.5), the people from the north (*BkI* 74 §2) and the Emperor obviously create strong ties between this work and *Beim Bau der chinesischen Mauer*, from which it is separated by only seven printed lines in the manuscript of the so-called sixth octavo notebook (s. Binder, 1975:221f.).

3　(p.145) In the Christian tradition, to which the Austro-Hungarian empire of Kafka's day belonged, the link between temporal and spiritual authority had been established since the conversion of Constantine in 312. In other traditions, such as the ancient Egyptian, Greek, Roman, Chinese and Japanese, the link had, at times, been even stronger, the temporal leader being regarded as an actual deity.

4　(p.146) According to Pasley (1971:204, n.18), the manuscript of this piece bears the title *Ein altes Blatt aus China*. Although the last two words were probably omitted by Kafka in order to broaden the work's implications and to associate the latter more closely with his own era, they do not make the title any the less arbitrary or banal. They do, however, lend added weight to the interpretation this study places on the figure of the Emperor.

Vor dem Gesetz

1　(p.146) The number of commentaries on this work exceeds even that on *Der Prozeß* (cf. A. Flores, 1976:178-185). Beicken (1974:273-286, esp. 279ff.) has reviewed a great many of them, but with an unjustified bias towards the views of Kobs (1970:esp. 524ff.), an attitude also strongly evident in the more recent survey and interpretation by Elm (1979). Among the more important analyses mentioned by neither Flores nor Elm are those by Binder (1966:199f.), Gray (1976:esp.175ff.), Sheppard (1977), Steffan (1979), Sokel (1980) and Pascal (1982:145-153). From the viewpoint of this study, the most valuable commentaries are those by Sokel (1967), Kudszus (1970), Gray (1976) and, especially, Heller (1974:84ff.), Stern (1976) and Sheppard (1977).

2　(p.146) Although Stern (1976) quite rightly insists on the immediate, socio-historical dimensions of the term 'law' in Kafka's works, and this study attempts not to neglect them, it is nevertheless clear from the unaging quality of the doorkeeper and the entire circumstances of *Vor dem Gesetz* (a door to the Law, etc.) that here Kafka's primary concern is with the term in its ultimate, transcendent sense (cf. Pascal, 1982:149).

3　(p.147) Others who essentially support this view include Pongs (1960:30ff.), Binder (1966:199f.), Thorlby (1972:67f.), Krusche (1974:41f.), Gaier (1974), Kuna (1974:132ff.), Rolleston (1974; 1976b), Corngold (1976), Sussman (1977:48ff.), Goodden (1977) and Steffan (1979: especially 144f.).

4　(p.148) Similar conclusions have been reached by many interpreters, including Emrich (1958:269), Allemann (1963), Sokel (1964:199ff.), Henel (1963;

1967), Politzer (1965:258), Baumer (1965:90f.), M. Greenberg (1968: 140ff.), Beutner (1973:212f.), Neumann (1975) and Sokel (1976a;1980). s.a. Beicken, 1974:176ff.

5   (p.148) Sokel (1967:273), Kudszus (1970:312f.), Krusche (1974:20) and Pascal (1982:150) all acknowledge a distanced, impersonalised or 'authorial' narrator in the work, but none of them notes the significance of his unobtrusive commentary and its advantaged knowledge.

6   (p.149) cf. Rosteutscher (1974:362): "Der Türhüter ist der Verhinderer, dessen Werk in unserer Zeit gerade den Suchenden verhindert, die Wahrheit im absoluten Sinne, d.h. als göttliche Lehre, zu sehen".

Schakale und Araber

1   (p.154) Of the commentaries discussed in Chapter 1, Flores lists only Tauber (1941) and H. Richter (1962). He also omits Emrich (1958:139f.), Weinberg (1963:46), Tomberg (1964:9), Binder (1966:330ff.) and Fingerhut (1969:149f.). Apart from Binder, who concerns himself exclusively with the work's narrative point of view, Emrich is the only one of these scholars not to allegorise the work in some way. According to him, the jackals are the expression of a self-contradiction in man which can be overcome only through death, but a death, "der Selbsterkenntnis, 'ein verständiges Tun', bedeutet und daher nicht mit dem leiblichen Tod identifiziert werden kann, sondern die Überwindung der empirisch beengenden Grenzen, den Sprung in eine universelle Existenz meint" (op.cit.:139). In addition to Tauber and H. Richter, other, sometimes tentatively allegorical interpreters of this piece among the scholars mentioned in Chapter 1 include Flach (1967:137f.), Gray (1973:134f.) and Neumann (1979:327ff.).

2   (p.154) In this context, it is interesting to note that in Grimm's entry on *Schakal*, he quotes two verse extracts from Grillparzer and Heine in which precisely the same equation occurs. Religious allegoresis of a different persuasion is to be found in Tauber (1941:71) and Weinberg (1963:46).

3   (p.154) The other forms of allegoresis include politico-ideological interpretations (H. Richter, 1962:144f.; Tomberg, 1964:9; Flach, 1967:137f.) and biographical reductions (Sokel, 1967; Fingerhut, 1969:149f.; Neumann, 1979:327ff.). In the latter, much is made of Kafka's remark to Milena, years later, that he was "endlos schmutzig, darum mache ich ein solches Geschrei mit der Reinheit" (*Bm* 208) and the links he draws between 'Schmutz', sexual intercourse and impediments to love (*Bm* 149,181f.).

Ein Besuch im Bergwerk

1   (p.154) Apart from Pasley (1965) and the scholars mentioned in Chapter 1, it would appear that only two others have published commentaries on this

text: W. Kraft (1968:47-49) and H. Kraft (1972:71). The latter regards the
theme of the work as "die Gegensätze zwischen den Klassen der Gesellschaft" (loc.cit.), with the *Kanzleidiener* causing the hierarchic order of
society to become "verfremdet, auffällig" (loc.cit.). The former, however,
construes the piece as a comment on levels of knowledge: "Dem vom Nichtwissen begrenzten Wissen des Wissenden entspricht das vom Wissen begrenz-
te Nichtwissen des Betrachters. Dieser erkennt, daß der Diener ohne Wissen
ist, und erkennt auch, daß die Macht des Wissens ihn erhebt. (...) Die dialektische Bewegung des Betrachters ist Unwissenheit, Wissen, Begrenzung des
Wissens. Die dialektische Bewegung der Wissenden ist Wissen, Nichtwissen
und statt Weisheit: Autorität" (op.cit.:49). Nevertheless, the dominant view
remains Pasley's allegoresis (cf. Binder, 1975:212f.; Neumann, 1979:339f.).

2   (p.154) H. Richter (1962:43) and Politzer (1962:94) wrongly talk about
eleven engineers.

Das nächste Dorf

1   (p.161) In addition to the previously mentioned commentaries on this
work, at least three others have been published. W. Kraft (1968:16f.) interprets the work as dealing with two different kinds of time, the quanti-
tative and the qualitative, the former denoting the long stretch of life, the
latter the ride to the nearest village, "welcher gleichnishaft mit dem ganzen
Leben identisch ist, dessen Maß Menschen nicht haben (...). In dem Ritt
ist beides gleich lang und die Kürze der qualitativen mit der quantitativen
Länge des Lebens identisch, und so ließe sich, qualitativ betrachtet, vielleicht auch umgekehrt sagen, daß auf jeder Stufe des Lebens der Mensch das
ganze Leben vor sich habe" (loc.cit.). Schlingmann (1968:128-131), on the
other hand, regards the work as being both paradoxical and parabolic, from
which he concludes: "Das verfremdende Licht, unter dem sich hier der Zeit-
begriff auflöst, weist auf etwas Außerzeitliches. Es wird ahnbar, daß man
sein Ziel eigentlich gar nicht mit Hilfe eines in der Zeit verlaufenden Weges
erreichen kann. Das Ziel liegt jenseits der Zeit, und der Großvater mit seinem 'Mangel an Zeitsinn' scheint ihm schon nahe zu sein" (op.cit.:130).
Philippi (1966:154) is discussed below.

2   (p.161) cf. Kafka's other comments on transience (e.g. *Hv* 115,116f.,125)
and the effects of war on man's relationship to time (*Gk* 175).

3   (p.162) About the grandfather's view of time, Philippi (1966) remarks: "In
seiner 'Zeit' haben Leben und Handlungen kaum noch Raum, so sehr ist sie
zusammengeschrumpft. Anstatt Leben zu ermöglichen, scheint sie es zu ver-
hindern" (op.cit.:154). While this is perfectly reasonable, he then adds the
unjustified footnote: "Das Erleben der Zeit als Korrelat der eigenen Be-
wußtseinswirklichkeit wird damit auf die Spitze getrieben, denn wo die
Zeit kein Handeln mehr erlaubt, weil sie dazu nicht ausreicht, ist sie selbst

nicht mehr durch das eigene Tun erlebbar und meßbar. Daß der Großvater dennoch 'Großvater' werden konnte, zeigt, daß sich schließlich hier das Bewußtsein ad absurdum führt" (loc.cit.). There are two main fallacies in this argument. First, the grandfather's comment does not present a vision of time that precludes all 'Handeln'; it excludes only that which is associated with resolution (*sich entschließen*) and the pursuit of some goal, that is, all those actions which imply a definite distance between resolution and realisation. Second, even if one's view of time were such as to preclude the possibility of action, this would not necessarily prevent any further experience of time, for time is not only "durch das eigne Tun erlebbar und meßbar". The totally paralysed, for example, can simply be and yet experience and measure time through that which goes on about them. Since time is inseparable from consciousness, it must always be 'erlebbar und meßbar' among the conscious. It is the quality of the experience and measurement that will differ, as Thomas Mann's narrator makes plain in *Der Zauberberg*.

Eine kaiserliche Botschaft

1 (p.162) Except for Politzer (1962:86f.) and H. Richter (1962:146-148), A. Flores (1976:164) lists none of the studies mentioned in Chapter 1. He also omits important commentaries on this piece by E. Heller (1948:206ff.), Anders (1951:71ff.), Brinkmann (1961:53-57), Baumer (1965:119f.) and, of course, Pascal (1982:164-167).

2 (p.163) The text in *BkI* differs from that in *Se* only in the following respects: (a) three cases of punctuation (*BkI* 78 *ll.*4,7,21); (b) the position of "noch" (*BkI* 78 *ll.*11-12); and (c) the omission of "ins Ohr" before "zugeflüstert" (*BkI* 78 *l.*29).

3 (p.164) Even here a vestige of hoping against hope remains and, with it, the implied wish that, in spite of the insuperable barriers, the message might still be delivered. As the speaker in *Beim Bau der chinesischen Mauer* concludes, after telling the parable-legend: "Genau so, so hoffnungslos und hoffnungsvoll, sieht unser Volk den Kaiser" (*BkI* 78). cf. Pascal, 1982:166 on the implications of the verb 'erträumen'.

Excursus: The Law

1 (p.165) e.g. Tauber (1941:124), Anders (1951:82ff.), Zimmermann (1954: 165ff.), C. Greenberg (1958:57), Brinkmann (1961:57), Politzer (1962:86), Philippi (1966:221), Bridgwater (1974:10f.). P. Heller (1971) also links Kafka's world-view with Nietzsche's thought, but maintains that Kafka's "distrust of temporal spheres of awareness is a corollary — not to his denial,

but to his total affirmation of the good, true, absolute — which Nietzsche considers to be arch-villains" (op.cit.:75). Osborne (1967) comes closer to the truth when he describes *Eine kaiserliche Botschaft* as "the quietly desperate cry of an agnostic yearning for a faith his reason will not allow him to accept" (op.cit.:45). However, probably the best available summary of Kafka's position is still that by E. Heller (1948:206; 1974:113f.): "Thus he knows two things at once, and both with equal assurance: that there *is* no God, and that there *must* be God."

2 (p.165) Anders' statements on this matter are actually rather confused. Earlier in his study he also calls Kafka an agnostic (op.cit.:48) and later a Marcionist (ibid.:87f.). His atheistic theory, however, is supported by Lukács (1958:45).

3 (p.165) Although it is true that, in his more philosophical works, Nietzsche vehemently rejects the notion of a God, especially of the Judaeo-Christian variety, one has only to read his *Dionysos-Dithyramben*, especially the *Klage der Ariadne*, which was composed after *Die fröhliche Wissenschaft*, to recognise the profound ambiguity in his position.

4 (p.166) e.g. *Ein Landarzt* (*Se* 125), *Beim Bau der chinesischen Mauer* (*BkI* 72).

5 (p.166) Emrich (1958:55f.), opposing Brod (1948:235; 1954:182), equates Kafka's notion of the Law with his ideas on 'das Unzerstörbare' (cf. *Hv* 44, 47,89,90,96,96f.; *Gk* 167) and identifies both with Tillich's concept of a "Gott über Gott" (op.cit.:56), although Kafka could not possibly have been familiar with the latter's theology. Basing themselves on the closeness between Kafka's aphorism: "Theoretisch gibt es eine vollkommene Glücksmöglichkeit: An das Unzerstörbare in sich glauben und nicht zu ihm streben" (*Hv* 47,96) and his remark to Brod in August, 1920: "Es gibt theoretisch eine vollkommene irdische Glücksmöglichkeit, nämlich an das entscheidend Göttliche glauben und nicht zu ihm streben" (*Br* 279f.), Foulkes (1967:50ff.) and Walther (1977:72ff.) also identify the 'Indestructible' with the Divine, the second explaining it in the neo-Platonist, Christian mystical sense of 'Gottheit' as opposed to 'Gott'. But what both fail to point out is that, in his letter, Kafka's statement is actually an attempt to paraphrase Brod's notion of paganism, a notion he explicitly rejects, so that there can be no question of equating 'das entscheidend Göttliche' with the 'Indestructible'. Others to deal with this concept in some detail are Reed (1965), who interprets it as synonymous with Schopenhauer's will to live, and Kobs (1970:346ff.), who construes it as an existentially unifying principle realised only in the dream state, when man is "bei sich und damit bei den Dingen, er ist recht eigentlich Ding an sich. Die geistige Welt des gelebten inneren Lebens und die Wirklichkeit der Außendinge sind miteinander identisch" (op.cit.:348).

Owing to the elusiveness of Kafka's thinking and the extreme generality of his few statements about this concept, it is doubtful whether its significance

216

within this total world-view will ever be explained with complete precision. However, in the light of other works from the same period as the aphorisms, it is possible to suggest a more likely, though necessarily more general interpretation than those already mentioned. It is true, as Emrich indicates, that the term is evidently related to Kafka's views on the Law, but the two cannot simply be equated. Rather, 'das Unzerstörbare' seems intended to signify an inborn, specifically human, largely intuitive and confused sense of lasting purpose and value, or at least of the need for them, in life. If this is true, then the concept also has associations with hope, which even in Kafka's world remains ultimately 'unzerstörbar', however 'unsinnig' (*Se* 135).

6 (p.166) In *Beim Bau der chinesischen Mauer*, the "oberste Führerschaft" assumes a similar significance (cf. *BkI* 72,74,75, and the effect of its leadership on the people: *BkI* 70,71). It would appear that Kafka also regarded Napoleon as such a leader (cf. Binder, 1974).

7 (p.166) cf. the court in *Der Prozeß*, which provides the most detailed and complex of Kafka's statements on this topic. A further equivalent of the 'Kaisertum' is to be found in the 'Adel' of the piece *Zur Frage der Gesetze* (end Oct., 1920). This association may seem to be contradicted by the statement: "der Adel steht außerhalb des Gesetzes (...)" (*BkI* 90). But it must be remembered that the Law referred to here is nothing more than the will of the nobles as imposed on the ordinary people. It is not the Law as ultimate Absolute. And since the people cannot even penetrate the mystery of the nobility, which is the "einzige, sichtbare, zweifellose Gesetz, das uns auferlegt ist (...)" (*BkI* 92), they are clearly in no position to go beyond it, so that the reader, dependent for information on a very limited, uncertain spokesman, is also prevented from establishing what the relationship between the nobility and the Law might be.

8 (p.166) Although Emrich (1958) is one of the very few critics to draw attention to the distinction between the 'Kaisertum' and the Emperor as mortal man (op.cit.:199f.), he misses this point and therefore arrives at the mistaken generalisation that, in Kafka's view, "das Verhältnis zwischen Menschheit und oberster Instanz seit jeher und zu allen Zeiten 'unklar' ist (...)" (op.cit.:202). From *Der neue Advokat* it should be evident that this is not the case. In Emrich's defence, however, it must be acknowledged that the historical perspective in *Beim Bau der chinesischen Mauer* is by no means unclouded. On the contrary, the whole chronology of the work is quite confused. At the beginning, the reader is told that the wall has been completed (*BkI* 67), though later (*BkI* 74) it would seem to be still going on. Similarly, the speaker says that he was 20 years old when the building began (*BkI* 69) and that the work was not to be accomplished "selbst in einem langen Menschenleben" (loc.cit.). Yet, the building evidently has been completed (s.a. *BkI* 75) and he is still very much alive.

9 (p.167) cf. couriers in aphorism 47 (*Hv* 44,89).

10 (p.167) s.a. *Beim Bau der chinesischen Mauer* and *Zur Frage der Gesetze*.

11 (p.167) e.g. the countryfolk in *Ein Landarzt*, the tradesmen and merchants in *Ein altes Blatt*, the imperial subjects in *Beim Bau der chinesischen Mauer* (s.esp. *BkI* 81).

12 (p.167) That these two stories were intended to portray punishments is evident from Kafka's letters (*Br* 134). The sudden change in Herr Bendemann towards the end of *Das Urteil* is a less acceptable form of the same process.

13 (p.167) s. *Vor dem Gesetz*, note 1 above.

14 (p.168) Walther also doubts that Kafka had read any of the Middle Platonists (op.cit.:76), but it seems extremely unlikely that in his strongly classical education he could possibly have failed to read at least some of one of the most prominent Middle Platonists, namely, Plutarch of Chaeronea. Furthermore, there is an extraordinary proximity between Kafka's repeated description of the creative artist's aim as raising the world "ins Reine, Wahre, Unveränderliche" (*Tb* 534; *Gk* 84) and Plutarch's reference, in his *De Iside et Osiride*, to the divine realm as "the region of the pure, invisible, and changeless" (Copleston, 1946:197). This proximity is not lessened by the fact that Griffiths (1970:243) translates the same passage as "the formless, invisible, dispassionate and holy kingdom", since he is using a modern, reconstructed Greek text unavailable not only to Copleston, but clearly also to Kafka and his teachers.

15 (p.171) cf. Emrich (1958:140), Fingerhut (1969) and Bridgwater (1974:118). The mistake in all three of these studies is that they treat all of Kafka's animal figures as if their nature and purpose were, in each case, the same, whereas this study attempts to demonstrate that such a view is unjustified.

16 (p.171) Fingerhut (1969:170f.) provides a convenient and accurate summary of the disagreement among Kafka scholars about the applicability of this term to Kafka's works.

Die Sorge des Hausvaters

1 (p.171) Although Pasley's previously mentioned allegoresis of this work has been questioned or rejected by Politzer (1965:151), Kobs (1970:80), David (1971), Gray (1973:128f.) and Beicken (1974:146f.), it continues to dominate critical opinion and discussion. cf. Pasley (1971:198f.), Bansberg (1974), Binder (1975:230ff.), Nicolai (1975) and Neumann (1979). Important alternative interpretations are provided by Bense (1952:63-67), Emrich (1958:92-96; 1968:112-120), Politzer (1962:96-98), H. Richter (1962:148f.), Philippi (1966:103ff.), Kassel (1969:68-72), E. Heller (1974:31f.) and Elm (1982:171ff.). Among English-speaking scholars there has also arisen a disagreement about the meaning of the title. Gray (1973:128) insists that it should be translated as "A Worry to the Caretaker", and Pascal

(1982:14,16,40) consistently refers to the work as "The Worry of a Care-taker". To interpret 'Hausvater' as 'caretaker', however, is to miss the whole point of the work, especially its last paragraph. This study therefore agrees with the Muirs, Pasley (1971:198) and E. Heller (1974:31f.) in construing 'Hausvater' in its familial sense.

2   (p.171) Although this word is now archaic, its revived use is made necessary by the corruption of 'fabulous'.

3   (p.174) Brod (1951/52:385), H. Richter (1962:149) and, above all, Backen-köhler (1970) have offered alternative etymological explanations of the word, but none of them is as convincing as Emrich's and they are all, in any case, entirely compatible with his.

Elf Söhne

1   (p.176) Apart from the relevant studies mentioned in Chapters 1 and 2, the only other detailed commentary on this work appears to be that by W. Kraft (1968:49-62), who concludes: "der Sinn des Ganzen ist versiegelt" (op.cit.:62).

2   (p.177) cf. Kafka's own doubts about marriage (*Tb* 310ff.; *Bf*; *Hv* 238), his letter to his sister Elli (*Br* 345f.), and his own undelivered letter to his father (*Hv* 162ff.).

3   (p.178) H. Richter (1962:149f.) makes very much the same point, but is wrong in suggesting that the eleventh son differs from all the others in being the only one who does not strive "sich in dieser oder jener Form mit der Gegenwart abzufinden und ihren Anforderungen zu genügen" (op.cit.:150). Compare, for example, the third son: "Auch fühlt er sich fremd in unserer Zeit; als gehöre er zwar zu meiner Familie, aber überdies noch zu einer an-dern, ihm für immer verlorenen, ist er oft unlustig und nichts kann ihn auf-heitern" (*Se* 141).

4   (p.178) cf. the discussion of *Allegorik* above.

Ein Brudermord

1   (p.179) A. Flores (1976) has no entry on this work at all. Yet, apart from the eleven scholars mentioned in Chapter 1, W. Kraft (1968:21-29) and H. Kraft (1972:70) have also published commentaries on it. By far the most useful study is that by H. Richter (1962:151-154).

2   (p.179) cf. Politzer (1962) who calls the work "a melodrama among mario-nettes" (op.cit.:94).

3   (p.180) In his autobiography, Brod surmises that Kafka adapted the name 'Schmar' from Flaubert's "Smarh, vieux mystère" (s. Binder, 1975:216), but it is difficult to see what light, if any, this sheds on the work.

4   (p.181) Apart from H. Richter (loc.cit.), W. Kraft (1968:28) and Binder (1975:216) are the only scholars to have recognised this allusion.

Ein Traum

1   (p.184) The entry on this work in A. Flores (1976:159) is extremely deficient, omitting nine of the scholars mentioned in Chapter 1 as commentators on the work, namely, Tauber, H. Richter, Politzer, Osborne, Flach, Kauf, Gray, Hibberd and, understandably, Kittler. Among others, the same entry also omits the studies by König (1954:111f.), Emrich (1958:296f.) and Sokel (1964:282-286; 1977:335-338). Although Sokel makes some very useful comparisons between this work and *Der Prozeß*, he still allegorises the piece as a veiled statement about Kafka's conception of his own art: "Die Funktion der Kunst ist es, nicht nur zu verewigen, sondern auch zu opfern. Sie verlangt das Opfer des Lebens" (Sokel, 1964:283; cf. 1977: 338). But, if this were true, the headstone engraver should be the one committing suicide, not Josef K. From the viewpoint of this study, the most valuable commentary is still Emrich's.

2   (p.186) That Kafka, himself, had frequently contemplated suicide before the composition of this piece is well attested by his diaries (*Tb* 171f.,266, 272,275,317,336f.,360f.) and a letter to Brod (*Br* 107ff.). Foulkes (1967: 21-25) discusses the matter in some detail.

3   (p.187) cf. Kafka's letter to Brod in mid-November, 1917, where he develops a very similar argument about his own failure to commit suicide (*Br* 195).

Ein Bericht für eine Akademie

1   (p.189) In his own, extremely perceptive analysis of this work, Sokel (1964) remarks that is has been "mit Unrecht von der Kritik vernachlässigt" (op.cit.:345). However, as Beicken (1974:307-312) and Neumann (1975:178f.; 1979:344f.) have shown, this is no longer the case, the latest detailed commentary being that by Pascal (1982:192-201). Nevertheless, most interpreters have allegorised the story in terms of Judaism (Brod, 1918:4f.; Rubinstein, 1952; Kauf, 1954; Beck, 1971:181-188; Gray, 1973: 135f.), Kafka's life and writing (Binder, 1966:387ff.; Fingerhut, 1969: 143ff.; Hibberd, 1975:83; Neumann, 1975; 1979:332ff.), philosophical or political ideology (Magny, 1942:89-92; Emrich, 1958:127-129; H. Richter, 1962:155-159; Bridgwater, 1974:127-131) and psychoanalysis (Kaiser, 1931; to some extent, Sokel, 1964:e.g. 330,334; Binder, 1979a:159). The most valuable studies are those by Sokel (1964:330-355), Philippi (1966: 116-147) and Pascal (1982:192-201).

2   (p.191) On this point, the present study agrees with Sokel's view (Sokel,

1964:348) rather than Philippi's heavy stress on Rotpeter's essential humanity (Philippi, 1966:127f.,137).

3   (p.192) Philippi (1966), overstressing the essential humanity of Rotpeter's nature, misses this point and thus construes the ape-man's reaction on this occasion, as well as his being in general, as comical (op.cit.:143f.).

4   (p.193) In a diary entry of 18th October, 1916, Kafka quotes from one of his letters to Felice (*Bf* 728ff.), in which the sentence occurs: "Ich, der ich meistens unselbständig war, habe ein unendliches Verlangen nach Selbständigkeit, Unabhängigkeit, Freiheit nach allen Seiten" (*Tb* 514; *Bf* 729). Perhaps this explains one of his earliest statements about the purpose of his own writing: "Aber jeden Tag soll zumindest eine Zeile gegen mich gerichtet werden (...)" (*Tb* 12). Binder (1975:228) and Spann (1976:125) are the only other scholars to have noted Kafka's self-quotation. On Kafka's real attitude to freedom, s.a. *Hv* 46,48,50,113,114,117f.; *BkI* 279f.,280,286f.

5   (p.193) Contrast Philippi, 1966:130ff., esp. footnotes 37 & 55; s.a. Sokel, 1964:344,349.

6   (p.195) Although Pascal (1982:199) agrees with this positive interpretation, most scholars do not, e.g. Tauber, 1941:73; Emrich, 1958:129; Politzer, 1962:92; H. Richter, 1962:159; Osborne, 1967:47f.; Fingerhut, 1969: 103ff.,143ff.; Kassel, 1969:149; Bridgwater, 1974:129; Beicken, 1974: 311; Neumann, 1975:175; 1979:334.

7   (p.195) It is Philippi (1964:142f.) who maintains that Rotpeter's situation is equivocal because of his position in the variety theatre, that is, because of his existence as an artist: "Diese Existenz ist als künstliche Daseinsform fragwürdig für den Künstler, der sich in der Scheinexistenz verwirklichter Freiheit — wie sie, von den Menschen aus gesehen, im Varieté vorgeführt wird — in einen neuen Zwiespalt von Sein und Bewußtsein der Scheinexistenz begibt, um diese als bewußt gestaltete eigene Lebensform den Menschen als wesentlich menschlich vorzutäuschen" (loc.cit.). For this to be true, one would have to know for certain (a) that Rotpeter regards all other variety performers in the same way as he regards the trapeze-artists, and (b) that the audience shares his supposed general view of variety artists, even to the extent of regarding him in the same way, that is, as part of a 'Scheinexistenz'.

But there is nothing in the text to confirm these assumptions. Since Rotpeter refers only to the trapeze-artists among his fellow performers, there is no way of knowing whether his attitude towards them extends to all other variety artists or not. Similarly, for all the reader is told, the audience may not even share his opinion of the trapeze-artists, let alone apply it to the other variety performers. Indeed, the very fact that Rotpeter has been invited by the academy to give his report is, in itself, an acknowledgment by at least part of the general public that, in his case, they do not share his alleged general view of the variety artist, that they actually regard him as being essentially humanised and not as merely pretending to be so. That, in spite of his essential humanity, he is nevertheless limited to performance in the variety theatre as an 'Ausweg' is a result of his undeniable oddity and rarity as an ape-man. It does not necessarily imply pretence on his or anyone else's part.

8   (p.195) Pascal (1982:196) quite wrongly translates this idiom as 'to take cover'.

9   (p.195) Because of the importance Rotpeter attaches to this idiom and the strongly ironic, even comic nature of his report, it is assumed here that there is a play on the literal and figurative meanings of the expression, as is so often the case in Kafka's works (cf. *Ein Landarzt*; *Die Sorge des Hausvaters*).

10 (p.197) Fingerhut (1969) takes as common knowledge the fact that "der Greiffuß des Affen gar keine Ferse besitzt" (op.cit.:105) and therefore construes this remark as Kafka's indirect, ironic commentary on Rotpeter. In doing so, however, he assumes that Kafka's zoological knowledge was as good as his own and that the author was concerned with zoological exactitude, when it is obvious from *Schakale und Araber* that neither of these suppositions is true, since it has also been common knowledge for a long time that jackals do not live exclusively on carrion.

11 (p.197) Although Philippi (1966) also stresses the broad significance of the tension in Rotpeter's existence, he relates it exclusively to the nature and realm of art, since he regards Rotpeter primarily as representing the artist in general (op.cit.:138,139,142). That such an interpretation is unjustified should be evident from the fact that, far from generalising the significance of his being as artist, Rotpeter explicitly draws attention to its singularity, when he distinguishes between himself and the trapeze-artists. Furthermore, if Philippi's interpretation were correct, then one would have to draw the extreme conclusion that Rotpeter actually regards all earthly creatures as artists, for, in speaking of the tension in his own being, he unequivocally states that it characterises "jeden, der hier auf Erden geht" (*Se* 148). As Pascal (1982:198) correctly observes, Sokel (1964) also "overestimates the significance of art in the ape's 'sublimation process'".

BIBLIOGRAPHY

Note: To facilitate the identification of quotations and references in the preceding text and notes, the original publication date of each work in the following list has been placed in brackets immediately after the name of the author(s) or editor(s).

Abbot, A.E. (1962): *Encyclopaedia of Numbers*, London: Emerson, 1962.

Ackermann, P.K. (1950): "A History of Critical Writing on Franz Kafka", *The German Quarterly*, 23 (1950), 105-113.

Allemann, B. (1956): *Ironie und Dichtung*, Pfullingen: Neske, 1956.

Allemann, B. (1963): "Kafka: 'Der Prozeß'" in Wiese, 1963: 234-290.

Allemann, B. (1963a): "Kafka: 'Von den Gleichnissen'", *ZfdP*, 83 (1963), 97-105.

Altenhöner, F. (1964): *Der Traum und die Traumstruktur im Werk Franz Kafkas*, Münster: Kramer, 1964.

Anders, G. (1951): *Kafka. Pro und Contra*, München: Beck, 1951.

Arntzen, H. (1963): "Franz Kafka: 'Von den Gleichnissen'", *ZfdP*, 84 (1963), 106-112.

Auden, W.H. (1963): "The I without a Self", in his *The Dyer's Hand and Other Essays*, London: Faber & Faber, 1963: 159-167.

Backenköhler, G. (1970): "Neues zum Sorgenkind 'Odradek'", *ZfdP*, 89 (1970), 269-273.

Bansberg, D. (1974): "Durch Lüge zur Wahrheit", *ZfdP*, 93 (1974), 257-269.

Baumer, F. (1960): *Franz Kafka*, Berlin: Colloquium, 1960.

Baumer, F. (1965): *Franz Kafka, Sieben Prosastücke*, München: Kösel, 1965.

Beck, E.T. (1971): *Kafka and the Yiddish Theater: Its Impact on His Work*, Wisconsin: Wisconsin U.P., 1971.

Beicken, P.U. (1971): *Perspektive und Sehweise bei Kafka*, Stanford University: doc. diss., 1971.

Beicken, P.U. (1974): *Franz Kafka. Eine kritische Einführung in die Forschung*, Frankfurt/M.: Athenäum, 1974.

Beicken, P.U. (1977): "Kafka's Narrative Rhetoric", in A. Flores, 1977: 178-187.

Beicken, P.U. (1978): "'Berechnung' und 'Kunstaufwand' in Kafkas Erzählrhetorik", in Caputo-Mayr, 1978: 216-234.

Beicken, P.U. (1979): "Erzählweise", in Binder, 1979/II: 36-48.

Beicken, P.U. (1979a): "Typologie der Kafka-Forschung", in Binder, 1979/II: 787-824.

Beißner, F. (1952): *Der Erzähler Franz Kafka*, Stuttgart: Kohlhammer, [4]1961.

Beißner, F. (1958): *Kafka der Dichter*, Stuttgart: Kohlhammer,[2] 1961.

Beißner, F. (1963): *Der Schacht von Babel. Aus Kafkas Tagebüchern*, Stuttgart: Kohlhammer, 1963.

Beißner, F. (1972): *Kafkas Darstellung des 'traumhaften innern Lebens'*, Bebenhausen: Rotsch, 1972.

Bense, M. (1952): *Die Theorie Kafkas*, Köln: Kiepenheuer & Witsch, 1952.

Beug, J. (1980): "The Cunning of a Writer", in Stern, 1980: 122-132.

Beutner, B. (1973): *Die Bildsprache Franz Kafkas*, München: Fink, 1973.

Bezzel, C. (1964): *Natur bei Kafka. Studien zur Ästhetik des poetischen Zeichens*, Nürnberg: Carl, 1964.

Bezzel, C. (1975): *Kafka-Chronik*, München: Hanser, 1975.

Binder, H. (1966): *Motiv und Gestaltung bei Franz Kafka*, Bonn: Bouvier, 1966.

Binder, H. (1967): "Franz Kafka und die Wochenschrift 'Selbstwehr'", *DVjs*, 41 (May, 1967), 283-305.

Binder, H. (1971): "'Der Jäger Gracchus': Zu Kafkas Schaffensweise und poetologischer Topographie", *Jahrbuch der deutschen Schiller-Gesellschaft*, 15 (1971), 375-440.

Binder, H. (1974): "Kafka und Napoleon", in Gaier/Volke, 1974: 38-66.

Binder, H. (1975): *Kafka-Kommentar zu sämtlichen Erzählungen*, München: Winkler, 1975.

Binder, H. (1976): *Kafka in neuer Sicht*, Stuttgart: Metzler, 1976.

Binder, H. (1976a): "Kafkas Schaffensprozeß, mit besonderer Berücksichtigung des 'Urteils'", *Euphorion* 70 (1976), 129-174.

Binder, H. (ed.) (1979): *Kafka-Handbuch in zwei Bänden*, Stuttgart: Kröner, 1979.

Binder, H. (1979a): "Leben und Persönlichkeit Franz Kafkas", in Binder, 1979/I: 103-584.

Binder, H. (1979b): "Bauformen", in Binder, 1979/II: 48-93.

Binder, H. (1979c): "Gustav Janouchs 'Gespräche mit Kafka'", in Binder, 1979/II: 554-562.

Blackmur, R.P. (ed.) (1934): *The Art of the Novel: Critical Prefaces of Henry James*, New York: Scribner, 1934.

Blunden, A. (1980): "A Chronology of Kafka's Life", in Stern, 1980: 11-29.

Booth, W.C. (1961): *The Rhetoric of Fiction*, Chicago: Chicago U.P., 1961.

Booth, W.C. (1974): *A Rhetoric of Irony*, Chicago: Chicago U.P., 1974.

Born, J. *et al.* (1965): *Kafka-Symposion*, Berlin: Wagenbach, 1965.

Böschenstein, B. (1980): "'Elf Söhne'", in David, 1980: 136-151.

Brandstetter, A. (1966): "Zum Gleichnisreden der Dichter: Hermeneutik einer Kafkaschen Parabel", *Zeitschrift für Studierende*, 21 (1966), 107-118.

Brettschneider, W. (1971): *Die moderne deutsche Parabel*, Berlin: Schmidt, 1971.

Bridgwater, P. (1974): *Kafka and Nietzsche*, Bonn: Bouvier, 1974.

Brinkmann, K. (1961): *Erläuterungen zu Franz Kafkas 'Das Urteil', 'Die Verwandlung', 'Ein Landarzt', 'Vor dem Gesetz', 'Auf der Galerie', 'Eine kaiserliche Botschaft', 'Ein Hungerkünstler'*, Hollfeld: Bange, 1961.

Brod, M. (1918): Review in *Selbstwehr*, 12 (Jan. 1918), 4f.

Brod, M. (1948): *Franz Kafkas Glauben und Lehre* in Brod, 1966: 223-299, orig. Winterthur: Mondial, 1948.

Brod, M. (1951): *Franz Kafka als wegweisende Gestalt*, St. Gallen: Tschudy, 1951.

Brod, M. (1951/52): *Ermordung einer Puppe namens Franz Kafka*, in Brod, 1966: 375-387, orig. *Neue Schweizer Rundschau*, 1951/52, 10: 613-625.

Brod, M. (1954): *Franz Kafka. Eine Biographie*, Frankfurt/M.: Fischer, 1966.

Brod, M. (1959): *Verzweiflung und Erlösung im Werk Franz Kafkas*, in Brod, 1966: 303-356, orig. Frankfurt/M.: Fischer, 1959.

Brod, M. (1966): *Über Franz Kafka*, Frankfurt/M.: Fischer, 1966.

Brooks, C. & Warren, R.P. (1943): *Understanding Fiction*, New York: Crofts, 1943.

Buber, M. (1950): "Kafka and Judaism", in Gray, 1962: 157-162, orig. in his *Zwei Glaubensweisen*, Zürich, 1950: 167-172.

Busacca, B. (1958): "'A Country Doctor'", in A. Flores/Swander, 1958: 45-54.

Camus, A. (1948): "L'espoir et l'absurde dans l'oeuvre de Kafka", in his *Le Mythe de Sisyphe*, Paris: Gallimard, 1948: 169-189.

Caputo-Mayr, M. (ed.) (1978): *Franz Kafka*, Berlin: Agora, 1978.

Chatman, S. (1978): *Story and Discourse. Narrative Structure in Fiction and Film*, Ithaca: Cornell U.P., 1978.

Church, M. (1963): *Time and Reality. Studies in Contemporary Fiction*, Chapel Hill: North Carolina U.P., 1963.

Cirlot, J.E. (1962): *A Dictionary of Symbols*, trans. J. Sage, London: Routledge & Kegan Paul, 1962.

Clifford, G. (1974): *The Transformations of Allegory*, London: Routledge & Kegan Paul, 1974.

Cohn, D. (1966): "Narrated Monologue: Definition of a Fictional Style", *Comparative Literature*, 18 (1966), 97-112.

Cohn, D. (1968): "Kafka's Eternal Present: Narrative Tense in 'Ein Landarzt' and Other First-Person Stories", *PMLA*, 83 (1968), 144-150.

Copleston, F. (1946): *A History of Philosophy*, vol. I, pt. II, New York: Image, 1962, orig. Westminster (U.S.A.): Newman, 1946.

Corngold, S. (1973): *The Commentator's Despair. The Interpretation of Kafka's 'Metamorphosis'*, Port Washington: Kennikat, 1973.

Corngold, S. (1976): "The Question of the Law, the Question of Writing", in Rolleston, 1976a: 100-104.

Corngold, S. (1976a): "The Hermeneutic of 'The Judgement'", in A. Flores, 1976a: 39-62.

Corngold, S. (1977): "Recent Kafka Criticism: From 'Groundless Subjectivity' to 'Homme Rhizome'", in A. Flores, 1977: 60-73.

Crick, J. (1980): "Kafka and the Muirs", in Stern, 1980: 159-174.

Dauvin, R. (1948): "Le procès de Kafka", *Études Germaniques*, Jan./Mar., 1948, 49-63.

David, C. (1971): "Zu Franz Kafkas Erzählung 'Elf Söhne'" in Ganz, 1971: 247-259.

David, C. (ed.) (1980): *Franz Kafka: Themen und Probleme*, Göttingen: Vandenhoeck & Ruprecht, 1980.

Deinert, H. (1964): "Kafka's Parable 'Before the Law'", *Germanic Review*, 39 (1964), 192-200.

Demmer, J. (1973): *Franz Kafka. Der Dichter der Selbstreflexion*, München: Fink, 1973.

Dentan, M. (1961): *Humour et création littéraire dans l'oeuvre de Kafka*, Geneva: Droz, 1961.

Dietz, L. (1965): "Drucke Franz Kafkas bis 1924", in Born *et al.*, 1965: 85-126.

Dietz, L. (1975): *Franz Kafka*, Stuttgart: Metzler, 1975.

Dietz, L. (1982): *Franz Kafka. Die Veröffentlichungen zu seinen Lebzeiten (1908-1924)*, Heidelberg: Stiehm, 1982.

Eastman, R.M. (1960): "The Open Parable: Demonstration and Definition", *College English*, 22 (Oct., 1960), 15-18.

Elm, T. (1976): "Problematisierte Hermeneutik. Zur 'Uneigentlichkeit' in Kafkas kleiner Prosa", *DVjs*, 50 (1976), 477-510.

Elm, T. (1979): "'Der Prozeß'" in Binder, 1979/II: 420-441.

Elm, T. (1982): *Die moderne Parabel*, München: Fink, 1982.

Emrich, W. (1954): "Franz Kafka", in Mann/Friedmann, 1954: 326-344.

Emrich, W. (1958): *Franz Kafka*, Bonn: Athenäum, 1958.

Emrich, W. (1960): *Protest und Verheißung*, Bonn: Athenäum, 1960.

Emrich, W. (1965): *Geist und Widergeist*, Frankfurt/M.: Athenäum, 1965.

Emrich, W. (1968): *Polemik*, Frankfrut/M.: Athenäum, 1968.

Emrich, W. (1978): "Kafka und der literarische Nihilismus", in Caputo-Mayr, 1978: 108-125.

Fietz, L. (1963): "Möglichkeiten und Grenzen einer Deutung von Kafkas Schloß-Roman", *DVjs*, 37 (1963), 71-77.

Fingerhut, K.-H. (1969): *Die Funktion der Tierfiguren im Werke Franz Kafkas*, Bonn: Bouvier, 1969.

Fingerhut, K.-H. (1972): Review of Kobs (1970) in *Germanistik*, 13 (1972), 392f.

Fingerhut, K.-H. (1979): "Bildlichkeit", in Binder, 1979/II: 138-77.

Firth, R. (1973): *Symbols Public and Private*, Ithaca: Cornell U.P., 1973.

Fischer, E. (1962): "Franz Kafka", *Sinn und Form*, 14 (1962), 497-553.

Flach, B. (1967): *Kafkas Erzählungen. Strukturanalyse und Interpretation*, Bonn: Bouvier, 1967.

Fletcher, A. (1964): *Allegory: The Theory of a Symbolic Mode*, Ithaca: Cornell U.P., 1964.

Flores, A. (ed.) (1946): *The Kafka Problem*, New York: New Directions, 1946.

Flores, A. (1976): *A Kafka Bibliography 1908-1976*, New York: Gordian, 1976.

Flores, A. (ed.) (1976a): *The Problem of 'The Judgement'*, New York: Gordian, 1976.

Flores, A. (ed.) (1977): *The Kafka Debate*, New York: Gordian, 1977.

Flores, A. & Swander, H. (eds.) (1958): *Franz Kafka Today*, Madison: Wisconsin U.P., 1958.

Flores, K. (1947): "The Judgement" in Flores/Swander, 1958: 5-24, orig. *Quarterly Review of Literature*, 3/4 (1947), 382-405.

Flores, K. (1977): "The Pathos of Fatherhood", in A. Flores, 1977: 254-272.

Foulkes, A.P. (1967): *The Reluctant Pessimist*, The Hague: Mouton, 1967.

Foulkes, A.P. (1977): "Speaking of Kafka", in A. Flores, 1977: 10-16.

Frenzel, E. (1963): *Stoff-, Motiv- und Symbolforschung*, 4. durchges. u. erg. Aufl., Stuttgart: Metzler, 1978.

Friedemann, K. (1910): *Die Rolle des Erzählers in der Epik*, Darmstadt: Wissenschaftliche Buchgesellschaft, 1965, orig. Leipzig: Haessel, 1910.

Friedman, N. (1955): "Point of View in Fiction: The Development of a Critical Concept", in Scholes, 1961: 113-142, orig. *PMLA*, 70 (Dec., 1955), 1160-1184.

Frye, N. (1957): *Anatomy of Criticism*, Princeton: Princeton U.P., 1957.

Frye, N. (1965): "Allegory" in Preminger, 1965: 12-15.

Fülleborn, U. (1969): "Zum Verhältnis von Perspektivismus und Parabolik in der Dichtung Franz Kafkas", in Heydebrand/Just, 1969: 289-313.

Fürst, N. (1956): *Die offenen Geheimtüren Franz Kafkas*, Heidelberg: Rothe, 1956.

Gaier, U. (1969): "'Chorus of Lies': On Interpreting Kafka", *German Life and Letters*, 22 (1969), 283-296.

Gaier, U. (1974): "*Vor dem Gesetz*. Überlegungen zur Exegese einer 'einfachen Geschichte'", in Gaier/Volke, 1974: 103-120.

Gaier, u. & Volke, W. (eds.) (1974): *Festschrift für Friedrich Beißner*, Bebenhausen: Rotsch, 1974.

Galloway, C.J. (1967): "The Point of Parable", *The Bible Today*, 28 (Feb., 1967), 1952-1960.

Ganz, P.F. (ed.) (1971): *The Discontinuous Tradition*, Oxford: Clarendon, 1971.

Garaudy, R. (1963): "Kafka und die Entfremdung", in Caputo-Mayr, 1978: 170ff., orig. "Kafka et le printemps de Prag", *Lettres Françaises*, 981 (1963).

Genette, G. (1980): *Narrative Discourse. An Essay in Method*, trans. J.E. Lewin, Ithaca: Cornell U.P., 1980.

Glicksberg, C.I. (1969): *The Ironic Vision in Modern Literature*, The Hague: Nijhoff, 1969.

Goldstücker, E. (1980): "Kafkas Eckermann? Zu Gustav Janouchs 'Gespräche mit Kafka'", in David, 1980: 238-255.

Goodden, C. (1976): "'The Great Wall of China': The Elaboration of an Intellectual Dilemma", in Kuna, 1976: 128-145.

227

Goodden, C. (1977): "Points of Departure", in A. Flores, 1977: 2-9.

Goth, M.J. (1971): "Existentialism and Franz Kafka: Jean-Paul Sartre, Albert Camus and Their Relationship to Kafka", in Zyla, 1971: 51-69.

Gray, R. (1956): *Kafka's Castle*, Cambridge: Cambridge U.P., 1956.

Gray, R. (ed.) (1962): *Kafka. A Collection of Critical Essays*, Englewood Cliffs: Prentice Hall, 1962.

Gray, R. (1973): *Franz Kafka*, Cambridge: Cambridge U.P., 1973.

Gray, R. (1976): "Kafka: A Critical Essay", in Kuna, 1976: 167-183.

Green, P. (1974): *Alexander of Macedon*, Harmondsworth: Penguin, 1974.

Greenberg, C. (1958): "'At the Building of the Great Wall of China'", in A. Flores/Swander, 1958: 77-81.

Greenberg, M. (1968): *The Terror of Art. Kafka and Modern Literature*, London: Deutsch, 1971, orig. New York: Basic Books, 1968.

Griffiths, J.G. (1970): *Plutarch's 'De Iside et Osiride'*, Cambridge: Wales U.P., 1970.

Hall, C.S. & Lind, R.E. (1970): *Dreams, Life, and Literature. A Study of Franz Kafka*, Chapel Hill: North Carolina U.P., 1970.

Hamalian, L. (ed.) (1974): *Franz Kafka. A Collection of Criticism*, New York: McGraw-Hill, 1974.

Hamburger, K. (1953): "Das epische Praeteritum", *DVjs*, 27 (1953), 329-357.

Hamburger, K. (1957): *Die Logik der Dichtung*, Stuttgart: Klett, 1957.

Harvey, W.J. (1965): *Character and the Novel*, London: Chatto & Windus, 1965.

Hasselblatt, D. (1964): *Zauber und Logik. Eine Kafka-Studie*, Köln: Verlag Wissenschaft und Politik, 1964.

Hayes, C. (1968): "Symbol and Allegory: A Problem in Literary Theory", *Germanic Review*, 44 (1968), 273-289.

Heldmann, W. (1953): *Die Parabel und die parabolischen Erzählformen bei Franz Kafka*, Münster: doc.diss., 1953.

Heller, E. (1948): "The World of Franz Kafka" in his *The Disinherited Mind*, New York: Meridian, 1959: 199-231, orig. *Cambridge Journal*, 11 (1948), 22ff.

Heller, E. (1974): *Kafka*, London: Fontana/Collins, 1974.

Heller, E. (1980): "Investigations of a Dog and Other Matters: A Literary Discussion Group in an American University", in Stern, 1980: 103-111.

Heller, P. (1966): *Dialectics and Nihilism. Essays on Lessing, Nietzsche, Mann and Kafka*, Amherst: Massachusetts U.P., 1966.

Heller, P. (1971): "Kafka and Nietzsche", in Zyla, 1971: 71-95.

Heller, P. (1974): "On Not Understanding Kafka", in Flores, 1977: 24-41, orig. *The German Quarterly*, 47 (1974), 373-393.

Henel, I. (1963): "Die Türhüterlegende und ihre Bedeutung für Kafkas 'Prozeß'", *DVjs*, 37 (1963), 50-70.

Henel, I. (1964): "'Ein Hungerkünstler'", *DVjs*, 38 (1964), 230-247.

Henel, I. (1967): "Die Deutbarkeit von Kafkas Werken", *ZfdP*, 86 (1967), 250-266.

Henel, I. (1979): "Periodisierung und Entwicklung", in Binder, 1979/II: 220-241.

Heselhaus, C. (1952): "Kafkas Erzählformen", *DVjs*, 26 (1952), 353-376.

Heselhaus, C. (1966): "Parabel", in *RL*, [2]III, 2. Lieferung, Berlin: de Gruyter, 1966: 7-12.

Heydebrand, R. von & Just, K.G. (eds.) (1969): *Wissenschaft als Dialog*, Stuttgart: Metzler, 1969.

Hibberd, J. (1975): *Kafka in Context*, London: Studio Vista, 1975.

Hillmann, H. (1964): *Franz Kafka. Dichtungstheorie und Dichtungsgestalt*, Bonn: Bouvier 1964.

Hillmann, H. (1965): "Franz Kafka", in Wiese, 1965: 258-279.

Hillmann, H. (1967): "Das Sorgenkind Odradek", *ZfdP*, 86 (1967), 197-210.

Hillmann, H. (1979): "Schaffensprozeß", in Binder, 1979/II: 15-35.

Hilsch, P. (1979): "Böhmen in der österreichisch-ungarischen Monarchie und den Anfängen der tschechoslowakischen Republik", in Binder, 1979/I: 3-39.

Honig, E. (1959): *Dark Conceit. The Making of Allegory*, Evanston: Northwestern U.P., 1959.

Hopster, N. (1971): "Allegorie und Allegorisieren", *Der Deutschunterricht*, 23 (Dec., 1971), 132-148.

Ingen, F. van *et al.* (eds.) (1972): *Dichter und Leser*, Groningen: Noordhoff, 1972.

Jahn, W. (1965): *Kafkas Roman 'Der Verschollene' ('Amerika')*, Stuttgart: Metzler, 1965.

Jahn, W. (1979): "'Der Verschollene (Amerika)'", in Binder, 1979/II: 407-420.

Järv, H. (1961): *Die Kafka-Literatur. Eine Bibliographie*, Malmö/Lund: Bo Caverfos, 1961.

Kahler, E. (1953): "Untergang und Übergang der epischen Kunstform", *Die neue Rundschau*, 64 (1953), 1-44.

Kaiser, H. (1931): *Franz Kafkas Inferno. Eine psychologische Deutung seiner Strafphantasie*, Wien: Internationaler Psychoanalytischer Verlag, 1931.

Kassel, N. (1969): *Das Groteske bei Franz Kafka*, München: Fink, 1969.

Kauf, R. (1954): "Once Again — Kafka's 'Report to an Academy'", *The Modern Language Quarterly*, 15/4 (Dec., 1954), 359-366.

Kauf, R. (1972): "*Verantwortung:* The Theme of Kafka's 'Landarzt' Cycle", *The Modern Language Quarterly*, 33 (1972), 420-432.

Kayser, W. (1948): *Das sprachliche Kunstwerk*, Bern: Francke, [4]1956.

Kayser, W. (1954): *Entstehung und Krise des modernen Romans*, Stuttgart: Metzler, 1954.

Kayser, W. (1956): "Das Problem des Erzählers im Roman", *The German Quarterly*, 19 (1956), 225-238.

Kayser, W. (1957): "Wer erzählt den Roman?", *Die neue Rundschau*, 68 (1957), 444-459.

Kerkhoff, E. (1972): "Noch einmal: Franz Kafkas 'Von den Gleichnissen'. Vorgreifliche Bemerkungen zu einer Deutung", in Ingen *et al.*, 1972: 191-194.

Kittler, W. (1979): "Integration", in Binder, 1979/II: 203-220.

Kitto, H.D.F. (1951): *The Greeks*, Harmondsworth: Penguin, 1967.

Kleinschmidt, G. (1968): "'Ein Landarzt'", in Weber *et al.*, 1968: 106-121.

Klotz, V. (ed.) (1965): *Zur Poetik des Romans*, Darmstadt: Wissenschaftliche Buchgesellschaft, 1965.

Kobbe, P. (1980): "Symbol", in *RL*, [2]IV, 3/4. Lieferung, Berlin: de Gruyter, 1980: 308-333.

Kobs, J. (1970): *Kafka. Untersuchungen zu Bewußtsein und Sprache seiner Gestalten*, hrsg. U. Brech, Bad Homburg: Athenäum, 1970.

König, G. (1954): *Franz Kafkas Erzählungen und kleine Prosa*, Tübingen: doc. diss., 1954.

Kraft, H. (1972): *Kafka. Wirklichkeit und Perspektive*, Bebenhausen: Rotsch, 1972.

Kraft, W. (1968): *Franz Kafka. Durchdringung und Geheimnis*, Frankfurt/M.: Suhrkamp, 1968.

Krusche, D. (1974): *Kafka und Kafka-Deutung: Die problematisierte Interaktion*, München: Fink, 1974.

Kudszus, W. (1964): "Erzählhaltung und Zeitverschiebung in Kafkas 'Prozeß' und 'Schloß'", *DVjs*, 38 (1964), 192-207.

Kudszus, W. (1970): "Erzählperspektive und Erzählgeschehen in Kafkas 'Prozeß'", *DVjs*, 44 (1970), 306-317.

Kudszus, W. (1977): "Changing Perspectives in 'The Trial' and 'The Castle'", in A. Flores, 1977: 385-395.

Kuna, F. (1974): *Kafka. Literature as Corrective Punishment*, London: Elek, 1974.

Kuna, F. (ed.) (1976): *On Kafka. Semi-Centenary Perspectives*, London: Elek, 1976.

Kurz, P.K. (1967): *Über moderne Literatur. Standorte und Deutungen*, Frankfurt/M.: Knecht, 1967.

Lämmert, E. (1955): *Bauformen des Erzählens*, Stuttgart: Metzler, [2]1967.

Lang, W. (1968): "Zeichen − Symbol − Chiffre", *Der Deutschunterricht*, 20 (1968), 12-27.

Langguth, C.W. (1968): *Narrative Perspective and Consciousness in Franz Kafka's 'Trial'*, Stanford: doc.diss., 1968.

Lawson, R.H. (1957): "Kafka's 'Ein Landarzt'", *Monatshefte*, 49 (Oct., 1957), 265-271.

Lawson, R.H. (1972): "Kafka's Parable 'Der Kreisel': Structure and Theme", *Twentieth Century Literature*, 18 (1972), 199-205.

Leistner, D.B. (1975): *Autor − Erzähltext − Leser*, Erlangen: Palm & Enke, 1975.

Leiter, L.H. (1958): "A Problem in Analysis: Franz Kafka's 'A Country Doctor'", *Journal of Aesthetics & Art Criticism*, 16 (Mar., 1958), 337-347.

Leopold, K. (1959): "Franz Kafka's Stories in the First Person", *AUMLA*, 11 (Sept., 1959), 56-62.

Leopold, K. (1960): "Some Problems of Terminology in the Analysis of the Stream of Consciousness Novel", *AUMLA*, 13 (May, 1960), 23-32.

Leopold, K. (1963): "Breaks in Perspective in Franz Kafka's 'Der Prozeß'", *The German Quarterly*, 36 (1963), 31-38.

Liddell, R. (1947): *A Treatise on the Novel*, London: Cape, 1947.

Liddell, R. (1953): *Some Principles of Fiction*, London: Cape, 1953.

Lubbock, P. (1921): *The Craft of Fiction*, London: Cape, 1921.

Lukács, G. (1958): *Wider den mißverstandenen Realismus*, Hamburg: Claasen, 1958.

Lyons, J. (1977): *Semantics*, vol. 1, Cambridge: Cambridge U.P., 1977.

Magny, C.-E. (1942): "Kafka ou l'écriture objective de l'absurde", *Cahiers du Sud* (Nov., 1942), 12-36.

Mahler, K.-W. (1958): *Eigentliche und uneigentliche Darstellung in der modernen Epik. Der parabolische Stil Franz Kafkas*, Marburg: doc.diss., 1958.

Mann, O. & Friedmann, H. (eds.) (1954): *Deutsche Literatur im zwanzigsten Jahrhundert*, Heidelberg: Rothe, ²1956.

Marson, E.L. & Leopold, K. (1964): "Kafka, Freud, and 'Ein Landarzt'", *The German Quarterly*, 37 (Mar., 1964), 146-159.

Martini, F. (1954): "Franz Kafka: 'Das Schloß'", in his *Das Wagnis der Sprache*, Stuttgart: Klett, 1954: 287-335.

Martini, F. (ed.) (1971): *Probleme des Erzählens in der Weltliteratur*, Stuttgart: Klett, 1971.

Metzger, M. & E. (1966): "Franz Kafkas 'Ein altes Blatt' im Deutschunterricht", *Kentucky Foreign Language Quarterly*, 13 (1966), 30-36.

Meyerhoff, H. (1955): *Time in Literature*, Berkeley: California U.P., 1955.

Mitchell, B. (1974): "Kafka's 'Elf Söhne': A New Look at the Puzzle", *The German Quarterly*, 47 (1974), 191-203.

Moffet, J. & McElheny, K.R. (eds.) (1966): *Points of View: An Anthology of Short Stories*, New York: Signet, 1966.

Muecke, D.C. (1969): *The Compass of Irony*, London: Methuen, 1969.

Muecke, D.C. (1970): *Irony*, London: Methuen, 1970.

Mühlberger, J. (1960): *Franz Kafka. Die kaiserliche Botschaft*, Wien: Stiasny, 1960.

Müller, G. (1947): *Die Bedeutung der Zeit in der Erzählkunst*, Bonn: Bonn U.P., 1947.

Müller, G. (1950): "Über das Zeitgerüst des Erzählens" *DVjs*, 24 (1950), 1-31.

MacQueen, J. (1970): *Allegory*, London: Methuen, 1970.

McDonald, C.C. (1966): "The Relevance of the Parable of the Sower", *The Bible Today*, 26 (Nov., 1966), 1822-1827.

Navone, J. (1964): "The Parable of the Banquet", *The Bible Today*, 14 (Nov., 1964), 923-929.

Neider, C. (1948): *The Frozen Sea*, New York: Oxford U.P., 1948.

Neumann, G. (1968): "Umkehrung und Ablenkung: Franz Kafkas 'Gleitendes Paradox'", *DVjs*, 42 (1968), 702-744.

Neumann, G. (1975): "'Ein Bericht für eine Akademie'. Erwägungen zum 'Mimesis'-Charakter Kafkascher Texte", *DVjs*, 49 (1975), 166-183.

Neumann, G. (1979): "Die Arbeit im Alchimistengäßchen (1916-1917)", in Binder, 1979/II: 313-350.

Nicolai, R.R. (1975): "Diskussionsbeiträge zu Kafkas 'Die Sorge des Hausvaters'", *Revue de Langues Vivantes*, 41 (1975), 156-161.

Nietzsche, F. (1874): "Unzeitgemäße Betrachtungen III" in *Sämtliche Werke. Kritische Studienausgabe*, hrsg. G. Colli/M. Montinari, München: dtv, 1980: 335-427.

Osborne, C. (1967): *Kafka*, London: Oliver & Boyd, 1967.

Pascal, R. (1956): "Franz Kafka" in his *The German Novel*, Manchester: Manchester U.P., 1956: 215-257.

Pascal, R. (1974): "Parables from No Man's Land", *TLS*, 3370 (1974), 611 f.

Pascal, R. (1977): *The Dual Voice*, Manchester: Manchester U.P., 1977.

Pascal, R. (1977a): "Critical Approaches to Kafka", in A. Flores, 1977: 41-50.

Pascal, R. (1980): "Kafka's Parables. Ways Out of the Dead End", in Stern, 1980: 112-119.

Pascal, R. (1982): *Kafka's Narrators*, Cambridge: Cambridge U.P., 1982.

Pasley, M. (1964): "Two Kafka Enigmas: 'Elf Söhne' and 'Die Sorge des Hausvaters'", *MLR*, 59 (1964), 73-81.

Pasley, M. (1965): "Drei literarische Mystifikationen Kafkas", in Born *et al.*, 1956: 21-37.

Pasley, M. (1966): "Asceticism and Cannibalism. Notes on an Unpublished Kafka Text", *Oxford German Studies*, I (1966), 102-113.

Pasley, M. (1971): "Kafka's Semi-Private Games", in A. Flores, 1977: 188-205, orig. *Oxford German Studies*, VI (1971), 112-131.

Pasley, M. & Wagenbach, K. (1964): "Versuch einer Datierung sämtlicher Texte Franz Kafkas", *DVjs*, 38 (1964), 149-167.

Pasley, M. & Wagenbach, K. (1965): "Datierung sämtlicher Texte Franz Kafkas", in Born *et al.*, 1965: 55-83.

Petsch, R. (1934): *Wesen und Formen der Erzählkunst*, Halle: Niemeyer, [2]1942.

Philippi, K.-P. (1966): *Reflexion und Wirklichkeit. Untersuchungen zu Kafkas Roman 'Das Schloß'*, Tübingen: Niemeyer, 1966.

Philippi, K.-P. (1969): "Parabolisches Erzählen: Anmerkungen zu Form und möglicher Geschichte", *DVjs*, 43 (1969), 297-332.

Politzer, H. (1934): "Nachwort" to Franz Kafka: *Vor dem Gesetz*, Berlin: Schocken, 1934: 75-80.

Politzer, H. (1939): "Franz Kafka. Versuch einer Deutung der Anekdote 'Gibs auf!'", *Jüdische Welt-Rundschau*, 13 (9. June, 1939), 5.

Politzer, H. (1946): "'Give It Up!'", trans. H. Lenz of Politzer, 1939, in A. Flores, 1946: 117-121.

Politzer, H. (1950): "Problematik und Probleme der Kafka-Forschung", *Monatshefte*, 62 (1950), 273-280.

Politzer, H. (1962): *Franz Kafka. Parable and Paradox*, Ithaca: Cornell U.P., 1962.

Politzer, H. (1965): *Franz Kafka, der Künstler*, Frankfurt/M.: Fischer, 1965.

Politzer, H. (1965a): *Das Kafka-Buch. Eine innere Biographie in Selbstzeugnissen*, Frankfurt/M.: Fischer, 1965.

Politzer, H. (ed.) (1973): *Franz Kafka*, Darmstadt: Wissenschaftliche Buchgesellschaft, 1973.

Politzer, H. (1973a): "Einleitung", in Politzer, 1973: 1-32.

Pongs, H. (1960): *Franz Kafka. Dichter des Labyrinths*, Heidelberg: Rothe, 1960.

Pouillon, J. (1946): *Temps et roman*, Paris: Gallimard, 1946.

Preminger, A. (ed.) (1965): *Encyclopaedia of Poetry and Poetics*, Princeton: Princeton U.P., 1965.

Quilligan, M. (1979): *The Language of Allegory*, Ithaca: Cornell U.P., 1979.

Ramm, K. (1971): *Reduktion als Erzählprinzip bei Kafka*, Frankfurt/M.: Athenäum, 1971.

Ramm, K. (1979): "Handlungsführung und Gedankenführung", in Binder, 1979/II: 93-107.

Reed, T.J. (1965): "Kafka und Schopenhauer. Philosophisches Denken und dichterisches Bild", *Euphorion*, 59 (1965), 160-172.

Reiß, H.S. (1956): *Franz Kafka. Eine Betrachtung seines Werkes*, Heidelberg: Schneider, 1956.

Reiß, H.S. (1956a): "Recent Kafka Criticism (1944-55) – A Survey", in Gray, 1962: 163-177, orig. *German Life and Letters*, 9 (1956), 294-305.

Rhein, P.H. (1964): *The Urge to Live. A Comparative Study of Franz Kafka's 'Der Prozeß' and Albert Camus' 'L'étranger'*, Chapel Hill: North Carolina U.P., 1964.

Richter, H. (1962): *Franz Kafka. Werk und Entwurf*, Berlin: Rütten & Loening, 1962.

Richter, P. (1975); *Variation als Prinzip. Untersuchungen an Franz Kafkas Romanwerk*, Bonn: Bouvier, 1975.

Rohner, W. (1950): *Franz Kafkas Werkgestaltung*, Freiburg i.B.: doc. diss., 1950.

Rolleston, J. (1974): *Kafka's Narrative Theater*, Pennsylvania: Pensylvannia State U.P., 1974.

Rolleston, J. (1976): "Strategy and Language: Georg Bendemann's Theater of the Self", in A. Flores, 1976a: 133-145.

Rolleston, J. (ed.) (1976a): *Twentieth Century Interpretations of 'The Trial'*, Englewood Cliffs: Prentice-Hall, 1976.

Rolleston, J. (1976b): "On Interpreting 'The Trial'", in Rolleston, 1976a: 1-10.

Rolleston, J. (1979): "Das Frühwerk (1904-1912)", in Binder, 1979/II: 242-262.

Rosteutscher, J. (1974): "Kafkas Parabel 'Vor dem Gesetz' als Antimärchen", in Gaier/Volke, 1974: 359-363.

Rubinstein, W.C. (1952): "'A Report to an Academy'", in A. Flores/Swander, 1958: 55-60, orig. *The Modern Language Quarterly*, 13 (1952), 372-376.

Rubinstein, W.C. (1967): "Kafka's 'Jackals and Arabs'", *Monatshefte*, 59 (1967), 13-18.

Salinger, H. (1961): "More Light on Kafka's 'Landarzt'", *Monatshefte*, 53 (1961), 97-104.

Sandbank, S. (1967): "Structures of Paradox in Kafka", *The Modern Language Quarterly*, 28 (1967), 462-472.

Schillemeit, J. (1964): "Welt im Werk Franz Kafkas", *DVjs*, 38 (1964), 168-191.

Schillemeit, J. (1966): "Zum Wirklichkeitsproblem der Kafka-Interpretation", *DVjs*, 40 (1966), 577-596.

Schillemeit, J. (1979): "Die Spätzeit (1922-1924)", in Binder, 1979/II: 378-402.

Schlingmann, C. (1968): "'Das nächste Dorf'", in Weber *et al.*, 1968: 128-131.

Scholes, R. (ed.) (1961): *Approaches to the Novel*, San Francisco: Chandler, 1961.

Seidler, H. (1959): *Die Dichtung*, Stuttgart: Kröner, 1959.

Sheppard, R.W. (1973): *On Kafka's Castle: A Study*, London: Croom Helm, 1973.

Sheppard, R.W. (1977): "'The Trial'/'The Castle': Towards an Analytical Comparison", in A. Flores, 1977: 396-417.

Sheppard, R.W. (1979): "'Das Schloß'", in Binder, 1979/II: 441-470.

Sokel, W.H. (1964): *Franz Kafka. Tragik und Ironie*, München: Langen-Müller, 1964.

Sokel, W.H. (1966): *Franz Kafka*, New York: Columbia U.P., 1966.

Sokel, W.H. (1967): "Das Verhältnis der Erzählperspektive zu Erzählgeschehen in 'Vor dem Gesetz', 'Schakale und Araber' und 'Der Prozeß': Ein Beitrag zur Unterscheidung von Parabel und Geschichte bei Kafka", *ZfdP*, 86 (1967), 267-300.

Sokel, W.H. (1976): "The Opaqueness of 'The Trial'", in Rolleston, 1976a: 56-59.

Sokel, W.H. (1976a): "The Programme of K.'s Court: Oedipal and Existential Meanings of 'The Trial'", in Kuna, 1976: 1-21.

Sokel, W.H. (1977): "The Three Endings of Josef K. and the Role of Art in 'The Trial'", in A. Flores, 1977: 335-353.

Sokel, W.H. (1980): "Freud and the Magic of Kafka's Writing", in Stern, 1980: 145-158.

Sörenson, B.A. (ed.) (1972): *Allegorie und Symbol*, Frankfurt/M.: Athenäum, 1972.

Spann, M. (1976): *Franz Kafka*, Boston: Twayne, 1976.

Stanzel, F.K. (1955): *Die typischen Erzählsituationen im Roman*, Wien: Braumüller, 1955.

Stanzel, F.K. (1959): "Episches Praeteritum, erlebte Rede, historisches Präsens", *DVjs*, 33 (1959), 1-12.

Steffan, J. (1979): *Darstellung und Wahrnehmung der Wirklichkeit in Franz Kafkas Romanen*, Nürnberg: Carl, 1979.

Steiner, C. (1978): "Kafkas 'Amerika': Illusion oder Wirklichkeit?", in Caputo-Mayr, 1978: 46-58.

234

Steinmetz, H. (1977): *Suspensive Interpretation*, Göttingen: Vandenhoeck & Ruprecht, 1977.

Stern, J.P. (1976): "The Law of 'The Trial'", in Kuna, 1976: 22-41.

Stern, J.P. (1976a): "Guilt and the Feeling of Guilt", in A. Flores, 1976a: 114-132.

Stern, J.P. (ed.) (1980): *The World of Franz Kafka*, London: Weidenfeld & Nicholson, 1980.

Stölzl, C. (1979): "Prag", in Binder, 1979/I: 40-100.

Strohschneider-Kohrs, I. (1971): "Erzähllogik und Verstehensprozeß in Kafkas Gleichnis 'Von den Gleichnissen'", in Martini, 1971: 303-329.

Struc, R.S. (1971): "Categories of the Grotesque: Gogol and Kafka", in Zyla, 1971: 135-154.

Sussman, H. (1977): "The Court as Text: Inversion, Supplanting, and Derangement in Kafka's 'Der Prozeß'", *PMLA*, 92 (Jan., 1977), 41-55.

Szanto, G.H. (1972): *Narrative Consciousness. Structure and Perception in the Fiction of Kafka, Beckett, and Robbe-Grillet*, Austin: Texas U.P., 1972.

Thieberger, F. (1953): "Erinnerungen an Franz Kafka", *Eckart*, 23 (1953), 49-53.

Thomson, P. (1972): *The Grotesque*, London: Methuen, 1972.

Thorlby, A. (1972): *Kafka*, London: Heinemann, 1972.

Thorlby, A. (1976): "Anti-Mimesis: Kafka and Wittgenstein", in Kuna, 1976: 59-82.

Tiefenbrun, R. (1973): *Moment of Torment. An Interpretation of Franz Kafka's Short Stories*, Carbondale: Southern Illinois, U.P., 1973.

Tillotson, K. (1959): *The Tale and the Teller*, London: Hart-Davis, 1959.

Tismar, J. (1975): "Kafkas 'Schakale und Araber' im zionistischen Kontext betrachtet", *Jahrbuch der deutschen Schiller-Gesellschaft*, 19 (1975), 306-323.

Todorov, T. (1977): *Théories du symbole*, Paris: Seuil, 1977.

Tomberg, F. (1964): "Kafkas Tiere und die bürgerliche Gesellschaft", *Das Argument*, 6 (1964), 1-13.

Vivas, E. (1948): "Kafka's Distorted Mask", in Gray, 1962: 133-146, orig. in his *Creation and Discovery*, New York: Noonday, 1948.

Wagenbach, K. (1958): *Franz Kafka. Eine Biographie seiner Jugend, 1883-1912*, Bern: Francke, 1958.

Wagenbach, K. (1964): *Franz Kafka in Selbstzeugnissen und Bilddokumenten*, Reinbeck: Rowohlt, 1964.

Walser, M. (1961): *Beschreibung einer Form. Versuch über Franz Kafka*, München: Hanser, [2]1963.

Walther, H. (1977): *Die Forderung der Transzendenz*, Bonn: Bouvier, 1977.

Warren, A. (1948): *Rage for Order*, Chicago: Chicago U.P., 1948.

Wäsche, E. (1976): *Die verrätselte Welt. Ursprung der Parabel. Lessing-Dostojewskij-Kafka*, Meisenheim: Hain, 1976.

Weber *et al.* (1968): *Interpretationen zu Franz Kafka*, München: Oldenburg, 1968.

Weinberg, K. (1963): *Kafkas Dichtungen: Die Travestien des Mythos*, Bern: Francke, 1963.

Weitzmann, S. (1970): *Studie über Kafka*, Tel-Aviv: Olamenu, 1970.

Wellek, R. & Warren, A. (1942): *Theory of Literature*, New York: Harcourt-Brace, [3]1949.

White, J.J. (1976): "Endings and Non-endings in Kafka's Fiction", in Kuna, 1976: 146-166.

Wiese, B. von (1956): "Franz Kafka: *Ein Hungerkünstler*", in his *Die deutsche Novelle von Goethe bis Kafka*, Bd. 1, Düsseldorf: Bagel, 1956: 325-342.

Wiese, B. von (1962): "Franz Kafka: *Die Verwandlung*", in his *Die deutsche Novelle von Goethe bis Kafka*, Bd. 2, Düsseldorf: Bagel, 1962: 319-345.

Wiese, B. von (ed.) (1963): *Der deutsche Roman*, Bd. 2, Düsseldorf: Bagel, 1963.

Wiese, B. von (ed.) (1965): *Deutsche Dichter der Moderne: Ihr Leben und Werk*, Berlin: Schmidt, 1965.

Zimmermann, W. (1954): *Deutsche Prosadichtungen der Gegenwart*, Düsseldorf: Schwann, 1954.

Zyla, W.T. (ed.) (1971): *Franz Kafka: His Place in World Literature*, Lubbock: Texas Tech.U.P., 1971.